CONTRADICTORY COOKBOOKS

Contradictory Cookbooks

Print, Protest, and Feminism in Women's Community Cookbooks

Ellen Barth

THE UNIVERSITY OF GEORGIA PRESS

ATHENS

Athens, Georgia 30602
www.ugapress.org

Set in Garamond by Westchester Publishing Services

Printed digitally

EU Authorized Representative
Easy Access System Europe—Mustamäe tee 50, 10621 Tallinn, Estonia,
gpsr.requests@easproject.com

Library of Congress Control Number: 2026012560
ISBN: 9780820380551 (hardback)
ISBN: 9780820380568 (paperback)
ISBN: 9780820380582 (ebook)
ISBN: 9780820380575 (PDF)

This book is dedicated to my grandma Gorny, with love.

CONTENTS

ILLUSTRATIONS

ABBREVIATIONS

CLUW	Coalition of Labor Union Women
CURE	Citizens United for Racial Equality
ERA	Equal Rights Amendment
NARAL	National Abortion Rights Action League
NOW	National Organization for Women
SCEF	Southern Conference Educational Fund
SF^3	Society for the Furtherance and Study of Fantasy and Science Fiction
WNPC	Women's National Press Club
YWCA	Young Women's Christian Association

CONTRADICTORY COOKBOOKS

Introduction

Women, Liberation, and the Contradiction of Community Cookbooks

In the late 1980s, there was a fight about cookbooks—specifically, which institution would receive the 858 cookbooks that made up the Andre L. Simon-Eleanor Lowenstein Collection of Gastronomic Literature, valued at roughly one million U.S. dollars. The process of donation was drawn out as research institutions vied for the assortment of rare books, which included a copy of the 1661 English cookbook *The Whole Body of Cookery*; an 1808 edition of Amelia Simmons's *American Cookery*, considered to be the first truly American cookbook; and Lydia Maria Child's classic *The American Frugal Housewife* from 1829.[1] Four years of negotiations and an intervention by Julia Child herself brought about a resolution, with the books eventually being split between the Mandeville Library of the University of California–San Diego and Harvard University's Arthur and Elizabeth Schlesinger Library on the History of Women in America, where librarian Barbara Haber was building up the cookbook collection.[2]

Yet, despite the budding field of culinary history, the fact that women's studies advocates and scholars had made significant and fruitful efforts to reclaim and reposition women's place in history, and an emerging underground third wave of feminism that was more comfortable embracing both femininity and feminism, Haber recalled that the books did not receive a unanimously warm welcome.[3] In the late 1980s, even as women continued to do the majority of cooking and meal planning in the home, the preparation of food remained a topic of contention and discomfort.[4] Opposing voices at the time felt that cookbooks, a material extension of the chore of cooking and women's unpaid domestic labor, were not appropriate in a library devoted to women's and feminist history in America.[5] According to Beth Potier, as Haber grew the cookbook collection at the Schlesinger Library, some of her colleagues "bristled at the idea that such tomes as 'Good Maine Food' or 'The Black Family Reunion Cookbook,'" a community cookbook published by the National Council of Negro Women, "should share shelf space with Betty Friedan's papers or the records of the National Organization of Women."[6]

This work, however, contends that cookbooks and in particular *community cookbooks*—self-published recipe collections that have often been put together by women's religious, charitable, and civic organizations to raise funds for good causes—deserve not just a space on the academic library shelf but also deeper consideration for how they have intersected with diverse women's lives. Although cookbooks are often considered to be conservative texts that uphold traditional gender roles, in the second half of the twentieth century, community cookbooks were produced and sold not only by the usual suspects—women's religious auxiliaries, PTAs, and charitable societies—but also by women engaged in both unpaid and paid careers outside the home, social justice activists, and second-wave feminists.

That feminists, activists, and professional women engaged in fundraising through cookbook making in the mid- and late twentieth century may be surprising to many—and understandably so. The books first became popular in the late nineteenth and early twentieth centuries, a time in which women's roles were highly restricted, limited in many ways to the home and family. Community cookbooks, typically compiled using the recipes and resourceful talents of clubwomen, connect to a history of charitable ladies' societies and women's covert political action. As books that operated in and for the public, community fundraising cookbooks from this era have been described as a "Trojan horse" for how they subverted limitations on women's public engagement and folded issues of politics into an unassuming culinary text.[7] In general, as texts and commodities, the funds of which might support such causes as temperance and women's suffrage, the books provide evidence of the ways women managed to influence the world beyond their homes when few other options were open to them.[8]

But while many women of the late nineteenth and early twentieth centuries might have felt the need to soften their political and civic intentions through a thoroughly domestic kind of literature, in the postwar period women's lives in America were no longer so circumscribed. After an initial return to the home in the 1950s, American women joined the paid workforce in ever greater numbers. Betty Friedan's concept and critique of the "feminine mystique," introduced in the best-selling book of the same name, had many women questioning their lack of fulfillment in the home in the 1960s, and, not long after, the women's liberation movement saw women demanding bodily autonomy, accessible health care, equal opportunities, and equal rights under the law. Within this movement women pushed to be seen as more than homemakers, mothers, and secretaries in the wider view of society, with feminist organizations releasing buttons declaring, "Women Make Policy, Not Coffee" and "Don't Assume I Cook."[9] Grassroots activism in the form of student and the civil rights movements propelled society away from ideas of charitable giving and ladies' societies that had been some of the main producers of fundraising cookbooks. In the 1970s a new ethos regarding fundraising was encapsulated in the slogan "change not charity," which underscored and offered a critique of the class divides that had marked much of American philanthropy up to that point. At the same time, the national market for cookbooks, which had always been large, experienced a boom in the second half of the twentieth century. During these decades cookbooks gradually shifted away from being primarily instruction manuals to glossy, impressive volumes that sat as comfortably on the coffee table as the kitchen table.

In short, none of these changes would seem to suggest that community cookbooks, with their strong connection to women's social clubs and charitable work, would continue to be a popular medium for women's personal, political, and activist engagement. In fact, some twentieth-century cultural critics even—erroneously—pointed to these new movements as reasons for the supposed decrease in community cookbook production in the second half of the twentieth century, focusing especially on second-wave feminism's role in dethroning the figure of the housewife. Sheryl Julian, for instance, wrote in the *Boston Globe* that "the women's movement that began in the 1960s was outspoken against women's roles in the household and didn't further the cookbooks cause."[10] Judith Weinraub, writing in the *Washington Post*, similarly commented that "in the '60s, the emerging women's movement began to make cooking almost politically incorrect. That," she comments, "plus the growing availability of packaged and frozen products caused community cookbooks to suffer."[11]

Taking these critics at their word, it would be safe to assume that community cookbooks began to lose favor at this time, being produced, if at all, only by conservative women as a way to maintain the status quo or perhaps to push back against the ideas of second-wave feminism.[12] Yet, between the years of 1950 and 1990, community cookbooks endured and even thrived. As church and regionally focused cookbooks continued to be produced by charity groups and women's auxiliaries, the self-publishing of community cookbooks was also taken up by career-focused women, women involved in radical political movements, and women fighting for the cause of second-wave feminism—groups and movements that seemed, at least on the surface, at odds with domestic and culinary pursuits.

Contradictory Cookbooks offers an exploration into these unexpected intersections of women's lives, taking a book historical focus to address the as yet underrecognized motivations and methods for women's production of community cookbooks in the second half of the twentieth century. The book's findings are drawn from analyses of hundreds of American community cookbooks, in both physical and digital collections, as well as research into American women's organizations archives, contemporary fundraising handbooks, news articles, journals, and newsletters.[13] By considering not only the contents of the cookbooks themselves but also a variety of primary sources that give insights into the agents, motivations, and aims of the publication process, this work uses publishing and book production as an access point into the history of women in America as well as a way to inform a more accurate twentieth-century publishing field and the place of women within it. The decades 1950 to 1990 are often characterized for women in America as a move out of the kitchen and away from traditional roles and in publishing for increased commercialization and conglomerization; this work argues, however, that the numerous informal community cookbooks self-published by various women's groups during these years complicate these characterizations while also attesting to the significant but often undervalued role everyday women have played in American book culture. As will be shown, between 1950 and 1990, compiling, editing, printing, selling, and marketing community cookbooks continued to be a powerful if rarely acknowledged way women improved their communities, exerted influence, negotiated existing boundaries to public life, rewrote histories, gained professional skills, and, generally, were a force to bridge vastly different aspects of their lives.

According to Alison P. Kelly at the Library of Congress, community cookbooks represent a "unique genre," with the books first appearing during the

U.S. Civil War as Northern women found innovative ways to contribute to the war effort. There are several key features that define community cookbooks and set them apart from commercially published cookbooks. First, community cookbooks—or fundraising, charity, compiled, or church cookbooks, as they are alternatively called—are produced to raise funds, typically for local causes. "Compiled by church committees, aid societies, improvement associations, poultry clubs, and social circles," Kelly writes, "they were published in support of projects ranging from libraries and free kindergartens to steeples and church carpeting."[14] Compilers of community cookbooks made use of a common text many women had knowledge of and easy access to—a recipe—and monetized it through book sales, thereby providing women with ways to exert influence on, affect, and help shape American society.

There are no hard and fast rules regarding the endeavors cookbooks could fund, and regional, national, international, and transnational interests have all been supported through community cookbook sales. In addition to their goal of raising funds, another feature of the books is that they do not have a single author but are written, compiled, and produced through communal efforts. The group involved in a book's production might be defined by, for instance, geography, religion, race, interest, profession, or club membership. In other words, the "community" represented in a community cookbook is always self-defined by the group involved in its production and, indeed, is perhaps more accurately described not as "community" but rather as "association," "society," "club," or even "network."[15] Two defining features of community cookbooks are that the labor that goes into their production is voluntary and no sole individual profits from the sale of a community cookbook. Instead, the funds raised through their sale are either funneled back into the organizing body or donated to a local or charitable cause. Unlike the polished and professional cookbooks put out by industry publishers, community cookbooks are a highly flexible genre, made to meet specific goals and often produced using inexpensive means. The less money that is spent on the production of the books, the more money that is gained through their sales. Finally, the recipes included in the books are usually contributed by people from within the organizing community and are typically individually attributed by name, in this way recognizing and creating a material record of the people that donated them.

Despite the sustained use of community cookbooks as fundraising projects to benefit communities throughout much of American history, the cookbooks, as many scholars note, have often been either dismissed or disparaged.[16] While interest in cookbooks as artifacts of popular and material culture has increased, attention to community cookbooks lags noticeably behind. Kelly writes that "whether they were seen as simple one-dimensional how-to manuals, or whether, like much domestic writing, they were simply deemed to be of little significance, community cookbooks were overlooked for even longer than standard cookbooks."[17] It is only really within the past few decades that community cookbooks have gained wider recognition and scholarly attention, with Hélène Le Dantec-Lowry making note in 2008 of a "growing interest" in cookbooks and culinary texts, which was, at that time, "somewhat new in America."[18]

A major contribution to knowledge about American community cookbooks is Anne Bower's 1997 edited compilation *Recipes for Reading: Community Cookbooks, Stories, Histories*, which looks specifically at community cookbooks as a genre that is separate and distinct from professional, individually authored cookbooks. Its contributors consider the literary, linguistic, cultural, and historical significance of the books, addressing a range of periods and national contexts. Yet, more than two decades on and despite the renewed interest in cookbooks noted by Le Dantec-Lowry, *Recipes for Reading* remains one of the few book-length works to focus squarely on community cookbooks. More often community cookbooks are addressed in sections of academic works dealing with American culinary and cookbook history, as well as articles in the fields of women's and rhetoric studies, with much of this attention being focused on books from the late nineteenth and early twentieth centuries.[19] On the other hand, and within this somewhat diminutive corpus, community cookbooks from the second half of the twentieth century have received comparatively little consideration. This aligns with existing bibliographies that take community cookbooks as their focus, which generally do not go beyond the year 1960, as well as copyright protection that makes both digitizing and accessing cookbooks of any kind from the 1950s and beyond incredibly difficult, as these books remain under copyright.[20] The obscurity and uneven documentation of sources on the large scale can make it difficult to see the presence and power of women in American publishing history, who, in the second half of the twentieth century, furthered new models of publishing outside of professional industry networks.

More than issues of access, though, community cookbooks continue to be ignored, dismissed, or marginalized as a genre. Bower lists several factors that have contributed to this situation, with the gender of their creators being chief among them. She writes, "The first and most obvious problem about community cookbooks is that they have usually been produced by ordinary women" and that "food, associated with women, has been seen as unworthy of serious study."[21] Moreover, club and associational women, the primary creators of community cookbooks, have a complicated status in American history. Lauded for their philanthropic efforts, clubwomen have at the same time featured as the butt of many jokes and less-than-flattering media depictions, from the missionary circle depicted in Harper Lee's *To Kill a Mockingbird* to the Ladies Auxiliary Dance Committee performing a tableau vivant in cinematic version of *The Music Man*. Kimberly Wilmot Voss has suggested that such "caricatures of these women [and] their flighty ways" are connected to stereotypical notions of gender roles, noting that the "mocking of women club members began almost as soon as women attempted to gather outside the home."[22]

The ambivalence toward women's associational work—respect for their benevolent deeds alongside mocking of their self-involved busybodying—reached a tipping point in the mid-twentieth century, as women's clubs began to lose much of their social status. Community cookbooks, as well, became the site of ridicule for both their representation of middle-class taste—the satirical song "Lime Jello Marshmallow Cottage Cheese Surprise" of 1980s novelty fame is a good example of this—and their seemingly outdated connection to clubwomen and benevolent charitable societies.

Attitudes toward community cookbooks from the second half of the twentieth century are bound up with issues of the status, gender, and cultural taste of their creators, as well as questions regarding how these identities are reflected in the material form of the books themselves. As informal and often amateur self-published creations, community cookbooks lack the characteristics that normally mark books as professional. This is especially true of books produced between 1950 and 1990, which have largely been, as one writer put it, "relegated to family jokes and memories."[23] Librarian Hans Rasmussen has been particularly vocal in his critique of the books, and, despite opening his article "Cataloging Community Cookbooks" with the claim that "for the purposes of scholarship, there is nothing at all wrong with such humble beginnings," he continuously points to the books' supposed flaws, from their "confusing layout" to their "murky publication credits." Rasmussen's issues with the books could be understood as professional frustration, given the very real challenges of cataloging books that do not conform to standard production and design conventions.[24] However, it is hard to read Rasmussen's critiques as being disconnected from gender-based stereotypes when considering comments such as "dividers commonly bear photographs of especially garish food collages heavy on lacquered hams, deeply stratified casseroles, and excessively-frosted sheet cakes that look like the product of a socially ambitious yet emotionally unstable WASP hostess on Prozac."[25] Such comments make plain the entangled issues of gender, class, taste, and material form at play in the reception of these books.

One field in which community cookbooks have found particular traction as primary sources is foodways studies, which is interested in "the eating habits and other food related cultural and social practices of a particular group, region, or historical period."[26] Community cookbooks are valuable to foodways scholars as they are thought to present a more accurate view of everyday food trends, and the books have been examined as sources to understand what Americans ate at certain points in history. Whereas professionally published cookbooks and food columns may be understood as more aspirational and influential in the foods they present to their readers, the recipes found in community cookbooks are contributed by amateur home cooks. Their recipes tend toward the everyday and often provide ways to cut corners, cut costs, or generally make life easier for the cook. For this reason the books are often thought to reflect a more honest picture of American domestic cuisine.

Likening the community cookbook to a kind of foodways "autobiography," Lynne Ireland writes that "much more than the magazines and cookbooks of the popular press which set standards and attempt to influence consumption, the compiled cookbook reflects what is eaten in the home."[27] Librarian Frank Boles notes the same, commenting that "fundraising cookbooks document what the locals were cooking, salt and all, at a specific time and place [and] that is what makes them valuable to historians."[28] This viewpoint is also reflected in the opening paragraph of the entry for "cookbook" found in the *Oxford Companion to the Book*, which states, "Cookbooks are collections of recipes, instructions, and information about the *preparation and serving of food*; they are also important social and historical records, offering a fascinating glimpse into an aspect of *daily life* that is by its very nature ephemeral. They provide information on issues such as the role of women in *the private sphere*, social attitudes to hygiene, and even the expansion of international commerce through the availability of ingredients such as spices or coffee."[29] In all these cases, the preparation of food in the private sphere is emphasized.

However, community cookbooks challenge these definitions, existing as they do between handwritten recipe books and professionally published cookbooks. Whereas manuscript recipe books might be passed down from generation to generation but never leave the kitchen, printed community cookbooks were produced in large quantities, with the intention to be sold and reach a substantial audience—albeit outside of mainstream publishing channels.[30] This is an important factor, as the financial motivations affected the contents and material aspects of the books, as well as how the books as artifacts are approached and received, reviewed and preserved. While foodways studies—which looks more or less exclusively at the recipe texts included in community cookbooks for traces of historical food trends and attitudes—are unquestionably worthwhile, they often fail to see the books in their entire complexity: as mediated objects that are produced and sold for specific purposes and which include much more than local food tastes. Foodways studies that deal primarily with the recipes and not their mediation or distribution through print keep community cookbooks in the kitchen, so to speak.

Book history, a field that engages with the production, distribution, and reception of material texts, is a useful lens for addressing the intersecting aspects of gender, production, materiality, and cultural memory at play in women's community cookbook production. Book history considers the role of books in society and the actors that have influenced this. It is, as Leslie Howsam has noted, "a way of thinking about how people have given material form to knowledge and stories."[31] Looking at cookbooks specifically, bibliographer Elizabeth Driver has argued that a book historical perspective is necessary if attempting to understand cookbooks as more than mere containers for recipes, stating that "to interpret accurately what they tell us about their time, . . . it is important to keep the books themselves at the center of the story."[32] Applying a book historical perspective to community cookbooks means never losing sight of community cookbooks as *books*, a medium for textual transmission but also an object of symbolic, cultural, and monetary value: at once a text, a container, and a commodity.

However, to date, few to no book historical works have examined American community cookbooks. In addition to the previously mentioned issues of gender, class, and taste that might affect the dearth of scholarship on community cookbooks in all fields, there are some additional causes that are likely reasons for this oversight within the field of book history. The time frame under consideration here, 1950 to 1990, which runs from roughly the postwar period to the rise of the internet as a major communications channel, has been, for whatever reason, largely uninteresting to many book historians. Remarking on this, Simone Murray wrote in 2021 that "until recent years, book history was averse to examining bookish phenomena from even the second half of the twentieth century, as though some decades' distance were required to render them suitable for academic study."[33] Connected to this, many of the print technologies used to produce community cookbooks between the 1950s and 1990s—the mimeograph machine, the typewriter, and the photocopier, technologies that could leave material productions washed-out, smudged, and reeking of alcohol—have also not received much attention from scholars, perhaps because they are considered, as Leah Price writes, "too old to be sexy but too new to be quaint."[34]

More than this, cookbooks, primarily in their function as instruction manuals, focus on the practice of food preparation, which is grounded in the tedium of everyday life. These characteristics have not commended the books to a vast array of scholars, book historians included. Although the field of book history is capacious in scope, the reality, as Price notes, may not always be as ambitious as intended: "Often, booklovers are thinking of a subset of books defined by a medium but also by a particular scale and a particular genre, one they assume to be read in a particular way. Call it Long-form Literary Print." Price further comments that cookbooks, as well as other nonfiction genres, are generally not "what we talk about when we talk about The Book."[35] David Finkelstein and Alistair McCleery offer some insight, linking this trend to the fact that, at least in the United States and United Kingdom, book history is often taught within university English departments. The two noted in 2005 that, "only slowly have some book historians in the United States and United Kingdom moved away from literary history to stress a wider engagement with a range of materials, from school textbooks to cartographic atlases."[36] In other words, the history of the book has tended to prioritize the literary over the instructional, and, although foundational book historian Robert Darnton conceptualized a holistic view of book history as one that includes "Shakespeare's sonnets" as well as "directions for assembling radio kits," books that focus on the practical and embodied, not to mention domestic and feminine, remain underresearched.[37] Textual productions associated with and made by women—such as scrapbooks, embroidery, and cooking manuals—are often unrecorded in historical records, undervalued, or, at times, unacknowledged as being "books."[38]

All that being said, in recent years the field of book history—an intensely interdisciplinary subject—has made impressive strides in addressing new moments and means of print history.[39] The Society for the History of Authorship, Reading and Publishing has, for instance, furthered conversations on decolonizing book history, and *The Papers of the Bibliographical Society of America* has published groundbreaking work in Black, liberation, and queer bibliography.[40] Furthermore, and most significant to the present work, research that examines women's as well as feminist print cultures has opened up the field in new and exciting ways.[41] This current work aims to contribute to the growing area of women's book history, adding to a body of book historical inquiry that considers the gendered dynamics and role of women within the history of the book.[42]

Cookbooks, so often connected to the traditional and the domestic, do not seem like a desirable medium for working women, women involved in radical political groups, or women fighting for the cause of feminism. However, as the following chapters show, these and many more women did take up cookbook self-publishing as a way to raise funds but also to learn employable skills, establish and further careers, engender support for grassroots political causes, generate local support for national movements, participate in feminist revisioning, and, generally, to create change within society and for themselves. Rather than tie women to the kitchen and to a one-dimensional domestic past, self-publishing and the adaptable community cookbook genre instead afforded women opportunities to bring vastly different aspects of their lives together and helped them move into futures of their own making.

Chapter 1 gives historical context to the genre of the American community cookbook and to the connection the books have to turn-of-the-century women's organizations. First appearing in the 1860s, community cookbooks were quickly taken up by a wide variety of women's groups, whose members, in some cases, used the domestic text as a subversive political tool. By the mid-twentieth century, however, the need for subversive domesticity was waning. In the wake of new social movements that were sweeping across the country, both the women's club and the community cookbook seemed to lose their cultural appeal. The final section of the chapter traces these shifts but also opens the door to questioning aspects of their accuracy.

Chapter 2 moves into the mid-twentieth century, making the claim that the increased popularity of the community cookbook genre can be linked to an increase in affordable and accessible self-publishing options, particularly to an array of competing commercial printers and binders as well as to the availability of at-home and office printing technologies. These affordable options eased the process of organizing, designing, and constructing the books and cut down on the largest cost: printing. That women used at-home and self-publishing options, such as stencil and spirit duplicators, draws connections to subcultural literary movements occurring at the same time. These new channels for printing offered chances at freedom of design and expression and gave cookbook compilers a variety of options they could make use of depending on the skills, energy, and available funds of their cookbook committees. Although an important factor, the availability of these printing options, however, can only partially explain why women continued to make community cookbooks during these years; changes in print technologies alone do not answer the question of why women who were connected to movements that were seemingly at odds with ideas of domesticity decided to make cookbooks.

The following three chapters, then, consider what attracted numerous women and women's groups to the project of producing and selling cookbooks, what they gained from being involved in these projects, and how that involvement sat alongside other social and cultural shifts. Exploring these issues reveals much about the tensions and anxieties in American society at the time, as well as the unacknowledged ways women have used self-publishing and charitable book sales to shape both society and their own futures. Each of the chapters focuses on a single "contradictory" pairing: women and work, profits and politics, and, finally, food and feminism. In doing so, and by taking women's production of community cookbooks into account, this work connects to broader book historical trends that ask for an intentional look at the technologies, networks, economic models, and print culture practices of women in the American publishing landscape; moreover, it fills a gap in historical research regarding the aims and motivations of women's alternative practices of cookbook production in the second half of the twentieth century.

Chapter 3 looks to contemporary news articles and fundraising handbooks to understand how women used community cookbooks to raise funds, gain skills, and in some cases used their new knowledge of books and publishing to move from unpaid to paid careers. Even if not transitioning into paid careers in the book industry, a number of groups created veritable publishing industries of community cookbooks based on volunteer labor. The success of these self-publishing endeavors did not go unnoticed by professional publishers, and the chapter reveals that during these decades self-published community cookbooks began to cross over into mainstream markets. In this way the books complicate commonly held perceptions of professional versus amateur publishing in the twentieth century.

Chapter 4 addresses the intersection of community cookbooks as commodities and political texts, looking within a selection of politically motivated cookbooks to understand how messages of political action were supported through culinary literature. While community cookbooks were a way for groups connected to radical social movements to raise funds, they also tapped into a wider market interest in political cookbooks, and this chapter considers community cookbooks as part of a broader cookbook landscape. Beyond being fundraising goods, community cookbooks also offered a way to spread political ideas to a broad readership and instruct readers on how to incorporate activism into their daily routines through activist recipes. As communal productions, cookbook projects also offered opportunities for groups to do activism at the local level.

Chapter 5 follows on from this political focus by exploring how community cookbooks were used by and within second-wave feminist groups. Although the second-wave feminist movement is often characterized as having had an uneasy or even hostile relationship with domestic duties and cooking, the chapter reveals that not all feminists felt the need to distance themselves from the act of cooking or the cookbook as an object. In fact, as the chapter shows through a study of feminist cookbooks, some of which are being addressed for the first time, several of the best-known and most influential feminist groups of the era—such as the National Organization for Women—had local chapters that produced fundraising community cookbooks. In these cases the books were valuable for how they acted at the local level, allowing feminists to raise funds, connect with and revision first-wave feminism, and push the boundaries of feminism by helping to finance, in at least one instance, a new literary award focused on gender exploration in science fiction and fantasy.

Together these chapters venture to the extreme edges of community cookbook production. They address how even the most unlikely of women's groups found creative, economic, political, and educational uses for a genre often associated with nineteenth-century women's charitable societies, to better understand why women who were deeply connected to and involved in the societal shifts taking place during these years were motivated to self-publish community cookbooks. While books from working women's organizations, civil rights activists, and feminist leaders may not be representative of overall community cookbook trends, these investigations reveal that, rather than being antithetical to these—sometimes radical—movements, the flexible genre of the community cookbook provided a way for activists, mothers, career women, homemakers, politicians, and feminists to join together, assert their influence, better their communities, shape policies, and, on their own terms, explore and define the spaces between these seemingly contradictory identities.

CHAPTER ONE

"What Else Can We Women Do?"

Women's Clubs and Community Cookbooks

COMMUNITY COOKBOOKS HAVE been called an "American phenomenon," with the books emerging in the United States at a key moment in the nation's history.[1] First appearing at a Civil War Sanitary Fair in the 1860s as a way to raise funds for charity, community cookbooks gained particular popularity at the turn of the century as part of the growing American women's club movement. From the 1860s onward, community cookbooks were a way for women to exert influence on society at a time when few other avenues existed for them. Through the production and sale of these books, women's clubs collapsed the public and private in distinct and profitable ways.

Although the first charitable cookbook published and sold in the United States was a singly authored volume of recipes, Lynne Ireland asserts that ladies' organizations and women's clubs, "not content with mere bandage-rolling," were inspired to take up cookbook making for charitable purposes almost immediately.[2] In the decades after the Civil War, as an increasing number of women's clubs and ladies' societies emerged, the community or compiled cookbook became an established genre. Throughout the years community cookbooks were created to meet a variety of needs, for example, to fund victims of the San Francisco earthquake in 1906, to provide aid to Belgian civilians in World War I, and to help women cook for their families during times of rationing in World War II. Moving into the middle of the twentieth century, however, the women's voluntary organization began to lose some of its cultural appeal. In light of the new social movements that gained force after World War II, such as civil rights, student movements, and second-wave feminism, women's clubs and their polite—if still often subversive—tactics of social influence seemed, some felt, old-fashioned and no longer necessary.

The following chapter sketches these historical moments: the Civil War emergence of the charity cookbook, the following postwar popularity of the compiled fundraising cookbook, and the supposed drop in popularity of the genre in the second half of the twentieth century as American activism changed drastically and feminism in particular had women moving out of the kitchen and into the workforce. However, the final section also brings some of these historical claims into question—particularly, that women's increased presence in the American workforce and grassroots political movements equated to less engagement with cooking and women's voluntary groups.

The Charitable Cookbook's Civil War Origins

The community cookbook as it is known today traces its history back to 1864, first appearing in the North during the Civil War at a women-run sanitary fair in Philadelphia. From the very beginning, the books were intimately tied to women's voluntary labor and negotiated participation in society. Although in the decades leading up to war pioneering women ran newspapers, published books, organized strikes, and campaigned for legislative change, on the whole and in society's perception, women remained chiefly wives and mothers, whose primary roles centered around the home. During this time in American history, nearly two million Black women were enslaved, marriage laws meant women were in essence "civilly dead," women of all backgrounds and races lacked the right to vote, and there was a widespread "taboo on female public speaking."[3]

At a time when strict societal rules limited their participation in public life, women were nonetheless motivated to find ways of engaging in the war effort. Evidence of this can be found in the 1867 book *Six Hundred Dollars a Year: A Wife's Effort at Low Living, Under High Prices*, in which the author, who goes unnamed, recounts a conversation she had in 1862 with her cousin Lucy:

> "For," as [Lucy] remarked, "what else can we women do, at such a time as this? We cannot fight ourselves, but can help those who can, and comfort those who have fallen, from wounds or sickness, by our sympathy, our prayers, and our offerings." . . .

> "Certainly, Lucy," I answered, "but who will take the lead?"
>
> "If there is no one else, then why not yourself?" she asked, emphatically. "These are not the times for any to lack courage when duty calls us. Come, I will go with you, and let us see what can be done now, this very day."[4]

After this rousing speech, the two women then go to speak to wealthy members of town and together form a Ladies' Aid Society to assist in the war effort.[5]

This example shows how women, restricted in how they could be publicly involved, nonetheless threw themselves into the war effort in a variety of ways, finding or creating their own opportunities for engagement. In the Northern states, many women participated through involvement in the United States Sanitary Commission, an organization that was modeled after Florence Nightingale's work to improve sanitary conditions for soldiers during the Crimean War. As part of the Sanitary Commission, women worked as volunteer nurses, sewed shirts and blankets, and organized homes for returning soldiers. During these years and, as Henry Whitney Bellows, the founder of the Sanitary Commission, commented, "Hundreds of women evinced talents there, which, in other spheres and in the other sex, would have made them merchant-princes, or great administrators of public affairs."[6]

In addition to these voluntary efforts, a chief way in which women participated was by raising funds for injured soldiers, for example, by learning to set type and putting out their own printed circulars that solicited funds from readers.[7] The most successful fundraising endeavor undertaken by women in the North, however, was the organization of Sanitary Fairs. These fundraising bazaars raised money through general entry fees, admission sales to special art exhibits and performances, and the sale of food and other goods. The fairs "pull[ed] people together around a common cause in a way that was immensely pleasurable," and offered amusement as well as distraction to visitors who could spend their money easily knowing that it was going toward a worthy cause.[8]

For many women voluntary work for the Sanitary Commission was an opportunity to employ the organizational skills they had learned as part of their engagement with other social causes, such as abolition and temperance.[9] By the time of the Civil War, and inspired by the popularity of world fairs, women in America had already held numerous fairs for the benefit of various benevolent causes, finding that "nothing could generate more money faster than a fair."[10] Women put this knowledge to good use in their organization of Sanitary Fairs across the North, with a single fair being able to raise up to $100,000 in funds.[11]

At the Civil War Sanitary Fairs, women made clever use of their position within society to raise funds: selling goods, organizing events, hosting popular tasting luncheons, and, in general, "actively producing a distinctive public sphere."[12] Due to their connection to women, earlier fairs were sometimes referred to as "ladies'" or "fancy" fairs, and, as Barbara Kirshenblatt-Gimblett points out, women were organizers not only of Sanitary Fairs but also an "attraction" that would bring in more visitors. "Indeed," she writes, "beautifully outfitted respectable women en masse in public was a 'brilliant spectacle,' as the male reporters of the period were fond of writing."[13] The presence of these kind "ladies," one reporter noted at the time, inspired men to purchase a little more freely than they otherwise might: "The ladies are irresistible creatures. . . . Unless one goes clad in an armour of cold selfishness and callous heartedness to attend one of these attractive exhibitions, he is sure to come away with his hat and his pockets filled with comical merchandise, and perhaps the loss of his [heart]." Both Beverly Gordon and Barbara Kirshenblatt-Gimblett argue that the frivolity of fairs was carefully and cleverly constructed, with Gordon asserting that this was, for women, "a powerful playing at being powerless."[14]

Although the women directly involved in the organization of Sanitary Fairs were often white and of middle-class means, Black women, although less often recognized for their efforts, also participated to support the Sanitary Commission. For instance, Susan Paul Vashon, a Black abolitionist from Missouri, organized a Sanitary Fair in Pittsburgh "for the benefit of black refugees."[15] Southern Black women also raised funds locally within their own networks and sent these funds on to the northern Sanitary Commission.[16] With the help of all these women, together the Sanitary Commission "earned and spent millions of dollars in aid of the soldiers." In the 1914 book *Lincoln: Addresses and Letters*, President Abraham Lincoln himself is quoted as saying at the close of one fair that "the chief agents in these fairs are the women of America. . . . I have never studied the art of paying compliments to women. But I must say, that if all that has been said by orators and poets since the creation of the world in praise of women were applied to the women of America, it would not do them justice for their conduct during this war."[17]

It was against this backdrop, in 1864 at the Great Sanitary Fair in Philadelphia, that a new kind of charitable cookbook is believed to have first appeared.[18] Books were a common fundraising object at Sanitary Fairs, with not only cookbooks but also souvenir catalogs of fair exhibits, books of poetry, and humorous books of caricatures accompanied by verse being available for purchase.[19] Although the book titled *A Poetical Cook-Book*, written by Maria J. Moss, was not the first cookbook to be sold during or for the Civil War with benevolent aims, it is nonetheless often cited as the first charitable or fundraising cookbook. While cookbook bibliographer Margaret Cook identifies two other Civil War–era cookbooks from Northern states, those books, again inspired by Nightingale and the British Sanitary Commission, were published for the purpose of instructing nurses on how to prepare healthy food for injured soldiers.[20] *A Poetical Cook-Book*, on the other hand, was sold at the fair to benefit a good cause, and, like the other humorous books sold at Sanitary Fairs, its contents were meant to entertain.

In contrast to these instructional cookbooks, Moss offered her book not as a remedy for the ill-nutrition of soldiers but rather as a way to lift spirits and raise charitable funds. As the name suggests, in addition to recipes, the book, as figure 1 shows, contained many poetic quotations, usually ones that dealt with food, beverages, and cookery, with the cookery-related words being helpfully italicized for emphasis. Original verses by the author were also included in Moss's cookbook, as were two rhyming recipes for "Stewed Duck and Peas" and "Oatmeal Pudding."[21] Like the Sanitary Fair, *A Poetical Cook-Book* was an amusing but also worthwhile distraction from the war. For these reasons the book is understood to be the first charitable or fundraising cookbook of this kind, paving the way for the many community cookbooks that would soon follow.[22]

However, unlike the many communally authored cookbooks that appeared after the Civil War's end, *A Poetical Cook-Book* had a single author and was in fact originally written "some years" before the fair.[23] Moss was involved in the fair's organization and donated her book to be sold for the purposes of raising funds. As Carol and John Fisher write, women attending the fair in Philadelphia might have seen in the cookbook something they themselves could emulate, "especially if other members of their group could

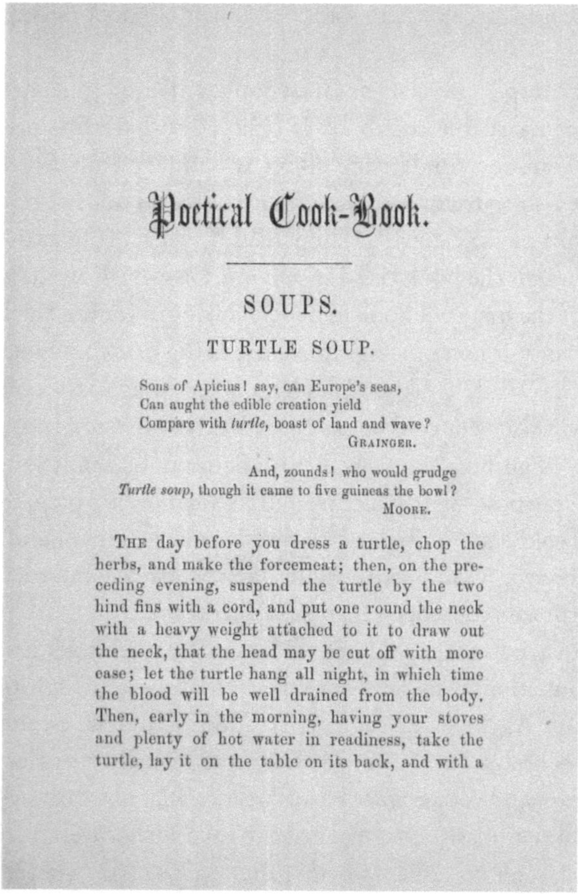

Poetical Cook-Book.

SOUPS.

TURTLE SOUP.

Sons of Apicius! say, can Europe's seas,
Can aught the edible creation yield
Compare with *turtle*, boast of land and wave?
GRAINGER.

And, zounds! who would grudge
Turtle soup, though it came to five guineas the bowl?
MOORE.

THE day before you dress a turtle, chop the herbs, and make the forcemeat; then, on the preceding evening, suspend the turtle by the two hind fins with a cord, and put one round the neck with a heavy weight attached to it to draw out the neck, that the head may be cut off with more ease; let the turtle hang all night, in which time the blood will be well drained from the body. Then, early in the morning, having your stoves and plenty of hot water in readiness, take the turtle, lay it on the table on its back, and with a

FIGURE 1. A page from Maria J. Moss's *A Poetical Cook-Book*, 1864. Katherine Golden Bitting Collection on Gastronomy, Library of Congress, Washington, D.C.

be enlisted to contribute some of their favorite recipes, making the project easier and less time-consuming."[24]

Rather than being the first community or compiled cookbook, *A Poetical Cook-Book* is perhaps more accurately described as the book that provided a model or template for community cookbooks. With its lighthearted tone, inclusion of poetic and artistic content, connection to a specific place and event, and its benevolent intention of raising charitable funds, in a variety of ways, *A Poetical Cook-Book* set the stage for the fundraising cookbooks that were soon to appear in great number. As with *A Poetical Cook Book*, the aim of these community cookbooks that followed on from Moss's book remained to raise money for charity. Poetry and humor—later often including the use of puns as well as a noticeable "passion for alliteration"—continued to be common elements.[25] That *A Poetical Cook-Book* was influential to the development of this genre can be seen in the tongue-in-cheek poem from Owen Meredith's *Lucille* that opens *A Poetical Cook-Book*:

We may live without poetry, music, and art;
We may live without conscience and live without heart;
We may live without friends; we may live without books;
But civilized man cannot live without cooks.
He may live without books—what is knowledge but grieving?
He may live without hope—what is hope but deceiving?
He may live without love—what is passion but pining?
But where is the man who can live without dining?[26]

This poem has continued to appear in numerous community cookbooks that followed, in differing and sometimes truncated forms, and long after ladies' benevolent fairs fell out of popularity.[27] These reoccurring instances of the poem in various community cookbooks throughout the decades are like a trail of breadcrumbs, leading back to that very first book.

Community Cookbooks and Women's Clubs

Not long after the end of the Civil War, in March 1868, the New York Press Club hosted an event at Delmonico's restaurant for author Charles Dickens, who was just finishing his tour of the United States. Although organized through the New York Press Club and ostensibly open to all of the city's press, when female journalists attempted to secure tickets, they were not automatically allowed to attend. Initially considering the women's request to be a joke, the Press Club replied to one woman journalist, Jane Cunningham Croly, or Jennie June, as she was also called, saying that she could in fact attend but only so long as she found enough women to pay the ticket price. Sent just three days before the event was meant to take place, the reply was, Cunningham later wrote, a "churlish and conditional assent" that amounted to a "practical refusal."[28]

As a result of this incident, Croly, unhappy with the treatment of women by the Press Club, decided to form one of the first secular women's clubs in America. Called "Sorosis," a term from botany that refers to a fruit with many seeds, the club offered women opportunities to learn, work on charitable causes, and come together with others who similarly felt "hungry for the society of women."[29] Sorosis, as well as the New England Woman's Club, which was formed the same year, led the way for many other clubs across the nation and began what has since been called the women's club movement. For her part Croly went on to become the founder not only of Sorosis but also of the General Federation of Women's Clubs.

Women's clubs were popular as they offered a socially acceptable way for women to participate in the public sphere, and, through their philanthropic efforts, clubwomen furthered community, national, and even international betterment. From 1870 on such clubs were formed and run through voluntarily effort and organized to suit local demand. "Everywhere," Croly wrote, "groups of women were found who eagerly seized the idea and shaped it according to their own conditions and needs."[30] And as women's clubs gained popularity across the nation, so too did the community cookbook.

The main producers of community cookbooks were women's clubs and their members, and the popularity of community cookbooks can be tied to this rise of women's groups in America. At a time when women were denied widespread access to employment and education, women's clubs provided a way for women to gain knowledge, skills, and personal connections. Involvement in women's clubs and ladies' aid associations was one popular and socially acceptable way for women to come together, and, in the decades after the Civil War, clubs gave women access to the public sphere and a means to influence their communities. Women met in dedicated clubhouses or even their own homes, blending household and voluntary work (see, for instance, figure 2).

Writing in 1898 about the history of women's clubs, Croly noted the usefulness of the club for women in America, stating, "The club, from the beginning, accomplished two purposes. It provided a means for the acquisition of knowledge, the training of power; and the working of a spirit of human solidarity, a comprehension of the continuity of life: its universal character of interdependence. It is not too much to say that this aspect changed the whole point of view of the woman who came under its influence. Her ideals were elevated, her trust in eternal goodness and its purpose strengthened, and her own possibilities as a social and intellectual force, brought out and gradually moulded into form."[31] Whether or not women were molded by their involvement in such clubs, they did join in large numbers. In 1906 membership recorded by the General Federation of Women's Clubs was five

FIGURE 2. Meeting of the women's club, Tygart Valley Homesteads, West Virginia, June 1939. Photograph by John Vachon. Black-and-White Negatives, Prints and Photographs Division, Farm Security Administration, Office of War Information, Library of Congress, Washington, D.C.

hundred thousand, with clubs "extending into almost every town and city in our own land."[32] In addition to the many federated clubs, women also created and joined their own locally formed clubs, with Janice Bluestein Longone noting that there were "literally hundreds of smaller groups"—a great number of which produced cookbooks—"to benefit every conceivable cause in the United States."[33]

Of the groups that published cookbooks, many had connections to local Protestant churches, and it is for this reason that the books are often associated with churches as a genre and sometimes called "church cookbooks." However, community cookbooks have, since the very start, been a type of book that has appealed to groups with different interests. Like the institution of the women's club itself, community cookbooks were a highly customizable as well as acceptable way for woman to raise funds and engage in life outside the home, and a wide diversity of women's organizations, clubs, and auxiliaries published cookbooks as fundraising projects. In the initial decades after the Civil War, an impressive variety of groups from a number of states compiled and sold community cookbooks. Between the years of 1860 and 1915, as Longone reports,

> There were a multitude of other organizations, causes, and groups, including Brethren Church, Business & Professional Women, Catholic Church (five from five states), cemetery associations, children's charities, Christ Church, Christian Church, Christian Temperance Union, Confederate Relief, Congregational Church, D.A.R., Dorcas Society, Eastern Star, Epworth League, fairs and expositions, granges, home economics and domestic science organizations, Homes for the Friendless, hospitals, Jewish charities (twenty-two from twelve states), King's Daughters, libraries, Lutheran Church, Moravian Church, Quaker groups, Reformed Church, Sanitary Commission and Civil War, schools (forty-eight from twenty-two states including Washington, D.C.), sororities, Trinity Church, Unitarian Church, United Daughters of the Confederacy, Universalist Church, vegetarian groups (four from three states); Women's Exchange (nine from six states), Women's Relief Corps and G.A.R., women's suffrage proponents, and YMCA and YWCA.[34]

The groups, therefore, ranged in the makeup of their membership as well as in their focus, from the arts to national political action.

Making use of women's everyday domestic knowledge and monetizing it through cookbook sales, women created a means through which they were able to exert influence on, affect, and shape American society. In general the reliance on preexisting recipe materials as the main source of community cookbook content made it possible for a range of groups to gather materials and produce books. The recipes included in these compilations did not need to be complicated or fancy—they did not even need to be original—but were instead lauded for being "tried and tested," a common title of many an early community cookbook. And by attaching contributor names to the individual recipes, such as in *The Cleveland Sorosis Cook Book* from 1916 (see figure 3), the person donating the recipe gave public assurance that the recipe included was good. Furthermore, including contributors' names personalized the books and served to embed them in a network of women's social ties. As Kirshenblatt-Gimblett puts it, community cookbooks "formalized the informal exchange of recipes among women [and] moved the culinary

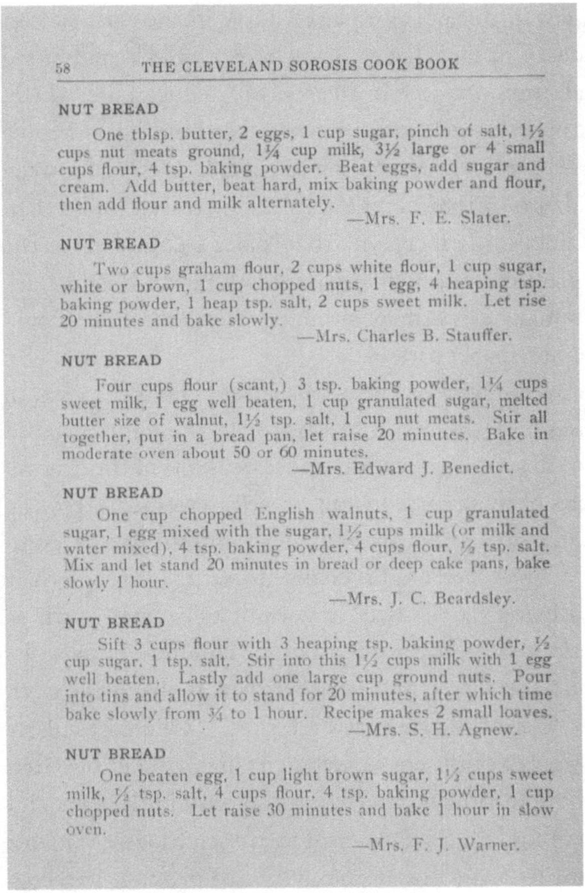
58 THE CLEVELAND SOROSIS COOK BOOK

NUT BREAD

One tblsp. butter, 2 eggs, 1 cup sugar, pinch of salt, 1½ cups nut meats ground, 1¼ cup milk, 3½ large or 4 small cups flour, 4 tsp. baking powder. Beat eggs, add sugar and cream. Add butter, beat hard, mix baking powder and flour, then add flour and milk alternately.

—Mrs. F. E. Slater.

NUT BREAD

Two cups graham flour, 2 cups white flour, 1 cup sugar, white or brown, 1 cup chopped nuts, 1 egg, 4 heaping tsp. baking powder, 1 heap tsp. salt, 2 cups sweet milk. Let rise 20 minutes and bake slowly.

—Mrs. Charles B. Stauffer.

NUT BREAD

Four cups flour (scant,) 3 tsp. baking powder, 1¼ cups sweet milk, 1 egg well beaten, 1 cup granulated sugar, melted butter size of walnut, 1½ tsp. salt, 1 cup nut meats. Stir all together, put in a bread pan, let raise 20 minutes. Bake in moderate oven about 50 or 60 minutes.

—Mrs. Edward J. Benedict.

NUT BREAD

One cup chopped English walnuts, 1 cup granulated sugar, 1 egg mixed with the sugar, 1½ cups milk (or milk and water mixed), 4 tsp. baking powder, 4 cups flour, ½ tsp. salt. Mix and let stand 20 minutes in bread or deep cake pans, bake slowly 1 hour.

—Mrs. J. C. Beardsley.

NUT BREAD

Sift 3 cups flour with 3 heaping tsp. baking powder, ½ cup sugar, 1 tsp. salt. Stir into this 1½ cups milk with 1 egg well beaten. Lastly add one large cup ground nuts. Pour into tins and allow it to stand for 20 minutes, after which time bake slowly from ¾ to 1 hour. Recipe makes 2 small loaves.

—Mrs. S. H. Agnew.

NUT BREAD

One beaten egg, 1 cup light brown sugar, 1½ cups sweet milk, ½ tsp. salt, 4 cups flour, 4 tsp. baking powder, 1 cup chopped nuts. Let raise 30 minutes and bake 1 hour in slow oven.

—Mrs. F. J. Warner.

FIGURE 3. A page from Cleveland Sorosis's *The Cleveland Sorosis Cook Book*, 1916. Library of Congress, Washington, D.C.

expertise of women from private interpersonal transaction into a coordinated collective enterprise."[35] This strategy was so popular that, by the turn of the century, printed community cookbooks were an established part of the American cookbook and fundraising landscape, with at least three thousand community cookbooks published by women in America from the Civil War to 1915.[36]

Selling cookbooks was not only a popular but also a reliable fundraising endeavor. Unlike traditional trade publishers that increasingly felt the need to "provide novelty at all costs" and make speculative—as well as risky—decisions, community cookbook compilers hit on a publishing model that was relatively stable and that could usually be counted on to raise substantial funds.[37] Technological advancements also played a role in the early success of community cookbooks. The fact that so many books could be published was a result of industrialization, evident in all areas of American life, which, for the book, meant the mechanized production of paper, binding, and typesetting, as well as steam-run presses. According to Scott E. Casper, between 1850 and 1880, the number of printers and publishers increased "more than fivefold." Even as book publishing increased, that "paled in number" to the printing of ephemeral print matter, such as pamphlets, playbills, and community cookbooks.[38] In many cases the printing of early community cookbooks was done by local newspaper presses.

Women's clubs collectively compiled and published cookbooks as a way to raise funds for the causes they deemed important, and the publication of cookbooks to raise funds in support of various causes was one of the innovative strategies and legacies of these enterprising American women. Growing out of in-person gatherings and primarily used as a fundraising tool, community cookbooks could affect meaningful change in society through their sales, with some causes being particularly important to women, such as Parent-Teacher Associations and proper nutrition for children, but also issues such as temperance, a social reform movement that "probably included more women than any other of the century's reforms."[39] One particularly popular institution for women of the era was women's literary clubs: gender-segregated clubs focused on reading that were popular with both Black and white women, typically of middle-class means. Literary clubs were valuable as women were, according to Anne Bower, "often limited in access to recognized status-bearing discourse forms such as poetry and fiction."[40]

However, even if focused primarily on literature, these clubs were, according to Elizabeth Long, "not merely local literary gatherings but a broad-based social movement."[41] Existing at a "meso" or "semipublic" level of society, women's literary clubs were sites of learning, but they also fostered self-expression, identity-formation, and the social activism of women.[42] Not only did literary clubs teach members how to effectively organize, but they also provided trusted spaces for interrogating the status quo through reading and discussion. For example, through examination of literary heroines, women in literary clubs "explore[d] women's identities and social roles."[43] Both Elizabeth Long and Elizabeth McHenry note that members of women's literary clubs were not just consumers of texts but also often producers.[44] Literary clubs could inspire textual production, and, within turn-of-the-century

Black women's clubs, McHenry states that this "resulted in the increased production and circulation of printed texts in the form of newspapers, magazines, pamphlets, and bound books."[45]

Community cookbooks were one such "bound book" that many women's groups and literary clubs produced, and the popularity of reading and literature as a way to gain independence may explain the abundance of poetry and quotations present in community cookbooks, going back as it does to the very first book in the genre.[46] In community cookbooks women found an outlet for their literary interests and a space to display their knowledge outside of the kitchen for their friends and peers.

The books were, then, useful to women in more ways than one, and, like the body of the women's club itself, the books as compiled texts could be crafted to suit a diversity of needs and aims. A reform-minded club might include a foreword explaining the evils of alcohol in their book; the rise in women's formal training in domestic science might be evident in discussions of health and recipes for nutritious eating; added poems could display erudition; and photographs, though rarely included during these early decades, honored and uplifted important members of the community.[47] Letters from politicians and celebrities were also a common method of letting readers know that the fundraising cause the purchase of the book contributed to was supported by people in high places.[48] Furthermore, the cookbooks often took on the function of historical documents. "From the very first days," Kelly writes, "community cookbooks recorded memories and history in addition to recipes."[49] As historical texts, the cookbooks listed dates of local events and names of club members and gave church and organizational histories. Books might also include historical recipes from past generations of women, with an example being the *Indian Cook Book*, through which a Native American women's club used the cookbook to preserve historical information on Native foods and preparation methods.[50]

The inclusion of all these features gave community cookbooks their special appeal. Cookbook producers understood that their cookbooks were about more than recipes alone, and that extra features, such as poetry and the recording of women's names, made the books even more desirable for purchase. In the 1891 *Alumnae Cookbook*, the compilers addressed this specifically within their cookbook's pages. The book includes a fictional "Overheard," a record of a conversation between a husband and wife (Mr. and Mrs. Public), about the merits of buying the book. "I thought you were already supplied with cookbooks, my dear," says Mr. Public, to which the wife, Mrs. Public, addresses the reader, "Now isn't that like a man?" Mrs. Public then explains to her husband—and the potential purchaser—how this cookbook is unique. The recipes in the book, she says, have been contributed by previous alumnae of the Philadelphia Normal School and that each is vouched for as "good" by its contributor. Mrs. Public further attests to the value of seeing her friends, now scattered across the country, represented on the pages, saying, "Turning at random the leaves of this little volume, I recognize the names of ladies, one of whom, I know, now lives in California, another in Minnesota, still another in Texas." This humorous addition of the "Overheard" illustrates the multifaceted appeal community cookbooks had early on. Not merely "a bundle of recipes like all the rest of its kind," as Mr. Public at first believes, community cookbooks differed by the fact that they benefited worthy causes, displayed women's skills and interests, materialized sentimental ties to social networks, and offered readers tested recipes that could be counted on.[51]

Finally, community cookbooks could influence society beyond the funds they raised through the spread of textual content. The making of a community cookbook gave women an activity to gather their efforts around, and, to quote Longone, "at a time when American women were without full political rights and representation, they found the community cookbook one very effective way to participate in the public life of the nation."[52] It does not seem incidental that these books, at times so fervent in their political aims and originating from a historical period that discouraged a woman from speaking publicly, are cookbooks. The 1915 *Suffrage Cook Book*, for example, advocated strongly for women's enfranchisement. The book is full of recipes, letters, and notes of encouragement, and figures from the women's suffrage movement receive special attention—such as a photograph of and letter from Margaret Sanger, an early proponent of birth control. But the book does not back away from or obscure its genre. Recipes are included from women involved in the movement, such as Jane Addams and, from abroad, British suffragette Lady Constance Lytton.[53] Moreover, the foreword makes plain that food is an essential part of society, one not to be overlooked: "Eating and drinking are so essential to our living and to our usefulness, and so directly involved with our future state, that these must be classed with our sacred duties. Hence the necessity for so educating the children that they will know how to live, and how to develop into hale, hearty and wholesome men and women, thus insuring the best possible social and political conditions for the people of this country."[54] Food and good nutrition were not seen as being separate from concerns of society, and the *Suffrage Cook Book* made the case that the political body was tied to the physical body of its citizens.

The cookbook genre provided a socially acceptable platform for social activism, and the publication of cookbooks allowed suffragists to craft what Jessica Derleth has described as a "feminine persona." According to Derleth, women used this textually constructed persona to demonstrate that "enfranchising women would not threaten the vital institutions of home and family."[55] Community cookbooks can then be understood as a subversive way that women who were not yet enfranchised engaged in and influenced the public sphere from the symbolic domain of the kitchen.

After women's enfranchisement the era of women's negotiated public engagement seemed—at least on the surface—to be slowly coming to an end. Although women's voluntary clubs continued to exist and community cookbooks continued to be published in the 1930 and 1940s—including, in these decades, books dealing with such concerns as how to cook on an extreme budget or according to war rations—the status of both of these began to change in the eyes of American society. "As long as women had virtually no access to the professions or business," Anne Firor Scott notes, "the leadership of voluntary associations was of an extremely high caliber."[56] However, as women brought their talents into new domains—including to professional fundraising—the perception of ladies' clubs and their charitable cookbooks no longer seemed as vital, necessary, or timely.[57]

New Social Movements After World War II

Although neither women's voluntary organizations nor community cookbooks ever disappeared, the political influence and social status of both seemed to diminish somewhat in the second half of the twentieth century, especially as, after World War II, "society changed almost beyond recognition."[58] Women's voluntary associations—such as popular Junior Leagues, groups "committed to serving their communities through worthwhile service projects"—and women's church auxiliaries continued to exist into these decades.[59] However, these groups were joined on the scene by "a bewildering proliferation of single-issue associations [many of which] included both sexes."[60] As such, women's voluntary associations were no longer as necessary a means for women's political expression. As one woman commented at the time about members of the women's Junior League "in 1974, the ladies seemed anachronistic."[61]

From the outside women's associations were increasingly viewed as conservative and populated with a privileged membership that, in some cases, might have done more to uphold class boundaries than break them down. Women's organizations were motivated, some argued, by a concept of noblesse oblige, or a societal obligation of the wealthy to give back to those in need, and for this reason often felt out of touch with the new wave of progressive social movements sweeping the country—including civil rights, the New Left student movement, and second-wave feminism.[62] Within feminist circles such clubs were sometimes seen as working against the interests of women; indeed, some were, and this tension can be seen in the 1985 satire-themed issue of the feminist magazine *Heresies*, in which a tongue-in-cheek piece written by "Virginia Cholesterol" discusses work in the fictional voluntary women's group Ladies Against Women (LAW).[63] With a reference to a "Phyllis," the piece is likely a thinly veiled commentary on conservative activist Phyllis Schlafly and her Stop ERA! campaign. As a result of antifeminist activists like Schlafly, who famously used homemade bread as a political lobbying tactic and who wrote in a 1986 Eagle Forum cookbook about her hope to "restor[e] traditional values," there was a feeling that women's groups and their cookbooks were increasingly "positioned as part of a larger political battle against feminism."[64]

Additionally, as men and women joined the fight for civil rights, women's clubs, which had historically favored "non-aggressive" strategies, seemed somewhat out of step with the times.[65] For example, in the parody recipe "Pie for a Suffragist's Doubting Husband" included in the *Suffrage Cook Book*, the reader is instructed to mix the "ingredients" "with tact and velvet gloves."[66] In contrast to this "velvet gloves" strategy of social influence, the leaders of many civil rights, student movement, and feminist groups favored direct action tactics, such as marches, public demonstrations, and sit-ins.[67] Although primarily nonviolent, these tactics aimed to confront the American public with issues of injustice, and, thanks in no small part to the efforts of these movements, the lives of women in America changed considerably over the next several decades.

While women of the 1950s and 1960s lacked many of the legal rights held by men—women, for example, needed a man's signature to get a credit card, discrimination based on gender was not outlawed at the federal level, and laws rarely protected women from sexual harassment and domestic violence—by the end of the 1980s, the legal and social position of women in America was drastically different.[68] The 1950s saw women return to the home and the kitchen, at least in the imagination of many Americans, with women again cast in the symbolic role as wives and mothers at the center of these family units.[69] Although the reality was often significantly different from the ideal, and economic demands meant that many women had no choice but to work outside the home at least part of the time, media depictions of women as well as women's limited legal rights served to reinforce these ideas.[70] The decades following, however, traced a road paved with legal, political, and social gains, seeing women join the workforce, politics, and activist movements in greater numbers.

With the Civil Rights Act of 1964, "discriminatory practices against African Americans, other minorities, and women began to erode in earnest."[71] Women had increased control over their health and bodies as the birth control pill became widely accessible in the 1960s and as the court case *Roe v. Wade* made abortion legal in all fifty states in 1973. These court rulings greatly affected the lives of women in America, and "one-third of the wage gains that women have made since the 1960s is the direct result of access to the birth control pill."[72] Greater control over family planning had educational and professional consequences for women in America, and "by 1970, 50 percent of single women and 40 percent of married women were participating in the labor force."[73]

Many of the changes taking place during these decades connected to and were furthered by women's activists and the women's liberation movement, which began to be discussed in America in the 1960s and gained force in the early 1970s. Within this new "wave" of feminism, women began to question and resist common gender norms, societal expectations, and legal inequalities.[74] Although inspired by the civil rights movement, the second wave of feminism, like the first, struggled with issues of representation and inclusivity. As Sara M. Evans has written, "Despite the intimate link between the movements for racial justice and for women's rights, the issues affecting women of color were treated as anomalies and frequently ignored," and lesbian women were also not always welcomed by members of the feminist "sisterhood."[75] A famous example of this is when Betty Friedan spoke of lesbians in the movement as a "lavender menace."[76] Yet, despite these tensions and struggles, the feminist movement—or movements, as it might more accurately be described—and women's rights activists helped bring about some of the most significant changes in the lives of American women in the second half of the twentieth century.

Women's organizations were founded to specifically combat issues that affected women, with the National Organization for Women (NOW), an incredibly visible force in the fight for women's rights, being founded in 1966. NOW had a broad statement of purpose, "to bring women into full participation in the mainstream of American society," but was sharply focused in its strategies. With an emphasis on providing equal employment opportunities, filing lawsuits in cases of discrimination, and creating opportunities for more women to work in the political arena, NOW worked largely within existing legal and political structures to ensure that women's rights were protected under the law.[77] The efforts of NOW and other feminist organizations were in many ways successful. By 1980 women made up 40 percent of the labor force, and 1992 was labeled by many in the press as "Year of the Woman" after a record number of women ran for and were elected to the U.S. Congress.[78] As women made these gains and a woman's "natural" role as wife, mother, and caregiver was questioned and as women moved into more public and political roles, there was an increasing belief—supported by some feminists—that cooking was an oppressive task, and an anticooking rhetoric emerged in many feminist debates and protests.[79]

There were, however, significant contradictions between what many of these new social movements espoused and what the realities of women's lives were. Within mixed-gender groups, women were not always empowered with leadership positions. In the group Students for a Democratic Society, founded in 1960, women did not always have equal status and found themselves performing roles based on their gender. With the organization led by verbose and charismatic men, women's voices were often overlooked or drowned out by louder, male voices, and similar comments have been made about misogyny and divisions of labor based on stereotypical gender roles within counterculture communes in the 1960s and early 1970s.[80] One woman involved in Students for a Democratic Society recalls that women "would sort of be expected to screw and make meals," also noting that women, not men, were typically the ones making copies. Considering that women were often in charge of typing and duplicating, it is perhaps not a coincidence that women used print as an outlet to express their concerns with the group, publishing a "Cassandra-like letter" in 1962.[81] A few years later, two female members of the Student Nonviolent Coordinating Committee, Casey Hayden and Mary King, published a similar open-letter titled "Sex and Caste," which called for more attention to women's issues within the group.[82] Even if women did not experience sexism within these social movements, they were likely to experience it as they moved into paid careers, as in the workplace the "self-confidence and organizational skills they learned in those other movements ran headlong into sexist expectations that they would automatically take notes or serve coffee."[83]

Despite the many gains of second-wave feminism and women's increased professional workloads, women's duties at home did not necessarily disappear or even significantly diminish as women increasingly joined the American workforce. Instead, working women often faced a "second shift," or, in other words, the "cooking, childcare, and cleaning that women still had to do once they returned home from their paid employment."[84] Cooking, then, remained a necessary and time-consuming part of life for many women, who were, to quote food critic and cookbook author Poppy Cannon, "engaged in frying as well as bringing home the bacon."[85] Even in the 1950s and 1960s, as the media continued to portray an idealized image of the "happy housewife," women were often faced with economic demands that meant they had no choice but to work outside the home. Erica Endrijonas describes the bind many women were in as such: "Buy processed foods but cook from scratch; be creative but follow directions precisely; accommodate all family members' preferences but streamline the food purchase and preparation process; work part-time but be a full-time homemaker; and do it all with little or no training."[86] Therefore, although the poles on what was socially expected had shifted across the decades—work or not work, cook or not cook—whether in the 1950s or 1980s, women were often tasked with having a job outside the home and also with taking care of domestic duties inside the home.

Finally, women's clubs, despite their diminished social status, remained important sites of community action and activism, particularly for women outside of major cities. Women's clubs offered women a way to take their skills—whether professional or domestic—and utilize them to make changes meaningful to them and their communities. More than this, women's clubs intersected with the new social movements of the era. Examining the ties between women's clubs after World War II and second-wave feminism, Melissa Estes Blair has argued that women's clubs "continued to allow women space to talk about their lives" and that "when the women's movement began sweeping the nation, . . . these organizations were primed to be receptive to its ideas and calls for action."[87] Similarly, as discussed in the following chapter, as new printing channels opened up publishing in accessible and affordable ways, the adaptable community cookbook was "primed" to be taken up by a multitude of groups for their own purposes while still being connected to the books' history as sites of women's knowledge production, community engagement, activism, and social participation.

CHAPTER TWO

From Cookie Cutter to DIY

Cookbook Printing After World War II

At the heart of this work is the supposed paradox of why, at a time of so many societal changes that seemed at odds with ideas of the domestic and culinary, women continued to create community cookbooks for charitable causes. Whereas early community cookbooks might have demonstrated women's subversive engagement through their use of culinary texts, community cookbooks from the middle and late twentieth century, on the other hand, offer a much more challenging narrative, in which women continued to turn to cookbooks as fundraising endeavors even after they were no longer as symbolically tied to the kitchen. Despite claims that the popularity of the cookbooks began to decline as women increasingly joined the American workforce and the women's movement, American library collections reveal that, between the years of 1950 and 1990, an enormous range of groups produced cookbooks for fundraising purposes—including, but certainly not limited to, books produced by beauty pageant contestants, military wives, Broadway casts, artist collectives, Jewish communities keeping kosher in Hawaii, refugee resettlement programs, and all-female barbershop choirs.[1] It seems, given this diversity of compiling bodies, that not only did community cookbooks remain popular with groups that had historically produced them but new groups—which had perhaps never sold a cookbook for fundraising purposes before—also began to take up cookbook self-publishing.

Individual publishing and organizational motivations are one way to address why groups—new and old—might have wanted to create and sell cookbooks, and later chapters look into why some of the most seemingly unlikely groups of the era made cookbooks. However, before the discussion of specific examples of individual compiling groups and their motivations, it is also necessary to look at the means of cookbook production, which affected how groups engaged in the self-publishing of community cookbooks. After World War II, significant changes took place in community cookbook production, with new options appearing as alternative and accessible channels for printing. A number of commercial printers and binders began to specialize in the production of fundraising cookbooks, offering package deals to compiling groups and breaking down the organization of cookbook projects into clear steps; added to this was the popularity and ubiquity of at-home and office printing technologies, which amateur producers could use to create cookbooks on even the thinnest of budgets.

This chapter first addresses community cookbooks as self-published books, which have since their emergence in the 1860s operated largely outside of the professional publishing industry and its channels of production and distribution.[2] The chapter then moves on to take a detailed look at the two new options for printing that began to appear and gain popularity in the late 1940s and early 1950s, considering how these material means of production affected content, longevity, and—importantly—sustained engagement with the community cookbook genre, arguing that accessible and affordable printing and binding options supported women's continued interest in fundraising through cookbook sales during these decades. Together the increased number of printing options offered groups more choice in how to produce their books than ever before.

Although the material output of such printing options is often considered to be formulaic or unimpressively amateur, as the following sections show, these printing options allowed women to produce cookbooks in ways that could match a variety of budgets and needs. More than this, groups would, as the final section details, move from one production channel to another between the printings or editions of their books as their circumstances, aims, and requirements changed. This flexibility made it possible for groups to keep their cookbook projects alive and to continue printing and selling cookbooks that might not have otherwise been feasible. Therefore, while the books produced using these methods may not always be perceived as the most beautiful or original, the existence of affordable channels of production can help to explain why increasingly "liberated" women in America continued to create charitable, fundraising cookbooks.

The Status of Self-Published Books

In 1982 Robert Darnton introduced a model that aimed to give a view of the different influences and agents that participate in the creation, distribution, and reception of printed texts. Called the communications circuit, the circular model maps the life cycle of a printed book as it moves in a linear fashion from agent to agent: author, publisher, printer, shipper, bookseller, and, last, the reader, within a field of economic, political, and social forces. Conceptualized as a holistic model, Darnton felt that "with minor adjustments, it should apply to all periods in the history of the printed book."[3] Some scholars of women's book history, however, have noted that the communications circuit, while perhaps applicable to vastly different periods, is "silent on the question of gender."[4]

In 2011, as a way to visualize the way gender plays a role in the processes of publishing, Katrina Melvin offered a revised communications circuit that makes just one small change to Darnton's model: moving authors out of the circuit of communication and placing them directly behind publishers. While a small adjustment, in this way Melvin makes a large statement about the role of publishers as gatekeepers, and through the model she attempts to depict the way publishers can be understood as guarding the gates of the circuit of communication: either blocking the way or allowing access.[5]

Melvin is by no means the first person to offer this kind of interpretation of industry publishers. In 1975 Lewis Coser, in the article "Publishers as Gatekeepers of Ideas," similarly described publishers as being "empowered to make decisions as to what is let 'in' and what is kept 'out.'"[6] Bibliographers Thomas Adams and Nicolas Barker have also argued for a greater recognition of publishing—not authorship—as the "point of departure" in the life cycle of the book, and Rachel Malik has gone further to suggest that publishing is itself a self-fulfilling practice that shapes, to a certain extent, what can be published.[7] Melvin's model, however, is unusual in how it illustrates the way mainstream publishing is not open and widely accessible to *women*—a situation that is worsened when thinking intersectionally.[8] The model asks, through one small change, that gender be considered as an influencing factor in how the decision to publish (or not publish) has historically been made.[9] The adjusted model also asks historians to consider how women might have otherwise found outlets for their textual pursuits and to search for their alternative routes to publication, such as through self-publishing.

Although underrepresented groups, such as women, have pursued ways of publishing outside of industry publishing channels—out of either necessity or their own simple desire to do so—often by making use of alternative technologies, the resultant productions are often seen as less professional and therefore less serious, valuable, or worthy of attention. That this is the case can be seen in discussions of publishing that often circle around the professional publishing industry, as though anything outside of this—independent publishing, vanity publishing, micropublishing, and self-publishing—is a deviant form.[10] Commenting on the perception of self-publishing, R. Lyle Skains writes,

> This prevailing attitude toward self-published authors, and even vanity presses, does not consider the many reasons people may have self-published, assuming only that they were not talented enough to make it in "real" publishing, or were too lazy to "pay dues," as it were, to get their work accepted in the royalty system. As can be seen by a simple browse of current self-publishing services, people self-publish for a variety of reasons, including local history or culture texts with limited audiences; family photo, recipe, or genealogy albums; education professionals producing learning materials; experimental projects without clear commercial avenues; and many other personal reasons that people create books outside the royalty system.[11]

Textual productions by women in America, as Jaime Harker and Cecilia Konchar Farr have noted, have often existed at the margins of established book industry models, produced in many cases within uniquely female networks and as part of feminine "shadow traditions." Such productions are made, they say, "outside of mainstream U.S. literary culture, where works by nonmale, nonwhite, non-straight, and nonprivileged writers reside." Operating outside of established and expected networks, however, affects the reception of women's material texts, and the authors go on to comment that "texts relegated to these shadows have been easily dismissed as less significant, less influential, and, emphatically, less beautiful."[12]

Community cookbooks are an example of how some books—and particularly self-published books by women—exist at the margins of many established publishing practices. The books do not, for instance, have a single author but are instead created by committees, compilers, editors, and recipe contributors; moreover, the books are not sold for commercial profit but rather to raise charitable funds. Further, as self-published books, community cookbooks are, in the majority of cases, not produced by professional publishers. Furthermore, and related to the "shadow traditions" discussed by Harker and Konchar Farr, community cookbooks produced for fundraising purposes have been variously discussed or dismissed for their physical form. Comments have been made regarding disorderly content and lack of editing, their "humble" or "modest" appearance, and their "murky publication credits"—aspects that relate to or can be explained by women's use of accessible channels of production that began to become popular during the second half of the twentieth century.[13]

The following sections detail changes that took place in the second half of the twentieth century in community cookbook production, taking a closer look at how the books were materially produced. Understanding the production methods and means of community cookbooks not only serves to spotlight women's alternative networks of communication but can also help answer the question of why women continued to make cookbooks during these years.

Commercial Cookbook Printers and Binders

Since their first appearance in the late nineteenth century and until the mid-twentieth century, community cookbooks were typically made through the assistance of printing services that provided the physical production of books. As Fisher and Fisher have noted, many early Missouri community cookbooks "were commonly printed at local print shops and at newspaper-printing facilities," and cookbooks included in the digital community cookbook collection at the Library of Congress, which contains books from the 1860s to 1929, show that this was a trend across the entire United States.[14] Many of the books in this collection list commercial printing companies and local newspaper presses—both of which offered their services for a fee—on cookbook title pages. The 1921 *Blue Hen's Chickens' Cook Book* from Milford, Delaware, was, for instance, printed by the local *Milford Chronicle* newspaper press; the 1913 *Central Congregational Church Cook Book* from Topeka, Kansas, was printed by the Trapp Print-Shop, also of Topeka; and the printers of the 1892 Chicago *St. Pauls Bazaar Kochbuch und Geschæftsfuehrer*, Fred Kressmann and Brother, are described in the book as "Commercial Printers, Lithographers and Blank Book Makers."[15]

Into the middle of the twentieth century, the self-publishing of community cookbooks continued to be facilitated in many cases by regional commercial printing companies. However, in addition to the continued reliance on general commercial printers, new options also appeared after the end of World War II, with one of the most significant changes being the appearance of commercial printers specialized in fundraising cookbooks. As Lynne Ireland has noted, by the 1980s community cookbooks were increasingly "published in standardized formats by regional printing and binding companies" that focused solely on printing fundraising, church, and charity cookbooks.[16] Between the years of 1950 and 1990, there were at least fourteen printers and binders that focused on community cookbook production (for a list of these printers, see appendix A). Tracing the history and development of these companies helps shed light on just what made these cookbook printers so attractive to women compilers and how the companies brought about changes to an established genre.

First appearing after World War II, many of the first printers of this kind had already been involved in the commercial printing business before the war. The earliest commercial printer focused on the production of community cookbooks seems to be Fundcraft, which began as a general printing business in the early 1900s. It was not until the 1940s, however, that the company printed its first cookbook for the local Methodist church. Other cookbook printers that emerged during these years included Bev-Ron Publishing Company, which was started around the same time, in 1947, just after the end of the war. Women's Clubs Publishing Company, whose name clearly reflects the company's marketing and sales strategy, was also in business by at least 1951. For these commercial cookbook printers and binders, the first decades after the war were ones of growth and expansion. In the 1950s Fundcraft "was the first printing company in eastern Kansas to purchase new offset printing equipment and add color printing to their cookbook printing methodology." The company grew enough in these decades to be able to purchase the rival cookbook printer North American Press, located in Kansas City, which had started business around 1945. With new printing equipment and the acquisition of North American Press, Fundcraft had the resources to print "more than 50,000 cookbook recipes each week."[17]

The commercial cookbook printers and binders that emerged during these decades differed from publishers in that they could be engaged for a set fee. Commercial printers and binders of fundraising cookbooks did not acquire books but rather printed them for a cost, and they were fairly indiscriminate about the books they helped create: recipes did not need to be tested or meet a certain level of quality, editing might take place but only for an additional fee, and the marketing of books was the sole responsibility of the compiling organization. Many of the most-used printers in community cookbooks were located in the Midwest, with women's groups from across the nation getting in touch and receiving books through the mail. Cookbook compiling associations making use of these services would send their recipes in by mail and later receive the bound book the same way.

Although the main task a of commercial cookbook printer and binder was, more than anything else, to bring a cookbook into physical existence, cookbook packages would also usually include the free indexing of recipes, content pages of standard weights and measures tables, and space allotted for information on local or group histories—a common feature in many community cookbooks from these decades. Moreover, for an additional fee, cookbook printers might offer limited assistance with layout and design, provide proofreading services, or include the option for a consultation call. Other extras offered on top of the basic printing and binding package could include standardized recipe forms for the collection of recipes, labeled envelopes for easy organization of recipes into categories, cover and divider page art for groups who did not want to submit their own artwork, and even suggestions for titles.[18] It is for this reason that a number of community cookbooks printed by these companies have identical or nearly identical titles—such as such as *Favorite Recipes* and *Butter 'n Love*—and cover art, making them difficult to distinguish from one another at first glance.[19]

Altogether commercial cookbook printers were equipped to take on many essential tasks in a cookbook's production and, moreover, provided compiling groups with a clear step-by-step process that they could follow. Significantly reducing the labor required of women compilers in producing a cookbook and demystifying the process of publishing, commercial printers contributed to a community cookbook landscape in which even a group with no prior publishing experience could easily compile, design, and publish a cookbook for fundraising purposes.

As companies like Fundcraft and Bev-Ron found success by shifting to the production of community cookbooks, new printing companies, interested in getting a piece of the community cookbook pie, joined the market in the 1970s and 1980s. Walter's Cookbooks, like Fundcraft, was not originally focused on cookbooks; however, the company moved into this area in the 1970s after its owner read an article in the *Wall Street Journal* about the profitability of cookbooks. Having previously been involved in direct mailing of catalogs, in 1971 he reportedly told his staff, "Look at this article. It says that for the first time in history cookbooks outsold the Bible. We're now in the cookbook business."[20] Jumbo Jack's Cookbooks started to print cookbooks in 1980, after the "owners of the local newspaper were approached by a nearby community to produce a centennial cookbook for their upcoming celebration," with the company initially printing just one cookbook per month.[21] Morris Press, which had been printing professionally since the 1930s, started its cookbook division in the 1980s as well. On their website the company explains this shift: "In the late 70s, commercial printing grew at a rapid rate due to a strong farm economy, until a recession hit in the early 80s. Recognizing the need for a broader sales base beyond the local market, Morris Press began a cookbook publishing division. In 1988, the decision was made to build a sales and production facility to meet the space requirements of the fast growing cookbook division."[22]

Commercial community cookbook printers and binders, though seemingly very successful in their business model, were, however, not always highly regarded for their material output. Writing on community cookbooks during these years, librarian Harriet Wintermute describes the books as having "formulaic, yet poor, composition," and cookbook advisers Helen Hays and Ellen Rolfes issued a warning to compiling bodies against using such printers. "*Beware*:" the two wrote, "a printing company may offer you the services of their designer. It sounds good, but you may find that all the books they print look alike."[23]

It is true that these printers tended to create books that had a standardized, at times almost "cookie-cutter," appearance. Books printed and bound by the company North American Press could, for instance, be almost identical in their appearance. Examples from the online collection Ephemerals: Cookbooks, Event Programs, and Directories made available on Internet Archive show four books with the title *Our Favorite Recipes* printed by North American Press, with their covers distinguishable from one another only by the name of the organization and photograph of a local landmark, usually a church; the layout, fonts, and even titles are otherwise largely the same.[24] Similarly, books held in the collection "Community and Church Cookbooks" from Northeastern Pennsylvania further show how the contents of books were also often similar in books printed by commercial printers.[25] For example, two books titled *Favorite Recipes from Our Best Cooks* printed by Circulation Service for groups located in Pennsylvania around 1977 are in many ways identical. In this case the covers differ, but all the photographic dividers are exactly the same and so too is much of the supplemental content—lists of equivalents and substitutions, cooking timetables, and ideas for how to use leftovers—offering an example of what Janice Bluestein Longone refers to as "canned" cookbook material.[26]

Yet, while many commercially printed cookbooks may be described as uninspiring and unoriginal, changes in production also had the effect of giving the compiling organization a degree control over the end product.[27] If opting to hire a commercial printer and binder, compiling groups could select from a number of customization options to communicate (albeit to a limited extent) the personality of their local organization—by making decisions about the cover image, the color of the binding, images appearing on section-divider pages, and in some cases the addition of quotes and expressions and advice, most often found at the bottom of the cookbook page. In the 1973 *Bergen Cook Book* by the church women of Bergen Lutheran Church and printed by General Publishing and Binding, advice and adages such as "the only food that never goes up in price is food for thought" and "housework is love made visible" appear every few pages.[28] Through these options for customization, women continued to be active participants in cookbook production as they compiled recipes, worked with printers, made artistic decisions, and chose supplemental content—a fact acknowledged by some printers more than others. Morris Press and Fundcraft, for example, fashioned themselves as publishers rather than printers and even went so far as to claim the copyright to the books they printed. Women's Clubs Publishing, on the other hand, clearly recognized the role women's organizations played in putting together these books, stating in the "Message from the Publisher" page found in many of their books, "This book has been published through the combined efforts of our company and the organization whose name appears on the cover."[29]

More than this, commercial cookbook printers brought about a significant change in how many community cookbooks were funded. One of the earliest printers of this kind, Bev-Ron—later renamed Cookbook Publishers—initially "contracted with community organizations to print their cookbooks at no cost, and sold advertising to local merchants to pay for the cost of production."[30] This was a standard practice for community cookbooks, and a book made before the 1950s might have an advertisement on nearly every other page. As the publishers of the 1925 *Midlothian Woman's Cook Book* write in their introduction, funds from advertisers "made possible" the cookbook's production.[31] On the other hand, early community cookbooks sometimes never managed to go into production due to lack of local advertising support.[32] However, this need for local advertisers to fund cookbook projects began to change in the postwar years. In the 1960s Bev-Ron made the decision to rely less on merchant advertising and on-the-road salesmen, and, instead of selling advertising space, Bev-Ron made the book itself the profitable commodity. As more commercial printers followed suit, the number of advertisements found in community cookbooks decreased dramatically. The result was that any group that could gather together enough funds to hire a cookbook printer could create their very own book—with or without local support.

Commercial cookbook printers and binders opened up one major and well-used avenue of cookbook production for women in the second half of the twentieth century, helping in no small part to increase the number of community cookbooks produced during these years. Such commercial printers, which focused primarily on the production of community and fundraising cookbooks, provided valuable services as they eased the production of cookbooks, from the initial phase of gathering recipes to delivering the completed books by mail. The inclusion of standardized content and even the facade of publisher might have been appealing to groups who aimed for a more professional and polished end product, even if the tradeoff was a community cookbook that was less of a reflection of its own local community.

Although often disparaged for their material output, the emergence of such printers and binders—such as Bev-Ron Publishing Company, Fundcraft, and Morris Press—was an important milestone in the history of community cookbook production and significantly affected the ways community cookbooks were produced. However, commercial cookbook printers were not the only newly accessible printing option to appear during these decades. As the next section explores, while a "revolution" of print connected to new duplication technologies allowed underground artists to produce more books, many community cookbook producers used the same DIY print technologies to create fundraising recipe collections.

At-Home and Self-Publishing Options

Although commercial cookbook printers provided one avenue of relatively affordable cookbook publishing for many groups, the cost of printing was nonetheless the main expenditure for most cookbook projects.[33] As Fisher and Fisher note, "Some organizers cut expenses by designing and duplicating their own cookbooks and covers."[34] For groups on a particularly tight budget, costs could be meaningfully reduced if women took on printing and binding duties themselves.[35] This option of duplicating one's own cookbook was made more feasible for a greater number of groups as the decades saw a noticeable rise of at-home print technologies, which could be cheaply purchased and which allowed groups to print at home in a variety of ways.

The increased access to affordable at-home printing technologies within community cookbook production between 1950 and 1990 can be placed as part of a more general increase of self-published works during the second half of the twentieth century. Printing technologies that enabled accessible self-publishing include typewriters; mimeographs and spirit duplicators; and, to a lesser degree, xerography or photocopying. Most of these technologies were invented well before the postwar period: The first commercial typewriter and the first mimeograph, for instance, both appeared in the nineteenth century, and photocopy technology was first introduced in the 1930s.[36] However, advances in their construction made these technologies more affordable, easier to use, and more widespread in the second half of the twentieth century. By the 1980s typewriters and duplicators were common sights in offices, churches, and many other business and community spaces. If not already available locally, such printing technologies could also be purchased for not terribly considerable sums. To give an example, in 1955 Marion L. Tallman wrote that it was cheaper to purchase a new mimeograph machine than to use a printing service for her school's annual publication, *Dial*. By choosing to have students print the annual on the newly purchased machine, costs were cut dramatically and no debt was incurred, something that Tallman notes was otherwise a rarity for such large school publications.[37]

Rob Banham describes this kind of copying technology as "direct printing," as it relies on "direct application of ink or toner to a substrate." Mimeograph duplication, a type of stencil duplication, made use of typewriters as a way to quickly create master stencils, which could then be used to create

FIGURE 4. Mimeographing the Farm Security Administration farmworkers' camp paper, Tulare County, California, February 1942. Photograph by Russell Lee. Black-and-White Negatives, Prints and Photographs Division, Farm Security Administration, Office of War Information, Library of Congress, Washington, D.C.

copies of a text. By changing the setting on a typewriter from type to stencil, a typist could use the typewriter keys to punch away space on an inserted stencil sheet, making the master. The sheet would be placed on a rotating inked drum (see, for example, figure 4), and, by pushing ink through the cut-away textual spaces onto a clean sheet of paper, a person looking to copy a text could quickly make a large number of identical copies—up to several hundred—in a relatively short amount of time.[38] Similar in process was spirit duplication, which also used a master sheet and was printed on a rolling drum, but which differed from mimeograph copying in that the master sheet itself contained the inked text to be transferred to later copies. As E. Haven Hawley notes, and unlike a mimeographed copy, "spirit duplication use[d] a second sheet bearing pigmented wax as a source of colorant rather than a stencil" and used aniline dyes, which were loosened from the master sheet for copying through application of an alcohol-based solvent.[39] By pressing a clean piece of paper against the dampened master, a copy was made.

This method of making copies was often used in offices, churches, schools, and community centers, for documents such as memos and worksheets.[40] While this mode of copying could also produce up to a few hundred copies, the technology had significant disadvantages as well. Copies made through spirit duplication would smell of alcohol, the loosening agent used in the printing process.[41] Printed texts would easily run or smudge, not only making the process messy but in some cases also leaving the human copier with a product that was difficult to read. The most common color ink for spirit duplication was purple, and copies made toward the end of a print run could be quite faded.[42] Despite such downsides, these technologies allowed printing to be more accessible than it had ever been before, enabling people to print materials without needing to go through a publisher, professional press, or local printer.

Although primarily designed for office use, such duplication technologies were quickly taken up for unintended and often subversive purposes and were part of what has since been named the "mimeograph revolution."[43] The era saw an explosion of unauthorized, underground, and radical printed productions in the 1960s and 1970s, thanks in no small part to the availability of duplicating machines.[44] In the introduction to their online bibliography, *From a Secret Location: Poetry, Little Mags, Small Presses, and Transient Documents from the Mimeo Era and Beyond*, Steve Clay and Rodney Phillips, for instance, write, "Direct access to mimeograph machines, letterpress, and inexpensive offset made these publishing ventures possible, putting the means of production in the hands of the poet. In a very real sense, almost anyone could become a publisher. For the price of a few reams of paper and a handful of stencils, a poet could produce, by mimeograph, a magazine or booklet in a small edition over the course of several days."[45] While the subversive creations of the "mimeograph revolution"—little magazines, poetry chapbooks, and fanzines—are perhaps the strongest associations with the technology, accessible print and duplication technologies were used by a broad range of producers, including community cookbook creators, who were looking to quickly and cheaply produce their own texts and books.[46]

Evidence of the use of such affordable copying technologies and trends in the production of community cookbooks can be found in the books themselves. In a number of community cookbooks, compilers make note of how the book was produced, either on the title pages or in introductory sections. Cookbook committees are often listed, at times described by the specific roles members played in the production process, such as typing or operating a mimeograph machine. To give one example, the introduction to the cookbook *Taste It Supper: Recipes from Forrest County Home Economics Alumnae of Mississippi Southern College* from 1961 thanks the two women responsible for collecting and compiling recipes as well as mimeographing copies of the book.[47] Similarly, in the 1977 Church of the Ascension cookbook, *Parish Cookbook: Festival '77, Garden of Eatin'*, the title page acknowledges the typist, Marion Dixon, and the individual who supplied the typewriter she used. In the latter instance, the typed pages were taken to be copied and bound by local printer Peter Kwik, who also added "spatter shields" to the final product. Although some groups did laboriously type every page of each cookbook they put on sale, duplicating copies with mimeographs or spirit duplicators could significantly lessen the amount of work that needed to go into to producing homemade books.[48] Cookbooks might even be sold to raise funds for purchasing printing equipment. In at least one documented instance, fundraising through cookbooks was used by the women of Greendale Peoples Church in Worcester, Massachusetts, to buy new church windows that had been damaged in a tornado and also to buy a mimeograph machine.[49]

In addition to listing the person responsible for running a mimeograph machine or doing the typing, cookbooks may also show material evidence of the printing technology used in their creation, with perhaps the most easy-to-identify option being the purple-colored ink of the spirit duplicator. Various organizations made use of this at-hand printing option, and books held in the Michigan State University's Cookery and Food Collection that were made using spirit duplicators include, for instance, *Amish Recipes: Some of "Our Favorites"* (1974); *Triune Business Girls Old and New, 1964–1976 Cookbook* (1976); *Czech Pastry*, by the American Bohemian Club (1950); *From Grandmother's Cookbook*, by Trinity Lutheran Church Women (1985); and *Smorgasbord Recipe Book*, by the Women's International League for Peace and Freedom (1969). A particularly noteworthy example from this collection is *The Green Book: Kitchen Tested Recipes from the Fairview Area*, compiled by the Fairview Parents and Teachers Association in 1970. Although it is unclear what, if any, specific significance the color green had to the book's compilers, in addition to including the word "green" in the title, they also chose to use the color for both the paper cover and the ink. However, by the time of printing the index at the end of the book, the green ink was, apparently, difficult to come by and the text changes abruptly from green to the more common purple.[50]

Like many of the books printed using office and at-home printing technologies, *The Green Book* additionally has a nonconventional binding—in this case, the book is bound by two plastic rings. Other common binding materials for cookbooks produced through at-home means include staples, string, metal ring fasteners, plastic binders, leather ties, and, most common of all, comb binding. Comb binding, also known as Cerlox binding, is a type of mechanical binding that uses fasteners to bind loose pages together (for an example of this type of binding, see the books in figure 5). Rectangular holes are cut into the pages, and the rings of a round plastic spine are inserted through the holes. These rings are plastic and flexible and can be opened up or removed at any time, which allows for the addition of new material to the book or reordering of pages. Comb was a highly popular binding choice for both at-home and commercial cookbook publishers, the latter of which sometimes touted the benefits of comb bindings within the self-advertising pages of their cookbooks—for example, noting how books with this binding would lie flat.[51] However, despite these supposed advantages, comb binding is not usually recommended for traditional publishing and bookselling. The plastic spine can easily be damaged, and, when facing out on a bookshelf, the spines do not display the title of the book. Another disadvantage to comb binding for traditional book sales is the difficulty of storing them vertically on a shelf. Comb binding is instead most frequently used for informal, short-lived, and professionally focused documents, such as course readers, homework packets, term papers, handbooks, and legal texts. Just as the mimeograph and spirit duplicator were printing technologies that many women and women's groups had at hand, so too did many offices and workplaces have binding machines for the informal binding of internal documents.[52]

These printing and binding options benefited community cookbook publishers, as they were affordable, keeping the cost of printing low, as well as accessible, being found in many offices, churches, and schools. In combination with the popularity of commercial cookbook publishers, the accessibility of at-home publishing technologies meant that women looking to publish a cookbook had a range of options at their disposal. If a group had a larger budget, they could cut down their workload by outsourcing the printing, binding, and some of the design—and perhaps even content—to a commercial

FIGURE 5. *Indian Cook Book* committee member Sadie Homer, with stacks of the finished books, date unknown. Courtesy of the Oklahoma Historical Society.

publisher. Groups with a tighter budget could still produce books by using printing options that were common and affordable. Both of these new printing and binding options, through their processes of production, changed the look and layout of many community cookbooks after 1950. More than this, the availability of multiple channels of production served to increase the popularity as well as the longevity of cookbook projects, and compilers were able to, as the next section addresses, move from one production method to another as needs dictated.

Any Group Can Publish

A closer look at the publishing history of select cookbooks made between 1950 and 1990 shows that a single compiling organization might change their production method depending on the resources available to them at a given time. While some groups were seemingly happy to stay with one printer for decades—for instance, the Freeman Junior College and Academy Women's Auxiliary used local printer Pine Hill Press for all eight editions of their cookbook *Pioneer Tradition, Modern Nutrition* between 1961 and 1989—other groups were compelled by internal or external factors to change the way their books were produced.[53]

In some instances groups initially created a book themselves, taking on the work of designing, typing, and binding, to then move to a commercial printer for a later edition once cookbook sales had increased and more funds were available. This was the case with the cookbook *Blue Print for the Cook*, by the Women's Architectural League of Detroit. First published in 1971, *Blue Print for the Cook* does not include any printer details. In such cases it can be assumed, if not absolutely determined, that the group produced the book using more at-hand printing methods. Five years later, however, and after the first edition proved to be a "'delicious' success," the second edition of *Blueprint for the Cook* was printed by Cookbook Publishers. At least two later printings of the book were also done through the commercial printer and binder.

In a similar example, the Sisterhood of Temple Beth Hillel-Beth El in Wynnewood, Pennsylvania, affiliated with the Women's League for Conservative Judaism, issued the "revised and enlarged" second edition of *Passoverama: A Collection of Favorite Recipes* in 1978. The first edition of the book, originally published in 1975, was reprinted and reportedly sold out the two following years. According to the New York Public Library holdings, the second edition was also reprinted at least once in 1980. A note in the 1978 book discusses the topic of book production and materiality, revealing a trajectory of cookbook printing by the Sisterhood that went from amateur and informal to more professional as time progressed. In the 1978 edition, the women write, "The first printing took place in 1975 in the basement of the synagogue. The collating was done around a table by Sisterhood women with their children playing in the corner. A second and third printing was done professionally and also sold out." At the same time, the 1978 edition gives credit to the women on the cookbook committee and lists their specific tasks, including editors, an artist, a layout designer, consultants, a typist, and a proofreader.

While in these instances groups were able to use sales from the more amateur books to fund further printings with a commercial company, this was not always the case. The compilers of the *Blue Denim Cook Book*, by the National Council of Jewish Women in Greensboro, North Carolina, felt the need to address the material condition of the cookbook they put out in 1975, giving readers a rare glimpse into how choices regarding production might be made. In the introduction to the book, which appears to be printed using stencil duplication and is bound by plastic rings, the compilers state that they initially intended for the book to be a second edition of their 1964 cookbook, *Council Cooking*. However, "inflation in the printing world prevented a commercial type reproduction of the original book and caused the chairmen to turn to a homemade version." And so, as Greensboro was the "largest producer of blue denim in the world" at the time, the women decided to use denim in the book's design as well as its name, using hand-painted denim for the book covers.[54] In this case a group moved from a commercial printer to self-printing using at-home methods, with accessible printing and binding options allowing the group to continue to produce a book when they might have otherwise been unable to do so due to lack of funds.

As these brief examples illustrate, a variety of printing and binding options can help to explain why women continued to create fundraising cookbooks in the second half of the twentieth century. While newly accessible printing and binding options made printing more affordable and in some instances more manageable, a variety of printing and binding channels also meant that cookbook compilers had a range of printing options to choose from. However, although this chapter argues that the continued interest in community cookbooks is due partly to the changing means of production, the possibility of accessible and affordable print does not equate to its use. That women continued to self-publish fundraising cookbooks must also be placed within the broad societal, political, and cultural changes taking place in the United States. In short, the existence of an affordable printing technology does not account for its use within certain communities and for specific purposes, and what must still be explained is why women—despite their increased presence in the workforce, engagement with new social movements, and supposed liberation from the kitchen and household duties—decided to self-publish and sell community cookbooks during these decades.

The following three chapters, then, aim to address these issues, taking a closer look at specific intersections of women's lives to better understand why, when it was perhaps most contradictory, a wide variety of women in America turned to cookbooks as a way to raise funds for good causes but also to affect change in their own lives. And, as the next chapter shows, while women were often interested in cutting down the cost of book production, they were not always worried about cutting down their own labor.

CHAPTER THREE

Women and Work

Between Paid and Unpaid Careers

As the previous chapter details, the many different printing and binding options available on the market could be used by groups with vastly different aims and budgets to produce cookbooks that were sold to raise funds and to better communities. However, although the books were easier to produce than ever before, the work that went into making community cookbooks was nonetheless considerable. Even if using a commercial printer that provided recipe forms and proofreading services, women producers of community cookbooks still needed to finance, manage, and organize the production of their books, with these labor-intensive tasks often needing to be done in addition to and alongside women's other domestic and professional duties.

Although, as has previously been discussed in chapter 1, after World War II women were "encouraged to return to their domestic roles as wives of returning GIs," many, nonetheless, were required by economic demands to seek at least part-time employment, and the following decades saw a noticeable increase in women (re)joining the labor force.[1] Cookbook historian Sarah Wassberg has pointed to such workforce demands as well as changes taking place in the publishing industry as two factors that caused a supposed drop in the popularity of the genre: "Community cookbooks began to decline first in cities around the 1970s and 1980s, as women began leaving the home and entering the workforce in bigger numbers, paired with the rise in commercially produced cookbooks and food magazines."[2] However, even within this cultural and economic climate and despite being a product strongly associated with voluntary women's groups, community cookbooks, in fact, remained a popular and profitable project for women in America, whether these women were engaged in professional careers or not. Drawing on contemporary newspaper articles and archival materials, this chapter explores the intersections between women's unpaid and paid careers within their community cookbook production. In addition to these sources, fundraising guides that circulated ideas for projects are also considered. Although rarely consulted within community cookbook research, fundraising guides provide valuable insights into the monetary and professional motivations of cookbook compilers at the time.

After first addressing Arlene Kaplan Daniels's concept of "invisible careers"—which argues for the recognition of women's activities in voluntary associations as part of fulfilling, sometimes lifelong careers—this chapter turns to the continued popularity of community cookbooks, arguing that these fundraising projects materialized women's labor and sacrifice in meaningful and profitable ways. Cookbook bibliographer Elizabeth Driver has described community cookbook producers as a "grassroots culinary network" and states that "the publishing project [was] a means by which women circulated their favorite tried and tested recipes."[3] In addition to the motivation of sharing favorite recipes, the project of publishing a community cookbook was also a way for women to further associational careers and to be part of successful community betterment projects. That community cookbook projects were complex and time-consuming was in fact a benefit for groups: The more visible labor an organization put into compiling and creating a cookbook, the more the book was worth as a fundraising object in a charitable gift economy. Additionally, at a time when more women were joining the American workforce, cookbook projects offered women a chance to gain useful—and possibly employable—skills by providing a "free education" in a variety of areas.[4] Some women took up careers in the book industry: working for or founding their own commercial cookbook printers, selling books in specialty shops, and parlaying cookbook project experience into cookbook consultancy.

Revealing complexities of the twentieth-century American publishing landscape and interrogating distinctions between professional and amateur book production, the cookbooks began to move into mainstream channels, with professional publishers buying rights to individual recipes or even entire books. Indeed, in contrast to Wassberg's claim that professional cookbook publishing and food magazines brought about a decline in community cookbook production, a number of community cookbook publishing groups worked with these agents, advertising their books in food magazines and selling book rights to professional publishers. However, despite the potential rewards of working with professional publishers, volunteers showed a passion for their projects that publishers were rarely able to match, and community cookbook producers often found that their own self-publishing efforts could be more monetarily successful as well as more personally rewarding. Junior Leagues in particular drew on their extensive networks as part of their sophisticated cookbook enterprises, in some cases raising over $100,000 in funds and selling books in numbers that rivaled or bettered those of traditional publishers. In short, as women's lives increasingly included various kinds of work—salaried, nonsalaried domestic, and voluntary—community cookbooks as projects afforded women with opportunities to create meaningful connections across these occupational areas of their lives.

Cookbooks and Invisible Careers

Women's community cookbooks produced between 1950 and 1990 reflect, in different ways, attitudes toward women and work. The topic of work, broadly understood, appears as a theme in many community cookbooks from this era, often highlighting women's invisible labor in the home. The interior space of community cookbooks gave women opportunities to express their feelings about work, with some contributors using the books to venerate women's domestic labor. For instance, Kennan Ferguson cites an example of a 1975 community cookbook that includes a "paean to women's domestic identity" from a male pastor, and a similar letter was included in the 1970 cookbook *Children's Choices*, which states, "Cooking is not drudgery, it is a kind of loving creativeness which makes the humblest home a castle."[5] Ferguson argues that such cookbooks did more than raise money, stating that they also celebrated women's knowledge and reinforced, in at least some cases, beliefs that a woman's place was in the home.[6]

In addition to these references to the value of women's unpaid domestic labor, community cookbooks were also used as a way for women to share time-saving tips and tricks in the kitchen and therefore cut down the labor of cooking and preparing meals. For example, in the undated *Cookbook* by the J. H. Kelson Bible Class, Bethel Baptist Church, the compilers write, "Some purposes of this non-profit cookbook project are (1) to help all of us prepare new and interesting meals, (2) to help future wives of pastors and missionaries to prepare quick, easy, either low-cost or fancy and 'do-ahead' dishes."[7] In this manner the book resonates with a number of professionally published load-lightening cookbooks specifically marketed to employed women, such as *Betty Crocker's Working Woman's Cookbook* (1982), *Better Homes and Gardens After Work Cook Book* (1974), and *The Working Wives Cookbook (Salaried or Otherwise)* (1963).

Although community cookbooks had long taken women's work in the home seriously, that a woman's work might be "Salaried or Otherwise" was not, however, widely recognized within American society. Community cookbooks were one means by which women could document and celebrate the value of their domestic work, through, for example, supplemental texts in their cookbooks that described how their labor facilitated the careers of their husbands, often in humorous ways. The 1976 cookbook *Not Bread Alone*, for instance, includes such marginal passages as "Women can never be as successful as men. They don't have wives to help them."[8] Similarly, in the book *"Will the Gentlemen Yield?": Or, What's Cookin' 'Round the Capitol!*, one contributor writes as part of an introduction to a recipe for "Baked Fish Fillets" that "I spent four happy years at Florida State and after graduation . . . began 'work' on my 'PHT' (putting hubby through) degree."[9]

In addition to discussing and documenting work within the home, community cookbooks were also testaments to women's voluntary work in their communities, an aspect of many women's lives that Kaplan Daniels dubbed in 1988 as "invisible careers." In her book of the same name, Kaplan Daniels argues that the term "career" had almost exclusively been used to describe the kind of work more likely to be done by men: salaried, set within a hierarchy of power, and sequential with definable stages of progression, which values as well as validates personal achievements. Because a woman's voluntary activity fell largely outside of this gendered definition, it was often not always as acknowledged as serious work.[10] However, and as Pamela Tyler later noted, "just as business and professional careers demand time, devotion, commitment, and skill, so to do invisible careers."[11]

As women joined the American labor force in greater numbers and were working both within and out of the home, it may be surprising that so many women continued to participate in voluntary fundraising projects. However, women's employment outside the home did not necessarily have as great an effect on women's voluntary organizations as might be assumed. Indeed, according to Kimberly Wilmot Voss, the women's club movement continued alongside paid employment opportunities after World War II. "Whether part of the paid workforce or not," she writes, "many American women were members of one or more women's clubs."[12] In fact, as late as 1996 there was evidence that employed women volunteered more than unemployed women. As such, Susan M. Chambré has argued for a nuanced understanding of women's careers, which is able to move beyond the concept of parallel power structures that defined so much of nineteenth- and early twentieth-century charitable associations and "apply to a volunteer work life that exists both parallel to and in interaction with a career that consists of paid work."[13] Chambré echoes scholars that have questioned the concept of separate spheres, arguing that the assumed divisions between public and private are, in fact, "intimately intertwined."[14]

Further, community cookbooks published during these decades show that women did not necessarily need to be part of a voluntary association to produce a cookbook, and, increasingly, women from all walks of life, with all sorts of interests and professions, published cookbooks—be it PTA members, missionaries abroad, day-care workers, or paid office workers. Indeed, it seems, wherever women went, community cookbooks went too, with one particularly noteworthy example being the 1986 *Teacher in Space Cookbook*, put together by finalists of NASA's ill-fated Teacher in Space program and including recipes from First Lady Nancy Reagan and teacher and *Challenger* astronaut Christa McAuliffe.[15] Professional women and professional women's groups were also putting out community cookbooks in greater numbers.[16] The Cookery and Food Collection at Michigan State University holds a number of books produced by professional women and professional women's organizations, with examples being the 1976 *Rapistan Girl Friday Recipe Book*; the 1976 *Triune Business Girls Old and New, 1964–1976, Cookbook*; and the undated Grand Rapids Chapter of the American Business Women's Association cookbook *We Knead Dough*. In these cases women's labor in producing the cookbook was voluntary and nonsalaried even as what united them together as a community—their careers—were paid.

These examples support Chambré's understanding of invisible careers as being able to move between both paid and unpaid work and even between different kinds of unpaid work: domestic housework and public volunteering. In the book *Peace de Resistance: A Cook Book*, for example, which was put together by Los Angeles members of the activist group Women Strike for Peace, the women write in the introduction, "It is true that we women of

WSP working for peace have walked thousands of miles, written plane-loads of letters to our president, our congressmen and the heads of state. . . . And at the same time, we've made hundreds of thousands of beds, changed a million diapers and cooked two million meals."[17]

The following sections explore how women used community cookbooks projects as part of their working lives—broadly understood—addressing how women used the books to materialize and monetize their voluntary labor, to gain new and professional skills, and to engage, for some, in increasingly sophisticated cookbook enterprises. Rather than specifically addressing the different voluntary and professional groups that produced community cookbooks between 1950 and 1990, the following sections instead explore one extreme edge of the "contradiction" of women's community cookbooks, detailing motivations for cookbook projects and mapping intersections between professional and amateur.

Visible Sacrifice and the Materialization of Labor

Despite the many changes taking place in women's lives in the second half of the twentieth century, when raising funds for a specific cause or within a nonprofit organization, community cookbooks remained a practical and profitable option. Fundraising guides aimed at nonprofits, libraries, and voluntary associations often included community cookbook projects in their list of suggestions, noting that the books were "good money-maker[s]."[18] At the same time, guides were careful to note that the creation of a cookbook was a laborious task. "The preparation of the material for a cookbook is very time consuming," Janell Shride Amos wrote in her book *Fundraising Ideas*, "and should not be undertaken unless the group has many good cooks willing to work on the project."[19] Not only good cooks were needed to make a cookbook project successful, but also good project leaders, bookkeepers, typists, and salespeople. As Driver has noted, "Making a book is a sophisticated activity" that requires "forming committees, planning the scope and execution of the work, gathering recipes, writing introductory text, soliciting artwork, photographs and poetry, and liaising with a printer or reproducing and binding the text themselves using humble materials such as ribbon and oil-cloth, selling advertisements, setting a price, selling copies, and recording expenses and revenue."[20] In short, creating a cookbook was no small feat. Just how time-consuming such a project was varied, but, writing in 1982, Bryan Miller reported that the average community cookbook project took roughly two years from conception to the final book's release.[21]

Although a fundraising project like a bake sale or raffle would have been much less demanding, both in terms of time and commitment, community cookbooks, nonetheless, remained a popular way for groups to raise funds, in part *because* of the many different tasks such a project required. As Joan Flanagan writes in *The Grass Roots Fundraising Book*, the diversity of tasks associated with producing a successful cookbook was useful for group morale because it "provide[d] a satisfying form of involvement" for volunteers.[22] The editors of the cookbook *Passing Through* by the American Women's Club of Korea acknowledge this in their introduction: "The purpose of this cookbook was to create a project in which all our members could participate." Community cookbook projects thus offered more opportunities for engagement than many other types of fundraisers, with the variety of different tasks involved in a cookbook fundraising project demanding a variety of people who had differing talents and skill sets. Such a diverse range of necessary skills was valuable to voluntary organizations, as keeping volunteers engaged was key to retaining them. More than this, a community cookbook project was suitable for volunteers at different stages of life, whether stay-at-home mothers or full-time professionals.[23]

For some women involvement in a community cookbook project meant tapping into their professional skills and personal connections, which might have otherwise gone unused. In the 1950s and 1960s especially, it was a general expectation that women would leave their paid careers once married, meaning that many unemployed women were in possession of skills, qualifications, and creative interests that they had few outlets for.[24] "The active clubwoman today," Dorothy Roe wrote in 1961, "may have been trained in a professional career, which she put aside after marriage, but found that running a house and caring for her children did not take all of either her time or her talents."[25] Community cookbook projects might, then, provide an outlet for these dormant talents, and, more than this, women's professional skills were an asset to cookbook projects. The cookbook *People Pleasing Recipes, 1871–1971* was, for example, overseen by a chairperson who had management experience from her previous job as secretary to a school principal and therefore "had some concept of what would be involved in such a project."[26]

The creators of the 1955 cookbook *Who Says We Can't Cook!* used their professional connections to draw attention to their book and its cause. Created by the Women's National Press Club (WNPC), the book was somewhat unique for the 1950s for how it positions its compilers and recipe donors as professionals. The illustrations, rather than depicting women at the stove or with a cooking spoon, instead show women working, such as one illustration of "a woman in a hat sitting on a trunk, typing."[27] The imagery supported the women's cause of industry inclusion, as, at the time of the book's release and in an echo of the motivations behind the formation of the Sorosis women's club, women were excluded from the National Press Club and its club building. Unsatisfied with this status quo, members of WNPC began to put pressure on their men-only counterpart, with some successes resulting in standing-room-only balcony admittance to the ballroom and access to the main dining room but not the bar. The cookbook was published as part of this organized push for equality and had the goal of raising money for a separate WNPC clubhouse while also bringing attention to the issue of segregation based on gender.[28] Professional women writers and reporters included recipes in the cookbook, and the book—unsurprisingly—received a fair amount of press coverage, with several articles appearing in the women's section of the local Washington, D.C., paper the *Evening Star*.[29]

Making use of at-hand talents, whether professional or amateur, and drawing on women's networks not only kept volunteers active and interested but meant that most groups realistically had the means to put a book together. As one organizer put it, creating a community cookbook was "a project that any woman's organization could launch for pleasure and profit."[30] More than this, though, the labor involved in creating the final cookbook might have also eased the burden of soliciting money, something that many volunteers struggled with. Writing on how to raise money for small public libraries, fundraising adviser James Swan, for example, advised that "some people would rather wash windows or clean bathrooms than go out and ask for money."[31] Instead, it is suggested that volunteers first give something of their own—time, energy, money—before asking something of others. Having already given something of themselves would make volunteers feel more comfortable asking for money, as the exchange, as a result, felt more equal. On this Flanagan writes, "Giving and asking go together for the leaders of a community organization. Giving first makes it easier for them to ask others for money."[32] Additionally, and within the logic of the volunteer-association gift economy, purchasers of a community cookbook might also feel they are getting more out of the transaction if volunteers have themselves donated something to it.[33] Community cookbooks, as material goods, serve this purpose by displaying the efforts of the organization involved. As such, the books become objects charged with personal meaning, which are more likely to inspire reciprocal giving: in this case the reciprocal act of purchasing the cookbook.

Sacrifice, and indeed visible sacrifice, was key, with Swan noting that "if you don't give what amounts to a sacrifice for you, others will sense a lack of commitment."[34] Women's voluntary labor in producing cookbooks was thus a good selling point, evidenced by the many articles written about community cookbooks during these decades, which often highlighted the labor, time, and sacrifice involved in producing the books. Sometimes including sample recipes meant to tempt potential purchasers, contemporary news articles spoke in laudatory and detailed terms about women's voluntary labor in the production of their cookbooks.

One such article is "Friendship Club Puts Out Friendly Cook Book," which appeared in 1951 in the *Wisconsin State Journal*. Alongside the article is a picture of the Friendship Club, a women's social club founded in 1949 with the goal of combating racial segregation at the grassroots level, with the photograph showing the club members around a table of unbound pages. The article explains that the women were involved in every stage of their soon-to-be-released cookbook's production: typing each page, hand-lettering each and every cover, taking the photograph that appears on the book's cover, and, an event happening at the time of photographing (see figure 6), binding the books by hand with string. As well as highlighting the work involved in producing the book, the article points out that the book, like many such cookbooks, would be released in time for Christmas.[35] Purchasers, therefore, might have seen not only a way to contribute to the worthy cause, on which these women had worked so hard, but also a way to pass along the gift to friends and loved ones in a loop of reciprocal giving so integral to gift economies. Another cookbook that advertised in time for a holiday—this time Mother's Day—is *Westchester County Tricentennial Cookbook, 1683–1983*. In a 1983 *New York Times* article about the book,

FIGURE 6. Four members of the Friendship Club stand around a table while assembling a cookbook, 1951. Photograph by Arthur M. Vinje. Courtesy of the Wisconsin Historical Society.

chairperson Alice O'Rourke, a wife of a prominent county executive and off-and-on-again nurse is interviewed.[36] O'Rourke says in the article that, as the project neared completion, she was working up to eighty hours a week on the cookbook and that she was, ironically, "so involved" she couldn't find time to cook.[37]

In the 1956 article "Press Club Cookbook Is Now 'Best Seller,'" women describe giving their literal blood to the project at hand. "From writing to selling," the article says, "the cookbook has been a strictly 'do-it-ourselves' operation." One of the tasks of this operation was filling mail-order requests, many of which came in before the Christmas holidays. Editor in chief of the cookbook, Josephine Ripley, is quoted as saying that the club women, some of whom worked on the cookbook after coming home from their paid jobs, would package roughly 1,500 books per night—a speed that damaged many fingers in the process. This injury was so common that Ripley reported the team motto as being "don't get blood on the books," going on to note that "bandaged fingers were a mark of distinction," as they showed volunteers' commitment to the project.[38]

Yet another article, this one appearing in a local Jewish newsletter of Houston, Texas, in 1976, puts a finer point on it. First describing the work that went into the cookbook *Let My People . . . Eat!*, the article then addresses the reader directly: "We urge you to take the time to discover what hard work and dedication can produce."[39] In these cases the work involved in producing a community cookbook was understood as a greater marketing tool than the recipes the books contained. Recipes were, in fact, in some ways incidental, and of all the articles mentioned earlier, only one includes a sample recipe from the promoted book, that being the recipe for "Delicate French Cookies" from the *Friendship Club Cook Book*.[40]

A final example comes from the 1971 article "A Community Creates a Cookbook," which intricately describes the process of producing the cookbook *People Pleasing Recipes*. Over nine pages the article details how the women in Waunakee, Wisconsin, gathered, organized, tested, and typed recipes to be included in their book. To cut down costs, the women did the layout for the book themselves, taking the oversized sheets to a local offset printer. When the final pages were returned, the women then used a rented binding machine to put the books together. The article also makes it clear that much of the work involved had to be managed alongside other, typically domestic, duties. Two of the nine images accompanying the article show women simultaneously working on the cookbook and caring for babies. One photograph shows a woman using a mechanical binder, surrounded by loose sheets of cookbook pages, as a baby plays on the floor; in another the cookbook chairperson, Virginia Adler, is seen "doubling as a baby sitter" while discussing the cookbook with two other women. Adler's juggling of her duties is addressed in the article itself, which states, "When contributions slowed down Virginia started round-robin envelopes. She went strolling with Todd in the buggy and dropped envelopes at block chairmen's houses. Each put in her own recipe and passed it to her neighbor. Virginia picked up the completed envelopes on later outings with the baby."[41]

In all these cases, there was an understanding that a woman's life was filled with many commitments, such as careers—both paid and unpaid—and that volunteering was a sacrifice to other demands. As well as offering diverse possibilities for engagement, community cookbooks also served as objects that made visible and physically materialized women's sacrifice, an aspect emphasized in the growing number of local and national feature articles on fundraising cookbooks. That the work that went into a community cookbook was considerable could be a benefit for fundraising, both easing the burden of asking for money and symbolically representing women's commitment to their cause. In addition to these benefits, and as the following section explores, community cookbook projects also offered women learning opportunities and a way to gain diverse skills.

A "Free Education"

The effort, time, energy, and talents required of volunteers to produce a community cookbook were not just good selling points for potential purchasers: These were also seen as important benefits of participating in a community cookbook project. Contemporary handbooks emphasized involvement in voluntary associations as a valuable learning experience for volunteers, and sources indicate that women might have joined voluntary organizations to extend their social influence and also to gain valuable—possibly employable—experience. Prudence Mackintosh addressed how widespread this was in an issue of *Texas Monthly* in 1979, writing that, "with divorce on the rise, even the most traditional women are assessing their marketable skills."[42]

Mackintosh is by no means alone in this observation, and, among other benefits of voluntary fundraising work, such as working at one's own pace, Flanagan lists "learning valuable and marketable job skills."[43] The book *How to Write and Publish a Classic Cookbook* also emphasizes that the prospect of gaining marketable skills would be a draw for many women who were considering to join a voluntary organization and that this could be a way to bring in new members. "Volunteers today are eager for skills that will help them in a paid or unpaid career," the authors write, "and a cookbook committee offers invaluable training."[44] Specifically, cookbook projects gave women opportunities to learn skills related to publishing, such as project management, design, advertising, marketing, and bookkeeping, and, crucially, to learn them alongside other women.

Although women were, at the time, the main users of office printing and duplicating machines in office environments, according to Kate Eichhorn, office printing and copying devices were advertised in such a way as to communicate the idea that the machines were "smarter and less costly than female laborers" and "that women and even girls can use them."[45] This gives an insight into the attitudes and gender biases that would have been prevalent in some professional settings. Even in explicitly liberal circles and outside of the typing pool, such as in the 1960s New Left student activist movement, stereotypical gender roles and misogyny played a part in the assignation of tasks. One woman involved in Students for a Democratic Society, for instance, recalled that "men tended to dominate all the discussions and women tended to run the mimeograph machine."[46] In these cases women were allocated what were thought to be simple tasks of typing and copying, but when it came to making decisions or managing projects, these roles were more often given to men.

Voluntary organizations and cookbook projects differed in that women were taking the lead—and expected to be competent—in all areas. "Today's typical clubwoman," Roe wrote, "is likely to know a lot about any subject she tackles, and if she doesn't know at the start, she finds out in short order."[47] In this way women involved in community cookbook projects engaged in something akin to what Cait McKinney has labeled "capable amateurism." According to McKinney, capable amateurism "rejects the negative associations 'amateur' can carry" and instead acknowledges women's "confidence in their capacity to get things done."[48] At the same time, women also gained confidence and skills through connections to professional women in the voluntary space. Women's clubs and voluntary associations brought professionals and nonprofessionals together in a supportive, and largely female, environment. In the book *Women Politicking Politely*, Wilmot Voss recounts how valuable such cross-career relationships among women could be, with one example being how newspaper editors of women's sections, who may have been involved in voluntary groups themselves, helped club women improve their writing and marketing skills. Workshops were, according to Wilmot Voss, held on the topic of "educating the women about how to create events and projects that would be worthy of newspaper coverage."[49]

The marketable skills learned and connections made as a result of participating in community cookbooks projects might, fundraising guides stated, be applied to paid careers.[50] Although such movement between voluntary and paid work is difficult to trace, there is evidence that, in at least a few instances, women began to work professionally on cookbooks, with some of these women taking their involvement in cookbook projects and applying it to careers in cookbooks and the book industry.[51] For instance, as well as being the main customers of commercial printing services, women also began to engage in this market as professionals, opening up new career paths in printing. The commercial printer Women's Clubs Publishing advertised in 1951 a position for a woman, found in the "Employment: Women" section of the *Indianapolis Star*. The job offered "$100–$200 A WEEK, Woman with car, free to travel, dignified position in advertising and public relations field. No experience needed. We train. LIFETIME OPPORTUNITY."[52] As the company's name suggests, women and women's clubs were the core market, and so the presence of female staff within the company might have been considered advantageous.

The fact that women were employed by cookbook printers could, as well, be used to market the printer and have it stand out from the competition. For example, the cookbook *What's Cook'n at Biltmore* contains a letter from Sara Lynne, the general manager of the Cookbook Department at G&R Publishing Company of Waterloo, Iowa. The letter from Lynne, which opens with "Dear Friend," asks readers to contact her if they or someone they know is interested in publishing a cookbook.[53] Such an advertisement for the printer at the back of the book is common in community cookbooks, with the space typically being used to show images of sample books and provide information on available products. This letter, however, is unique in that it takes the angle of a female "friend" and taps into ideas printers had about community cookbook compilers: that they might respond positively to a friendly, more intimate approach from another woman.

Whether or not Sara Lynne was a real employee at G&R Publishing Company or a clever advertising persona, in the tradition of Betty Crocker and Aunt Jemima, at least one commercial printer was founded and run by women. The cookbook printer General Publishing and Binding was started in 1962 by Phyllis Harris and Dorothy Surratt in Iowa Falls.[54] The company seems to have been a successful commercial printer, especially in the 1970s, even in one instance going so far afield as to produce the 1976 *Al Hasa Saudi Arabia Cookbook*, published for an international group with American members in Saudi Arabia.[55] Harris and Surratt also used their status as two women in a male-dominated industry to advertise for their books and bring in customers. Advertisements such as this one appeared in their books and highlighted the role women played in the company: "We hope you are enjoying using this Cook Book and find it useful in your kitchen. This book was printed by GENERAL PUBLISHING AND BINDING of Iowa Falls, Iowa, which is a Company that was founded by two women who are dedicating their time to printing Cook Books for Churches and other organizations at a cost that they can afford to pay."[56]

In addition to joining the commercial printing market, a few women made professional inroads through bookselling. As the popularity of cookbooks grew, specialty cookbooks shops, some focusing on selling community cookbooks only, began to appear in the 1980s.[57] Helen Jump of Zionsville, Indiana, for example, ran a bookstore specializing in community cookbooks. Jump worked with women's organizations to stock her bookshelves, and, in addition to the physical store, ran a newsletter, the *National Cookbook Registry*, on the topic of cookbook collecting.[58] A similar store was opened in 1982 in Tappahannock, Virginia, called the Charity Cookbook Collector, which also put out a semiannual newsletter. The Charity Cookbook Collector used the newsletter to let readers too far away to visit the brick-and-mortar store know about interesting books, and it also offered the option to order books through the mail.[59] In this approach the shop owners not only capitalized on growing interest in fundraising cookbooks but also replicated subscription-model book clubs, such as those by the Book-of-the-Month Club and the Better Homes and Gardens *Cook's Catalog*.[60]

Just how women might have transitioned the skills gained from community cookbook projects to paid careers can be seen in the example of Kathy Reising, who transitioned her Junior League cookbook experience into a cookbook consulting agency. Originally involved with community cookbooks by cochairing a cookbook project for the Junior League of Milwaukee, by 1989 Reising, with her company Cookbook Resources USA, was working "with charities by representing their regional cookbooks at major trade and gift shows."[61] A similar example comes from the Hays, Rolfes and Associates consulting company of Memphis, Tennessee, founded by Helen Hays and Ellen Rolfes. The two women had worked together on a cookbook project for their local Junior League and decided to move into professional consultancy. One of their popular services was hosting community cookbook seminars for cookbook producers. A promotional flyer put out three years after the company's founding lists over 130 organizations from all over the United States that had taken part in their two-day (eventually two-and-a-half day) cookbook seminar, which gave participants a chance to learn about a range of skills related to community cookbook projects, such as selecting a printer, writing job descriptions, marketing cookbooks, and basic bookkeeping. Also highlighted in the flyer was the "atmosphere of creativity and informality" for exchanging ideas and questions with other women.[62] These seminars show how seriously many women's groups across the nation took their cookbook projects and demonstrate that, at least for Hays and Rolfes, community cookbooks could be part of a professional career.

In the "Author's Note" to their book *How to Write and Publish a Classic Cookbook*, the two outline this career trajectory: "Hays-Rolfes had its beginnings with volunteer jobs. In 1976 we found ourselves as chairman and vice-chairman of the cookbook committee of the Junior League of Memphis, which at the time had two very successful cookbooks on the market. It quickly became apparent that what had first seemed like just another volunteer placement was actually the opportunity to learn the national publishing business—a free education in cookbooks, marketing, and office systems. And we *loved* it." In addition to other dedicatees, which include their "associates" (their children), the two thank the Junior League of Memphis, who, they say, trained them.[63]

For Hays and Rolfes, their positive experience with a Junior League cookbook project led the women not only to become cookbook consultants and seminar leaders but, additionally, to expand into participation in the American Booksellers Convention, creating an advertising catalog and distribution list for self-published organizations and in 1985 founding their own press.[64] In 1989 Ellen Rolfes was also connected to commercial cookbook printer Wimmer, and she later moved on to work as cookbook "midwife" for numerous cookbook projects, several at Doubleday.[65] In these instances the women took the skills they had learned through their volunteer jobs and successfully transitioned them to a paid career in the book industry.

Cookbook Projects as "Veritable" Businesses

In community cookbook publishing, it has so far been shown that women's invisible, voluntary careers overlapped with their paid, professional careers. But an interesting aspect of community cookbook production in the mid- to late twentieth century—and one that is rarely addressed—is the middle ground such projects created within the broader landscape of American publishing. Without earning any personal profits, community cookbook creators began to work with professional publishers, blurring the distinction between amateur and professional publishing at a time often characterized for conglomerization and professionalization.[66] Yet while these interactions with publishers seem to indicate a move toward professionalization and support these characterizations, in some instances women made the choice to go back to self-publishing, finding that their own efforts in bookmaking and bookselling could be more rewarding—and potentially more successful—than those of professional publishers.

It is first important to establish that community cookbooks could be big sellers between 1950 and 1990, a fact that began to make a number of both commercial printers and professional publishers interested in community cookbooks. As informal and "humble" in appearance as so many community cookbooks are, it is easy to assume that the books were always printed in small batches and raised only modest sums. While this is certainly the case for many cookbooks, it is not the case for all. In her chapter in *Recipes for Reading*, Barbara Kirshenblatt-Gimblett hints at the enormous range in print runs community cookbooks could have. On the results of a self-conducted survey of Jewish community cookbook producers in the 1980s, she says some runs were "as small as 250" and others "as large as 25,000."[67] But even this "large" number might be a conservative figure of community cookbooks' sales and earning potential. In 1975 Jon Nordheimer wrote in the *New York Times* about Jerome, Arizona, which, only a few years previous, had been in dire straits. "When Jerome's ancient water main began spouting leaks and needed replacement," he wrote, "the town fathers decided a bond issue to finance the cost of new pipe was too much for the 600 residents." Not content to rely solely on the town's "fathers," Jerome's women proposed a cookbook, the proceeds of which would go toward fixing the water main. According to Nordheimer's report, people in the town initially "scoffed that it couldn't be done," but three years later, twenty-four thousand feet of the new water main had been funded by cookbook sales alone. The article does not state exactly how much more money the project required; however, it was noted that the completion of the project would "take the sale of only 71,000 more copies."[68] That such a large number would be described as *only* seventy-one thousand books not only speaks to the community's faith in the cookbook but also hints at how popular and profitable community cookbooks could be.[69]

Although production numbers of community cookbooks are overall difficult to determine, some commercially printed and bound cookbooks list the number of book printings in their frontmatter and in this way give rare glimpses into the sales figures as well as the longevity of the books. The cookbook *Pots, Pans and Pioneers II*, for instance, by a Louisiana chapter of the Telephone Pioneers of America and printed by Cookbook Publishers, records 120,670 copies printed between 1979 and 1987.[70] To give that number a bit more context, in 1985, Caryn James wrote in the *New York Times* that "for a new [cook]book even 20,000 copies can be a solid success" and that "the most popular, profitable cookbooks rarely sell 200,000 copies."[71]

Community cookbooks were, as the previous sections demonstrated, receiving more media attention during these decades, both in local and national press. The Junior League of Boston, for instance, advertised their 1980 cookbook *Presenting Boston . . . a Cookbook* in both the *New Yorker* and *Gourmet* magazines.[72] Publishers and printers made note of the popularity and selling power of community cookbooks during these decades, with commercial printer S. C. Toof and Company, for instance, moving firmly into the commercial cookbook printing sphere in the 1980s, printing mainly Junior League cookbooks. It is a move that seems to have been, at least in the short term, an economically sound decision; in 1983 the company expected to make $1.5 million from cookbooks alone.[73]

Big-name professional publishers also began, during these years, to buy the rights to community cookbooks, with the books increasingly crossing over into mainstream markets.[74] A 1982 article in the *New York Times* made note of this trend for publishers, reporting, "It is not unusual for large publishing houses to buy rights to community cookbooks. Doubleday, which has published Junior League books in San Francisco, Houston, New Orleans and Pasadena, Calif., says it is considering many more community publications." Cookbook editor at Doubleday, Louise Gault, noted that the books had "very large sales potential, greater than many professional groups."[75]

There were a variety of ways that community cookbooks could cross over into professional publishing, and one strategy was for a publisher to purchase single recipes for reprint. This was the case with *Presenting Boston . . . A Cookbook*, which had recipes from the book purchased by Time Life and the Betty Crocker corporation to appear in their cookbooks.[76] The Junior League also had recipes reprinted in the David McKay Company cookbook *The Eastern Junior League Cookbook*, which brought together the "best" recipes from regional Junior Leagues.[77] The publisher Quail Ridge Press, started in the 1970s, used a similar model: collecting recipes, many from community cookbooks, and republishing them in a state-by-state collection of cookbooks for their "Best of the Best" series.[78] In at least two cases, a David McKay Junior League compilation cookbook was later picked up by the publisher Ballantine.[79]

Agreements such as these for republishing recipes brought in money and attention to the cookbook project without requiring a great deal of effort from committee members. In other cases publishers would republish an entire book under their own imprint. The book rights for *The Taste of Gloucester: A Fisherman's Wife Cooks*, by the Fishermen's Wives of Gloucester and Cape Ann League of Women Voters were, for instance, purchased by Yankee in 1979. A similar example is the book *Calico Pantry*, which was picked up by Cornerstone Library for reprinting and national distribution.[80] In both these cases, the women self-publishers were allowed to continue selling their own editions, with Yankee agreeing to leave the whole North Shore to the Gloucester women to sell the original cookbook.[81]

But despite the potential such crossovers seemed to promise, moving to a traditional publisher was not always a sensible or profitable decision for voluntary groups. Community cookbooks, once picked up by professional publishers, often lacked the marketing and sales passion volunteers brought to the project. Hays and Rolfes reported that the self-publishers of at least one of the community cookbooks in their directory chose to end their relationship with a large national publisher in part for this reason; specifically, they felt that the publisher did not promote the book enough.[82] While the average cookbook published professionally, one commentator noted, sells for a year to eighteen months and "then sinks without a trace," women involved in community cookbook projects, on the other hand, saw their own books as long-lasting money makers for their communities.[83] Limited only by their own energy and enthusiasm, community cookbook self-publishers were keen marketers and promoters of the books they had spent so much time creating and which benefited their own communities, and it is for this reason that many community cookbooks endured for decades, long after a professional publisher might have given up interest. "While commercial publishers promote their books for only a season or two," Hays and Rolfes commented on the situation, "good community books 'transcend time.'"[84]

Junior Leagues in particular made community cookbook publishing into an art form during these decades, rivaling professional publishing by steadily churning out new cookbooks, as well as reprints and revised editions of their best-selling books.[85] Junior Leagues trace their history to 1901 in New York City but quickly spread across the United States and gained particular popularity in the American South, where, for many women, membership in a Junior League "established [the women] in their communities, promoted their husbands' careers, and insured their social standing." The aims of the organization were "to develop responsible young women to work for the betterment of the community," and charitable work in the community was and continues to be an important aspect of membership. Involvement in a Junior League was also a mark of status, and membership was largely restricted to prominent white, Christian women.[86] Thanks in no small part to their networks and status, Junior League cookbooks were some of the most popular of the decades, in at least a dozen cases selling well over one hundred thousand copies.[87]

The number and popularity of Junior League cookbooks was already worth remarking on even in the 1970s. In 1977 Mimi Sheraton wrote in the *New York Times*, "Not too surprisingly, the South, with its many women's clubs and its tradition for good cooking and pride in family heirloom recipes, produces a disproportionately high number of fund-raising cookbooks."[88] A few years later, another article reported that "Junior League chapters in America run a veritable publishing industry through their cookbooks, more than half a dozen of which net more than $20,000 annually."[89] Looking specifically at cookbooks from Missouri, Carol and John Fisher have also commented on the profitability of Junior League chapter cookbook publishing: "Junior League cookbooks have sold millions of copies, raising considerable sums of money for causes in the organization's communities."[90]

To give a specific example of just how profitable the "veritable" business of Junior League cookbooks publishing could be, the book *River Road Recipes*, first published in 1959 by the Junior League of Baton Rouge, Louisiana, is often acknowledged as one of the most successful American Junior League cookbooks, both in terms of longevity and sales figures. In 1982, over two decades after its first release, the book was raking in "profits of $100,000 to $150,000 a year."[91] As of 2016, the book had sold 1.4 million copies and been reprinted eighty times.[92] According to one report, the 1976 second edition, *River Road Recipes: A Second Helping*, also "sold like gumbo at Mardi Gras."[93]

Junior Leagues made use of the extended national network of Junior League chapters to sell and advertise their books. Archived correspondence records show that many Junior Leagues set up cookbook exchanges—sending letters to other chapters, often on official cookbook letterhead, to inquire about having their books displayed in other cities, as a way to increase both awareness and sales. Exchanged books were sold in chapter thrift shops, boutiques, and book fairs and through other fundraising activities.[94] Wilmot Voss makes note of this trend in her discussion of the Junior League of Tampa's *Gasparilla Cookbook*, published in 1961 to raise funds for the league's headquarters: "Copies were available in hotels and sold to other junior league clubs across the country." Returning to charity cookbook roots, the book was also sold at the New York World's Fair, where Jackie Kennedy was photographed carrying a copy.[95]

However, the real secret to this widespread success was thanks, in large part, to the fact that cookbooks were being sold both locally as well as nationally through the mail, relating Junior Leagues and women's voluntary associations more widely to what Corinna Norrick-Rühl has labeled "book-distribution institutions."[96] These two distribution streams aided in the books' success, and selling directly to consumers through the mail was a strategy taken up by many cookbook publishing groups. Addresses were often included in promotional materials, letting potential buyers know who to contact with their order; and a typical community cookbook featured mail-order slips, usually found at the very back of the book. Readers could mail back the filled-in slip with their address (or the address of a friend), along with the money to pay for the book. This was all sent to the address listed, more often than not that of a single cookbook committee member, and then purchasers would wait for their book to arrive in the mail. A photograph of the 1969 *River Road Recipes* cookbook committee shows the women gathering to fill the many mail-order requests they had received, packaging their books into envelopes to be sent to the purchaser by mail (see figure 7).

Making it possible to mail order the books increased distribution circles, which would otherwise be limited to local shops, churches, and sales booths at community events. Books like *Who Says We Can't Cook!* were, as a result, able to reach beyond local networks to get nationwide distribution. Indeed, many of the books previously mentioned in this chapter found mail-order distribution to be key to their success. The WNPC cookbook was, for example, described in 1956 as a "mail-order sensation," with orders of up to five thousand cookbooks a month—so many that the club eventually hired a secretary to handle the orders.[97] Similarly, the cookbook committee for

FIGURE 7. *River Road Recipes* cookbook committee, 1969. Courtesy of the East Baton Rouge Parish Library.

People Pleasing Recipes had such a large number of mail orders that they began to meet weekly to fill them.[98] In short, women across the country were engaged in the increasingly sophisticated "veritable" business of cookbooks, bypassing and in some cases outselling cookbooks by professional industry publishers. Here again community cookbooks complicate distinctions between professional and amateur.

More than this, community cookbooks projects, as part of women's "invisible careers," affected women in subtle and often intangible ways. These benefits to the women themselves—benefits that sales and print numbers cannot begin to describe—help to explain women's continued interest in cookbook projects during decades that saw increasingly diverse demands on their time and energy. Through their voluntary involvement, to quote Tyler, women "earned rewards that, though not bankable, were nonetheless valuable. They gained prestige, experience, a sense of virtue, feelings of efficacy, public recognition, outlets for talents, mental and emotional stimulation, and the rewards that come from working with others towards a desired goal."[99] Kaplan Daniels also makes note of this, with one woman in her study speaking of the "psychic income" of participating in voluntary, unpaid work that benefits a community. And in their book, Hays and Rolfes similarly discuss the importance of "ego satisfaction" in community cookbook projects.[100]

D-M Withers has described similar trends in women's collective learning as "world-making activisms." As Withers argues, these activisms, such as learning to operate printing technologies, "created social contexts that supported de-skilled, feminised classes to substantially intervene, shape and re-build their environments."[101] Although Withers is discussing women involved in the women's liberation movement and their very intentional efforts to reshape the social and political environments of women, connections can nonetheless be made to producers of community cookbooks—women who attempted to improve their communities through book production and, in the production of those books, were able to make changes in their own lives.

For O'Rourke of the *Westchester County Tricentennial Cookbook*, involvement in the community cookbook project inspired her to broaden her horizons and consider a career as a cookbook author. "Despite the ordeal" of the Westchester cookbook, in 1986 she reportedly wanted to work on another cookbook, this time with her own recipes on display. Although there is no evidence that O'Rourke did ever author her own cookbook—it likely "remain[ed] a dream" due to her commitment to her husband's political career—involvement in the community cookbook project nonetheless had an effect on how she viewed her life.[102] O'Rourke said as much herself, stating that "before the cookbook project [her life] centered around her children." A connection to Withers, in this case, can further be made in how O'Rourke was inspired by the cookbook project to engage with new technologies, in particular, computers. According to an interview in 1983, "When a member of the cookbook committee, Linda Parcelli, volunteered to organize all the recipes on her home computer, Mrs. O'Rourke found the process so fascinating that she promptly signed up for a computer course."[103]

To return to Chambré and attempt to understand how women's volunteer work interacted with professional careers, this chapter shows that women saw many opportunities to bring these different aspects of their lives together in and through their cookbook projects. And although it is worth recognizing the largely unacknowledged role women's voluntary labor played in the American cookbook landscape, O'Rourke serves as a reminder that it is equally important to recognize how this labor fit into and became milestones of women's nonsalaried, invisible careers. As Tyler notes, "Their work changed the community, but their work also changed them."[104]

While this chapter has addressed why women continued to produce community cookbooks even as more women moved into paid employment, it has not significantly addressed the contents of the books themselves. The following chapter looks at cookbooks produced by politically aligned groups connected to new social movements, examining why such groups might have been motivated to produce cooking literature and how political goals could be financially as well as textually supported through these fundraising cookbooks.

CHAPTER FOUR

Profits and Politics

Fundraising Cookbooks at the Grassroots

COOKBOOKS HAVE BEEN described by some as objects that reinforce the status quo, with Jill Nussel, for example, writing that community cookbooks are "explicit emblems of women's relegation to the domestic sphere, maintaining institutionalized patriarchal systems and serving the core of that system."[1] However, since first appearing in the 1860s, community cookbooks have been used as commodities sold to support social and political change, with the genre first stemming from women's desire to do good during a time of civil war. Over the decades the charitable funds raised by community cookbooks played a part in supporting community, social, and political change, from immigrant assistance to the cause of women's suffrage.

In the second half of the twentieth century, grassroots action connected to civil rights and social justice movements began to reap societal, cultural, and legal rewards. Ideas about charitable giving were replaced by direct action tactics that aimed to create long-lasting social change. Yet, even within this new political era, community cookbook continued to be produced, and women connected to grassroots social movements saw community cookbooks as a means through which they could support and spread political ideas. At this time, in addition to the ever-present church or synagogue cookbook and the regionally focused cookbook, there were suddenly New Left, antiwar, and Black Power cookbooks, as well as cookbooks supporting racial integration and civil rights. Surprisingly, during an era of protest, civil rights, social movements, and radical politics, the genre of the charitable community cookbook was a popular—and profitable—way to support grassroots political change.

Using archival records, contemporary news articles, and the community cookbooks themselves, this chapter addresses how women compilers and editors began to make greater use of the interior space of community cookbooks to support political change and raise funds.[2] Although scholars such as Donna R. Gabaccia, Sherrie A. Inness, Isaac West, and Rafia Zafar have discussed the political and cultural importance of community cookbooks for women in the twentieth century, they often do not address the economic and fundraising considerations that are an integral part of these books, nor do they give significant attention the books' appearance as goods within a broader publishing market.[3] This chapter, then, brings the financial back into the fold by connecting community cookbooks to the enormous changes taking place in the mainstream cookbook market, in which readers had a growing appetite for political cookbooks.

An American market for cookbooks that highlighted and supported political views made raising funds through community cookbooks a profitable endeavor for struggling grassroots groups. Furthermore, through the use of paratexual elements, such as forewords, illustrations, photographs, interviews, and marginal asides, groups interested in furthering social change embedded sometimes radical ideas within the historical genre of the charitable cookbook. Doing so softened political messages and presented a kind of "palatable" politics to readers who were more and more turning to cookbooks for their reading pleasure. Finally, for groups that historically lacked mainstream representation and were subject to cultural erasure, community cookbooks offered not only the space to communicate grassroots political ideas but also a way to *do* political work at the grassroots: through the project of making and self-publishing a community cookbook.

A Market for Political Cookbooks

That community cookbooks compiled and sold by grassroots political organizations were able to raise significant funds and attract interested readers and donors needs to be understood as part of a new era for American cookbook publishing, in which a growing market for personal, culturally relevant, and politically themed cookbooks had readers hungry for more than recipes alone. Beginning in the 1950s, the market for cookbooks was transformed from one in which a small number of all-purpose cookbooks were guaranteed successes to a market saturated with ever-more specialized and elaborate cookbooks competing for space on bestseller lists. What resulted was a "cookbook explosion," with the cookbook market growing at a nearly alarming rate.[4] According to reports in *Publishers Weekly*, there were 47 new cookbook titles published in 1956; in 1973 that number had grown to 365 new titles published.[5] Just a decade later, by 1984, that number had doubled, with "an average of over two cookbooks . . . published daily." In monetary terms that equaled roughly $286 million in cookbook sales for that year.[6]

This "cookbook explosion" in the mid-twentieth century can be linked to several key factors. Societal changes that affected greater interest in cookbooks included the rise of a middle class that enjoyed more leisure time as well as a decline in paid household cooks.[7] The popularity of the dinner and cocktail party was another reason that women turned more and more to cookbooks during these years, as they searched for new recipes to delight their guests.[8] Books were published with entertaining specifically in mind, and many cookbooks often dedicated a section or two to the topic.[9] The best-selling *A Date with a Dish: A Cookbook of American Negro Recipes*, by *Ebony* magazine's first food editor Freda DeKnight, begins, for instance—after a guide of household tips—with a section on appetizers and advice for hosting a stress-free cocktail party.[10] The rapid growth of the publishing industry was another factor in this growing market for cookbooks, with advances in printing technologies and photography making it more affordable to print in color and with photographs.[11] Additionally, shifts in sales strategies brought books into new consumer locations, such as supermarkets, drugstores, and department stores, with cookbooks being marketed, as one publisher remarked, "like toothpaste."[12]

During these decades and as part of these changes, the genre shifted away from cookbooks as primarily instruction manuals to cookbooks as lifestyle and entertainment books. As "the idea of the cookbook as aesthetically pleasing, with sensually stimulating photographs" grew, cookbooks were no longer only about how to prepare food.[13] Instead, cookbooks were a genre that a growing number of "arm chair cooks" turned to for imaginative inspiration and cultural information.[14] In addition to interest in gourmet, American, and "authentic" international cuisines, a popular trend was cookbook as travelogue, offering readers a way to vicariously experience a place by imagining (and consuming) its food and traditions.[15] In these cases innovative recipes were only one of several necessary elements required to draw in readers. As one cookbook collector commented, "I like any cookbook that isn't just recipes."[16] Cookbook editors, apparently, felt similarly, with a cookbook editor at the publishing house Alfred A. Knopf noting in 1981 that the kind of cookbook they were interested in "teaches you something new" and "opens up a new dimension or a new world."[17]

Readers and editors looked for books that offered unique touches and a friendly, conversational voice—what Megan J. Elias describes as a "personality-driven narrative."[18] Susan J. Leonardi's influential article "Recipes for Reading: Summer Pasta, Lobster à la Riseholme, and Key Lime Pie" commented on this new era of narrative-driven cookbooks. Writing in 1989, she addressed how cookbooks, generally understood as a nonnarrative genre, had begun to include narrative strategies, such as adding a clear authorial persona as well as a "cast of characters" the author may draw on.[19] Leonardi argues through the words of *Heartburn* protagonist Rachel Samstat that such cookbooks do well because "they're very personal and chatty—they're cookbooks in an almost incidental way."[20]

Food and cooking also began to take on political dimensions that had previously been less present in the cookbook genre. Zafar, for example, has noted that post–World War II it was increasingly difficult to separate politics from food and eating, and the increase in published cookbooks connected to the health-food movement, natural eating, vegetarianism, and soul food attests to this.[21] One of the best-selling cookbooks of the 1970s was the vegetarian *Moosewood Cookbook*, by Mollie Katzen, who was part of the Moosewood collective and restaurant of Ithaca, New York. Her book, Warren Belasco notes, had the "hand-lettered, chatty, and somewhat disorganized" aesthetic of many commune cookbooks, as well as offering recipes for "how to live well without wasting the earth's protein resources."[22]

For some of these cookbooks, food was the "cultural material" of the cookbook text, which could be connected to various social and political ideologies.[23] *The Beat Generation Cook Book*, for example, satirized the genre of the cookbook to ridicule and reject middle-class cultural values.[24] Offering recipes like "Pablo Picasserole," which makes enough to "fill a lampshade," the cookbook playfully engaged with the context of food to form a kind of irreverent protest.[25] "Food," Elias says of *The Beat Generation Cook Book*, "was not the point."[26]

For other politically minded cookbooks, food was indeed the point, evidenced by a growing number of hippie-influenced vegetarian and health-food cookbooks that hoped to challenge consumerist practices, the prepackaged food industry, and globalization.[27] Books like *Diet for a Small Planet* (1971) and *Dick Gregory's Natural Diet for Folks Who Eat: Cookin' With Mother Nature* (1974) focused on the environmental and moral issues connected to the consumption of meat. For comedian and civil rights activist Gregory, a vegetarian diet was a natural extension of the peaceful protest tactics of the civil rights era. In his cookbook he wrote, "The philosophy of nonviolence, which I learned from Dr. Martin Luther King, Jr., during my involvement in the civil rights movement, was first responsible for my change in diet."[28] At the same time, Gregory's book might also be described as incidentally a cookbook, with only a few recipes spread throughout thirteen chapters, and perhaps not a *cook*book at all, considering the raw diet it advocates.

Vertamae Smart-Grosvenor's *Vibration Cooking, or The Travel Notes of a Geechee Girl*, while not a vegetarian cookbook, is similar for how it embeds recipes and food in a social discourse. The book begins with a chapter titled "The Demystification of Food" and the words, "In reading lots and lots of cookbooks written by white folks it occurred to me that . . . there is no reference to black people's contribution to the culinary arts. White folks act like they invented food and like there is some weird mystique surrounding it—something that only Julia [Child] and Jim [Beard] can get to do." Offering recipes for dishes like *Harriet Tubman Ragout* surrounded by diary-like passages that spoke about being a Black woman in America, *Vibration Cooking* was one of a growing number of popular cookbooks that questioned the establishment and status quo through thoughtful commentary and personality-driven narrative but also through alternative practices of eating.[29]

While cookbooks that presented oppositional views were not a complete novelty of the times, it is noteworthy that such cookbooks began to receive mainstream attention.[30] In their study of vegetarian cookbooks from 1800 to 2006, Laura J. Miller and Emilie Hardman note that, whereas vegetarian cookbooks were once difficult to access, beginning in the 1970s such books were being published by mainstream publishers and available in bookstores and even being reviewed in the mainstream press.[31] *Moosewood Cookbook*, for example, had sold a half a million copies by 1982, the year Katzen released her next vegetarian cookbook, *Enchanted Broccoli Forest*.[32]

On the whole community cookbooks were well placed to feed into these growing cookbook trends: already coming out of regional communities with unique identities and foregrounding individual voices through contributor names and personalized recipes. To use Lisa Mastrangelo's word, community cookbooks create "snapshots" of the communities that make them, and these snapshot elements could serve to draw in readers looking for more specificity in their cooking and reading materials.[33] Community cookbooks, to a certain extent, may have even helped inspire such trends, and Elias, for instance, has noted that corporate cookbooks would sometimes mimic the style of community cookbooks for promotional purposes.[34]

At the same time, community cookbook producers began to see that, to sell books and raise funds, their cookbooks needed to offer something special and highlight the differences that would distinguish them in an already saturated cookbook market; they needed some kind of "gimmick" to draw readers in.[35] As Lucy Saunders wrote in 1989 in *Publishers Weekly*, "Community/regional titles are said to enjoy wider distribution and influences when they are inventive."[36] Increasingly, community cookbooks—thanks to mail-order distribution, national cookbook-collecting lists, and news articles on regional cookbooks found in nationally distributed newspapers—were reaching audiences beyond their own compiling communities, and inventiveness could help expand that reach. Consultants Helen Hays and Ellen Rolfes also emphasized that for community cookbooks "the secret of their success lies in their diversity."[37] In their book *How to Write and Publish a Classic Cookbook*, the two write that, when coming up with a cookbook theme, compilers should embrace that diversity. "Look for what separates your book from all its competition," they advised "and build upon that specialness." In that vein they recommended choosing a "unique and unifying theme," which might be personal taste or a regional identity, and sprinkling reminders throughout the book in titles, illustrations, histories, and themed recipes.[38]

For many groups the unique theme chosen was that of the fundraising cause itself. That community cookbooks were sold not for individual gain but for community betterment was a natural way to differentiate these cookbooks from others and to potentially enhance sales.[39] Although community cookbooks did not, perhaps, directly compete with singly authored, professional cookbooks, there were, as the previous chapter details, increasing overlaps between these markets. This blurring between professional and amateur was helped by articles on community cookbooks in national newspapers, cookbook-collector lists, mail-order distribution, and the republishing of community cookbooks by professional publishers. At the same time, the strategy of emphasizing fundraising causes was taken up by groups across the country who produced books such as *We Knead Dough*, by the Grand Rapids Chapter of the American Business Women's Association, and *Stay for Lunch*, a book that benefited the Crippled Children's Hospital and School Auxiliary in Sioux Falls, South Dakota. In these books readers were reminded of the theme through, for example, the title and inclusion of illustrations, with the book *Stay for Lunch* including numerous pictures drawn by children at the hospital.[40]

Political parties on both sides of the aisle increasingly self-published cookbooks that monetarily supported their party and reinforced a sense of community through the added features related to their political theme. The 1967 *GOP Cookbook*, published by the Republican Women's Club of Lubbock, Texas, for example, interspersed images of cartoon elephants in the kitchen with recipes and letters from Republican VIPs. Writing about community cookbooks like the *GOP Cookbook*, Kennan Ferguson says that the books "strengthen party identification, organization, and fundraising."[41]

In the second half of the twentieth century, groups connected to the political and social movements of the era also self-published and sold community cookbooks to finance various progressive causes and therefore support social and political change. Using extra materials that surrounded recipes—such as forewords, illustrations, and marginal asides—cookbook compilers used their political cause as a theme, one that might help differentiate the book, attract readers, and increase sales. As well as seeking funds, compiling groups also hoped to change minds and inspire activism through the contents, but also through the making, of their cookbooks. As is explored in the following section, the books found success by highlighting rather than hiding their—sometimes radical—political goals, feeding into the new era for unique and socially relevant cookbooks.

"Extra Ingredients" Enhance Cookbook Sales

Although it seems unlikely that a cookbook genre founded by benevolent and often well-to-do "ladies" would be taken up for radical political aims in the second half of twentieth century, community cookbooks were in fact produced by members of grassroots political and social movements in the 1960s and 1970s. Self-published community cookbooks connected to such movements include books by the People's Fund of Philadelphia, the Women's International League for Peace and Freedom, Citizens United for Racial

Equality, the Southern Conference Educational Fund, the Japanese American Citizens League, the National Council of Negro Women, Women's International League for Peace and Freedom, and the Peter Maurin Neighborhood House. Profits from cookbook sales went toward the progressive causes of, for instance, racial integration, civil rights, affordable housing, assistance for prisoners, and gay activism. Additionally, cookbook sales helped support the compiling organizations themselves, many of which were in a constant battle for survival.

For the People's Fund of Philadelphia, raising money "was a continuous scramble."[42] Established in 1970 with a motto of "change, not charity," the People's Fund eschewed traditional modes of charity and was part of an emerging trend toward social-change philanthropy.[43] Using a democratic and participatory funding model, the People's Fund aimed to address the root causes of injustice and inequality.[44] Alongside fundraising initiatives that included operating a food cart and hosting a benefit concert, sales from their 1976 *The People's Philadelphia Cookbook* helped keep the People's Fund in a position to fulfill their mission to advance change and attempt to "end human suffering."[45]

Similarly, at the Peter Maurin Neighborhood House in Oakland, California, and despite state as well as foundational funding for a selection of their projects, finding the money to pay the bills was "an ever present burden."[46] Named after Peter Maurin, cofounder of the anarchist-leaning Catholic Worker Movement, the Neighborhood House offered services such as a soup kitchen, co-op nursery, and adult literacy classes in the impoverished and majority-Black community of West Oakland. Their *West Oakland Soul Food Cook Book*, first published in 1965, supported, according to cookbook editor Dorothy Kuffman, paying off the mortgage on the nursery. Like the People's Fund cookbook, the *West Oakland Soul Food Cook Book* was one fundraising initiative of many, with others including the sale of soap, quilts, and plate dinners; the hosting of dances; and "all sorts of things to meet the monthly note."[47]

Cookbooks, then, were just one avenue of funding that groups pursued, with the projects nearly always being led by female editors and compilers, even within mixed-gender organizations. The books, in some cases, only partially supplemented funds raised through more traditional channels, such as paid memberships, individual donors, and foundational support. The civil rights organization Southern Conference Educational Fund (SCEF), for example, had a mission of "dismantling racial segregation in the South" and was largely supported by individual donations.[48] The organization did, however, also raise money through art auctions and the selling of printed goods like calendars.[49] While their 1973 cookbook, edited by SCEF members Ruth Goldberg and Lenore Hogan, might have brought in more attention than funds, archival records of Citizens United for Racial Equality (CURE) show that in some instances community cookbooks could succeed when more traditional fundraising avenues failed.

Minutes from CURE's monthly board meetings reveal that the traditional fundraising approach of reaching out to donors was not finding great success. CURE was a nonprofit organization founded in 1968 in San Diego, which aimed to combat racism in the white community and support racial equality at the local level.[50] A cookbook was not on their agenda until member Melba Margolis brought up the idea for *The Integrated Cook Book* project in August 1970. With the book initially appearing low on the roster in the summer and fall reports, the board soon realized the potential it had for its organization. The November 1970 board meeting notes that the book was nearly ready for release; just the next month, and as fundraising brought in a mere hundred dollars, almost all of the first thousand copies of the cookbook had already been sold. The board voted in the same meeting to have more copies printed immediately.[51]

That December the book raised $2,137 in funds for CURE.[52] Although never quite reaching that monthly sum again, *The Integrated Cook Book* continued to sell steadily, and in the same report where the board considered moving the book to a "prestige" publisher for future reprints, the fundraising report was not as encouraging: "very slow," it stated, "many rejects." In 1971 the cookbook began to be sold at local stores and was promoted at national fairs, and, over the next several years, it brought in monetary funds that the group relied on for its survival.[53] In the September 1973 report on the organization's finances, the cookbook seems to have been the sole hope for keeping the organization afloat. "Conclusion:" the report reads, "we must raise between $250 and $300 a month over the next 8 months, and hope that cook book sales yield enough to leave a surplus into 74/75."[54]

Politically aligned community cookbooks like *The Integrated Cook Book*, which raised funds—big or small—to support social movements, were successful in part due to the heightened interest in cookbooks overall but also because they used their political motivations as a unique and saleable theme. Titles were one clear way a political theme could be communicated to readers—such as with the Women Strike for Peace's *Peace de Resistance* cookbook and SCEF's *SCEF Recipes: A Radical Cookbook*. Increasingly, political themes were also visible within the pages of the cookbooks, through what Danielle Nielson calls "ancillary material."[55] Similar to the concept of paratext introduced by French literary theorist Gérard Genette, ancillary materials in community cookbooks are defined by Nielson as "the forewords, epigraphs and editorial notes that make clear the sponsoring organisation's espoused values."[56]

The compilers of *The People's Philadelphia Cookbook* made good use of these ancillary materials or, as they called them, "extra ingredient[s]." As well as an introduction that lists the many cooperating groups that were to be funded by the cookbook sales—including groups such as the Black Panther Party and *Yellow Seeds*, an independent Chinese American magazine—the cookbook is notable for its inclusion of several interviews with "good cooks" who also happen to be local activists. Ostensibly centered around food and eating, these interviews also provide insights into the cooperating groups funded by the book and their aims. For example, an interview with gay activist Michael Goldberger introduces the aims of the Gay Activist Alliance as well as Goldberger's recipe for "A Very Gay Meatloaf," which appears in the book and was inspired by recipes from Craig Claiborne and "gay sister" Alice B. Toklas. In another example an interview with Rafia Rivers, member of the Puerto Rican Socialist Party, just a few pages later casually mentions FBI surveillance while explaining sofrito.[57]

In a similar fashion, *SCEF Recipes* includes lengthy contributor biographies after recipes, nearly all of which go well beyond the contributor notes typically included in community cookbooks. The contributor biography for Anne Braden, former executive director of SCEF, tells, for example, the abridged version of her and her husband's attempt to sell their house in a white neighborhood to a Black family, which resulted in the house being bombed and the Bradens charged with sedition. These biographies tell the story of SCEF, its members, and its actions and enhance the book through this content. As readers dip into the book to find recipes or read histories, they are drawn into a personal discourse that tells the story of this unique organization and are reminded of its specific goals. "There are many cookbooks," the compilers write in the foreword to the book, "but there is only one SCEF. Our approach to food, like our approach to . . . all problems of living in these United States, has developed on a base of dissent, realism, innovation—call it radicalism."[58]

In *The Integrated Cook Book*, the topic of integration is communicated mainly through the inclusion of diverse cuisines, which connected to popular mainstream cookbook trends in ethnic cooking and cookbooks as travelogues. However, through marginal asides like "Good Cooks Come in All Colors," "Black Eyed Peas are Beautiful," and "Travel is fatal to prejudice," the book places these trends clearly within a political context of segregation and race relations. Furthermore, signatures and recipes from supporting politicians and activists, such as Elizabeth Duncan Coontz, the first Black president of the National Education Association, bring a celebrity element to the book while reminding the reader of the given topic: human rights and racial integration.[59]

The illustrations and hand-lettering of text added to the beauty and personality of the book while also connecting it to a tradition of commune and politically motivated cookbooks. Illustrations highlight the different cuisines and cultures included the book—such as a Navajo crop guardian, a cup of Chilean mate tea, or a Mexican piñata—with some giving subtle nods to the topic at hand, for instance, silhouettes in national traditional dress that hold up protest signs. As well as a foreword titled "Let's Break Bread Together," the book also has the rare addition of a conclusion, which brings food and the issue of integration succinctly together. The book finishes with these words: "We *can* learn to love each other's cooking. We *can* learn to love each other."[60]

Such materials enhanced the books' appeal and helped differentiate them in a market bursting at the seams with new cookbooks on ever-more specific topics. Being able to draw attention to unique features was also a way to increase the sales potential by attracting readers and donors. A flyer for *The Integrated Cook Book* urged readers to buy the book to "help foster understanding and brotherhood" but also makes most prominent note of its special features. The flyer lists,

beautifully hand drawn and lettered
interesting reading
gourmet recipes
exotic menus

as well as

Recipes from well-known persons[61]

In a similar vein, Dorothy Kuffman wrote letters to the *Catholic Worker* to describe and promote the *West Oakland Soul Food Cook Book*, and an advertisement for the book also appeared in the left-wing, underground newspaper the *Berkeley Barb* in 1968.[62] Although first released in 1965, the book was soon reissued in 1968 as an enlarged edition and this time was "profusely illustrated."[63] The many illustrations of the neighborhood and residents of West Oakland that are included in the book have made it a classic within soul food literature by offering, as Toni Tipton-Martin has described, "a snapshot of a community struggling with dilapidated housing, overcrowding, hunger, and homelessness and trying to make its way back to stability."[64] The illustrations show the realities of life in the West Oakland community and also foreground the services supported by the Neighborhood House, with depictions of men reading, women typing, and children taking part in group activities. The advertisement for the *West Oakland Soul Food Cook Book* in the *Berkeley Barb* gave information on local stores carrying the book and how to purchase it through the mail, and illustrations from the book also appear.[65] This visual preview gave purchasers a taste of what they could expect inside the book: captivating, unusual, and politically meaningful content.

These features underscored the fundraising causes, making the books unique and therefore meeting the desires of a growing readership of cookbooks while, at the same time, helping to financially support social change. Extra features clarified the theme of the cookbooks, raised money for its worthy cause, and fed into contemporary trends for cookbooks. However, as the next section explores, cookbook recipes and materials were also used to disseminate and communicate political ideas to a new readership—a motivator that was in some cases more important to compiling groups than raising funds.

Outreach and "Palatable" Politics

Grassroots organizations connected to social movements saw the challenge of raising funds to be, in many respects, less daunting than the systemic issues being faced by underprivileged communities. Harriette S. Atkinson of the Peter Maurin Neighborhood House in West Oakland wrote in the *Catholic Worker*, "Often . . . our funds are very low. Nevertheless, many of us believe that operating funds are the least of our worries. Gifts and donations seem easier to come by and appear more readily when we need them than do solutions to the many problems our existence to the neighborhood present to us."[66] Community cookbooks remained useful to fundraising groups as productions that could raise funds but also because the books provided a space for relevant reading materials that could textually support the fundraising cause. Connecting to mass market cookbook trends that blurred genre distinctions between cooking manual and lifestyle guide, the community cookbook editors who were connected to these sometimes radical groups used their books to spread political messages outside of their regular channels. The inclusion of political and educational material within cookbooks was a way for compiling groups to introduce readers to political ideas, and even actions, through a genre not typically associated with politics. In this way the books became both a vehicle and venue for change.

For some groups the communicative function of cookbooks and their ability to reach broad audiences was just as valuable as their fundraising potential. In general radical and alternative publications typically circulate within small networks, with close relationships between creators and readers.[67] Cookbooks, however, were useful to groups interested in social change, as they were disseminated in different circles than the typical printed output of newsletters and political pamphlets. Selling cookbooks was a way to reach out to new audiences who might not have otherwise taken part in activist causes, and, with a cookbook market interested in unusual and socially relevant cookbooks, the traditional format of the charitable cookbook was an attractive offer to many nontraditional groups looking for a broader reach. Indeed, according to fundraising expert James Swan, one of the only reasons to sell goods for fundraising is to reach outside of existing circles.[68] Furthermore, through the reputation of cookbooks as conservative literature, grassroots political organizations might appeal to a wider number of readers and donors if publishing a cookbook.[69]

For CURE the ability to reach a broad audience was one of the main motivations in producing a cookbook. In 1970, according to their meeting minutes, the board members looked ahead to the new decade, asking themselves about the group's identity, goals, and upcoming strategies. Their newsletter came up, with the group noting that, although a newsletter could not solely motivate people to act, it could serve as a final push to those who were already considering action. CURE, like many grassroots organizations, understood the value of print in supporting social movements, seeing print as an essential platform or forum for the dissemination of ideas and opinions.[70] In their 1970–1971 annual report, the group states that the cookbook was produced for the purpose of community outreach and education: "A committee of volunteers produced the Integrated Cookbook, which subtly reaches persons that otherwise are difficult to reach." The next year's report details the success of that outreach, mentioning that cookbooks had been bought by regional libraries and school districts but making no mention of how much money was raised through book sales.[71]

This strategy of using cookbooks to "subtly" reach out to new groups was favored by numerous compiling bodies at the time, especially by groups with minority identities. *The Arab/American Girl Scout Cookbook*, by the Michigan Metro Girl Scouts Council in Dearborn, Michigan, is an example of how cookbook compilers often aimed to engage communities outside of their own specific ethnic backgrounds. With the book produced as part of the local Arab Outreach Program, its compilers state that they "hope that part of their heritage can be shared with those who wish to gain more knowledge and insight into the Arab Culture."[72] Similarly, in publishing the 1975 cookbook *Happy in My Stomach / Tôi vui trong lòng*, the YMCA Refugee and Resettlement Services hoped to sell the books nationwide and, chiefly, to "help Americans know and understand their new neighbors."[73] In this manner the community cookbook could perform, to use Lola Milholland's words, "a form of cultural diplomacy."[74]

More than just any saleable product, cookbooks, as textual documents, presented a way to embed political ideas within the "palatable" context of the cookbook.[75] Many groups had a clear focus on providing information and changing minds. "In our approach to fund-raising," the People's Fund wrote in their cookbook, "we try to educate people about the conditions in our society which cause these problems, stressing the need for fundamental social change."[76] Kuffman similarly commented that the *West Oakland Soul Food Cook Book* could easily be used as part of a Black studies curriculum, and, in a presale advertisement for their cookbook, CURE described the book as "different, useful, educational, attractive, easy to mail," and "even a gentle persuader for your biased friends!"[77]

Part of the palatable approach was interspersing political content—poems, slogans, questions and answers, interviews, and biographies—in a genre rarely associated with the political. As Ferguson states, "[Cookbooks] do not seem political because the demands they make upon us do not seem to be ones concerned with power or authority. They do not declaim, as do manifestos. They do not constrict, as do laws. They do not command accord, as do arguments. . . . Even their narrative form is different from that of most books: they fail to tell a story, and one dips into them depending upon one's time, appetite, and taste."[78] But, as Jessica Derleth and Sherrie A. Inness have argued, creative use of cooking literature is a way that women have made use of a subjugated position to advocate for political, social, and communal change throughout history.[79]

Derleth has explored how this strategy of embedding political content in cookbooks was taken up by early twentieth-century suffragists, who tapped into a widespread public interest in cookbooks and used the charitable cookbook as a way to "share recipes, raise money, and advance their political arguments."[80] Suffragists were often accused of threatening the traditional home and family, an opinion that is recorded in antisuffrage postcards, which often depicted scenes of exhausted husbands forced to do housework or care for their children or cowering in front of their domineering wives. In both cases the message to men seems clear: Suffrage would disrupt gender roles in an unfavorable way.[81] Community cookbooks were used to soften the suffragist image and show that expanded rights for women could coexist with domesticity. That being said, suffrage cookbooks did not shy away from politics, and Andre Chevalier has likened the books to Trojan horses: a means by which ideas could illicitly enter the domestic sphere through the pages of a cookbook.[82] The 1915 *Suffrage Cook Book* is an excellent example of this, with content in support of suffrage appearing between most recipes. Indeed, suffrage cookbooks are some of the most multimodal (with numerous photographs, letters, and poems) and multifaceted of their era, on the one hand, softening political messages through the use of the culinary genre and, on the other hand, using the textual space to communicate highly political and contested ideas.[83] In these ways suffrage cookbooks can be said to foreshadow the many grassroots activist cookbooks that were to come.

Like the suffragists before them, grassroots organizations in the second half of the twentieth century capitalized on the widespread interest in cookbooks to get their ideas into American homes, with some groups continuing to use community cookbooks as a way to bring together discussions of domesticity and politics. These books gently questioned what women's work in the home and as mothers might include, suggesting that activism and protest were essential duties. Women Strike for Peace was one organization that used motherhood as a mobilizing as well as a protest tactic. Focusing on issues that affected mothers and families, primarily on nuclear disarmament and peace activism, the women involved in Women Strike for Peace used their status as white, middle-class, suburban mothers in what historian Sara M. Evans has called "politicized domesticity."[84] In an article about the 1969 Los Angeles Chapter of Women Strike for Peace's cookbook, *Peace de Resistance*, Isaac West examines the way the book "opened a space for women to position themselves as activists without having to worry about disrupting their motherly positions." West goes on to note that within the book "activism is recast as a vital action of caring for the family."[85]

Another cookbook to connect motherhood with protest is the Oregon Chapter of Friends of Children of Vietnam's *"Chosen Moms" Cook Book*. Published sometime in the 1970s, the purported purpose of the cookbook was to encourage the adoption of orphaned Vietnamese children. The book uses motherhood as an entry point into the topic of adoption but also into the war itself. Largely through what West calls "textual fragments," which surround and support the recipe content, the cookbook offers its protest through photographs and poetry that evoke the horrors of war.[86] The book opens, for example, with a photograph of a young child with a prosthetic leg above a poem by Vietnamese poet Phuong Trieu, titled "The School on the Front Line."[87]

Cookbooks could often include such surprising and confrontational content. As Gail Chester notes, "radical publications are in the business of communicating their ideas to their intended audience, and ingenuity is required to achieve this."[88] Inventive and unusual content in grassroots cookbooks included interviews with activists, question-and-answer sections, poetry, and illustrations and photographs, such as those in *"Chosen Moms" Cook Book*, which bring readers face-to-face with casualties of war in a book about adoption. These elements push at genre as well as organizational boundaries for cookbooks. They acknowledge, to some extent, that the books were only "incidentally" cookbooks, a fact supported by the inclusion of a list of local ethnic restaurants in *The People's Philadelphia Cookbook*, for readers "who were given this cookbook as a gift and hate to cook."[89] The CURE cookbook also plays with these conventions by repurposing the mail-in order slip commonly found at the back of community cookbooks. As discussed in the previous chapter, these mail-order slips were a common and convenient way to sell more books, but in the case of the CURE cookbook, the space was used as a membership form, which readers could cut out and send in to join the fight for equality.

Grassroots community cookbooks asking for social change had, then, a historical precedent with suffrage cookbooks, but they were also part of a trend of "the book as a new kind of object and social space in the 1960s," in which it "was no longer just a place to record and store texts and images but a spatiotemporal entity in its own right, with the potential for actions."[90] Through instructions on how to do activism that are cleverly hidden within recipes, grassroots cookbooks could turn readers into activists. In *The Integrated Cook Book*, for example, the editors playfully engage with cookbooks as instructional manuals to ask their readers to act for human rights. They do so by blending recipes for food with recipes for action. In integrating instructions for recipes and instructions for activism, they create a new category of activist recipes, the purpose of which is to make activists out of everyday cooks.

Such activist recipes resemble the "action recipes" described by Abby Dubisar, which offer step-by-step instructions on how to do activism and are found amid more traditional recipes for preparing food.[91] However, the activist recipes in *The Integrated Cook Book* go a step further to blur the distinction between main and ancillary content. No longer "textual fragments" or frames for the main dishes, the political message of activism becomes incorporated in part of the meal. To give an example, the recipe for dumplings in CURE's cookbook includes cooking instructions that end with "while the chicken is stewing, pick up the phone and call your city councilman or a school board member and tell him how you feel about human rights." Or, at the end of the recipe for "Instant Russian Tea," there is this suggestion: "How About: Inviting your neighbors over to drink a cup of tea and to organize a dialogue group or a social action group?" And in a space that resembles the oft-included "extra recipes" section, the book prompts readers not to use the space for additional recipes but rather to write a letter in support that they had "been putting off." Through these unique activist recipes, the cookbook as manual puts forward the idea that activism, like cooking, is a skill that can be learned. The compilers, furthermore, provide readers instructions and space for their own action and confront them with possible excuses, prompting action with the words, "Do it right now!"[92]

Recipes that incorporate the topic of activism are also found in the second edition of the Los Angeles Women Strike for Peace cookbook, *Peace de Resistance*. Examples include

> Did you rush off to demonstrate with such enthusiasm that you forgot to take something out of the freezer for dinner? Here's the solution to that problem. We wish it were this easy to solve problems like war and Peace.

or

> A rich relative coming to dinner? Want to serve him on his ear and *then* ask for a large contribution to WSP? Serve caviar in aspic with the drink before dinner.

and as part of the recipe for "Maple Bavarian Cream":

> While we're on the subject of sweets, how about sweet-talking your Congressman by writing to him regularly. No postage stamp necessary if mailed in the United States. Postage will be paid by addressee.[93]

Through such integrated recipes for cooking and activism, the books treat social action as a daily task, one as essential, simple, and quotidian as preparing food and eating. More than mere instructional manuals for food preparation, *The Integrated Cook Book* and the second edition of *Peace de Resistance* were manuals on how to integrate social activism and engagement into everyday life.

Cookbook compilers adapted, in these cases, the genre of the cookbook as well as the recipe to meet their own political ends. Women compilers and editors who were connected to the civil rights and social movements of the day used the contents of books to support, advocate for, and enact social change. Community cookbooks were useful to grassroots political organizations, as they could reach groups outside of existing circles, educate readers on political issues, and even provide instructions for action. Being a way to frame food within cultural contexts for political aims and embed political messages in a nonthreatening genre, cookbooks were chosen for their palatability and ability to potentially reach new audiences. In addition to these motivations, the next and final section of this chapter explores how community cookbook projects allowed women and groups to not only represent and spread political ideas but, through the act of making cookbooks within a community, to do political work at the grassroots.

Cookbook Projects as Political Acts

Food, as Leslie Howsam has remarked, "like other cultural forms, can be the site of oppression, repression"—but also "resistance."[94] For groups that lacked mainstream representation and suffered from stereotyping and cultural erasure—such as Black, Indigenous, and Asian American communities—self-publishing community cookbooks opened up a path to publishing where few others existed. As well as raising funds to support communities and political aims, the books provided accessible and affordable channels for minority women to (re)present their communities in print and created chances to do activist work at the grassroots. In these ways the cookbooks were not necessarily connected to radical political organizations but rather were radical in the sense of "getting to the roots of problems in society."[95]

In the postwar era, community cookbooks by ethnic and racial minority groups began to appear in greater numbers. Before these decades community cookbooks—and published cookbooks generally—by Indigenous, Black, and Asian American women were incredibly rare. Yong Chen, for example, reports that it was not until the 1960s that more than twenty cookbooks by Chinese Americans were published in a single decade.[96] Similarly, only a handful of fundraising cookbooks by Black women's associations were published in the United States before 1955.[97]

The rise in cookbooks by racial and ethnic minority groups connected to cookbook trends in ethnicity, soul food, and "authentic" cuisines but also to the new avenues of affordable and accessible publishing described in chapter 2. In *Secret Ingredients*, Inness writes that community cookbooks were "more open" to racial and ethnic minorities because of numerous and affordable options for publishing.[98] Self-publishing was undoubtedly a practical consideration for many groups looking to raise funds through cookbook sales, but it was also a political one. "Self-publishing," as Colleen Higgs has said, "is a kind of activism, of taking into your own hands, not waiting around for someone who is a gatekeeper to say 'yes' or 'no.'"[99] The self-publishing of community cookbooks allowed underrepresented groups to exchange knowledge without needing to seek the permission or capital of mainstream publishers.

The value of self-publishing is specifically addressed in the Navajo *Ch'iyáán 'íít'íní binaaltsoos*, or "Cookbook." Until the end of World War II, few Native or Indigenous American community cookbooks were published, with one of the only known examples being the *Indian Cook Book*, by the Indian Women's Club of Tulsa, Oklahoma, published in 1933.[100] *Ch'iyáán 'íít'íní binaaltsoos*, published in 1986, addresses this dearth of textual resources on Native food culture and preparation. Produced by the Navajo Curriculum Center at Rough Rock Demonstration School in Nevada, the book's foreword speaks of the role the book serves in the community. "The present volume," it says, "fills a void in a topic area in which few materials exist." By self-publishing the book and using local, at-hand talent for the gathering of recipes and illustrations, *Ch'iyáán 'íít'íní binaaltsoos* met a contemporary need for the accurate and respectful preservation of traditional foods and food preparation, with the book acting as "a critical part of educating young Navajo people."[101]

For Black women in particular, self-published recipe books provided a space to preserve and share knowledge on their own terms. Although Black women had long been cast in the role of talented cook in the United States, being immortalized in corporate figures such as Aunt Jemima, their knowledge and expertise were largely excluded from—or had been appropriated by—dominant white cultural memory.[102] Even into the mid-twentieth century, many community cookbooks drew on the stereotypical "mammy" figure as a shorthand for white Southern nostalgia and belonging to the American mainstream.[103] As such, cooking and food could not be separated from this history, and, as Zafar has noted, Black women who entered into the culinary domain were forced to (re)engage with the "ghosts of American racism."[104] Nonetheless, in the second half of the twentieth century, Black women turned to the cookbook genre as a way to foreground their own talents, voices, and communities. In doing so, as Doris Witt argues in *Black Hunger: Soul Food and America*, they mobilized cookbook literature "for political ends."[105]

Black women and other underrepresented groups raised funds through self-publishing of community cookbooks, with the books also often supporting the "ulterior missions of community preservation and perseverance." Looking at cookbooks produced by the civil rights organization Japanese American Citizens League, Tamio Spiegel has addressed how fundraising cookbooks were a venue for Japanese Americans to rewrite and recast their history in a cultural arena steeped in stereotypes about "authentic" Japanese culture.[106] While mainstream cookbook authors and publishers began to celebrate the ethnic diversity of American foodways during these decades, minority communities were sometimes viewed as "unreliable sources." Liora Gvion writes, "After years of detaching immigrants from their culinary heritages in order to assimilate them and change their food and eating habits, writers started looking to immigrants for the culinary knowledge of their countries of origin. They argued that in the process of Americanization, second and third-generation immigrants had lost their cultural roots. It was therefore their duty to supply the immigrants with authentic recipes from their home country."[107]

Japanese American Citizens League cookbooks like *East-West Flavors* and *Nisei Kitchen* resisted such characterizations and made space for a unique Japanese American cuisine, one that incorporated Chinese dishes and American staples alongside traditional Japanese foods.[108] The books allowed for a writing back to the cultural and culinary mainstream as well as a rebellion "against dominant white stereotypes."[109] The compilers of *Nisei Kitchen* furthermore made it clear in their book that their aim was to preserve their cuisine and customs so that they might be passed on and survive. In the book's dedication, they write, "We NISEI, the second generation, lovingly transmit the miracle of life and richness of heritage to our children, the SANSEI, or third generation."[110] By the same token, Asian American community cookbooks were increasingly being created for Asian American communities.[111] Without the need to explain their cultural practices to other groups or cater to mainstream tastes, the books had the opportunity to forward what Rosalyn Collings Eves has described as "cultural countermemories."[112]

Preservation of endangered knowledge was often a key focus of community cookbooks published by minority groups. Indeed, many community cookbooks from Black and Indigenous American compiling associations are as much historical archives as cooking manuals. The 1951 book *Cherokee Cooklore: Preparing Cherokee Foods* (see figure 8), for example, preserves traditional food knowledge through recipes with English and Cherokee names, and it also includes an unconventional recipe format for "Bean Bread" that uses newly available printing technologies to record traditional preparation methods. Over forty pages and twenty photographs, the recipe is presented through the quoted voice and photographically demonstrated instructions

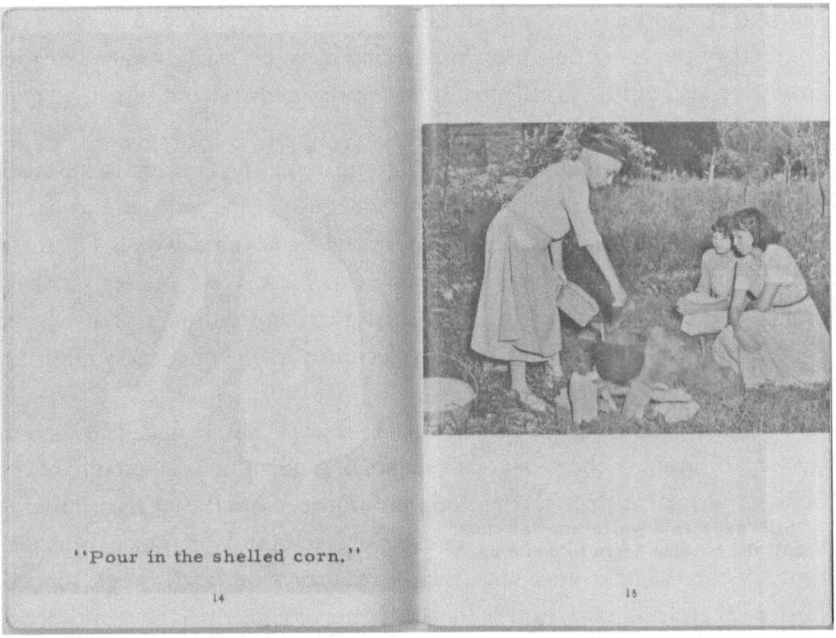

FIGURE 8. Two pages from Mary Ulmer Chiltoskey and Samuel E. Beck's *Cherokee Cooklore: Preparing Cherokee Foods*, 1951. Courtesy of the Museum of the Cherokee People.

of Aggie Lossiah, granddaughter of Cherokee chief John Ross. The reader follows Lossiah as she goes to the corn field for ingredients, uses a traditional pestle, or *ka no na*, to beat the corn to flour, and finally serves the finished product to a hungry crowd.[113] The recipe in the book not only presents the ingredients and methods of cooking "Bean Bread" but also records the traditional means of learning food preparation—from an experienced elder, who instructs in their own voice, step-by-step—and in this way the book attempts to safeguard and preserve this particular cultural experience.

Similarly, *The Historical Cookbook of the American Negro*, published by the National Council of Negro Women, is much more than a collection of recipes. Edited and compiled by historian and activist Sue Bailey Thurman, the 1958 book introduces and contextualizes the food traditions of Black Americans by mixing recipes with historical content. Thurman was part of a "cadre of black Christian intellectuals and activists."[114] At the National Council of Negro Women, she was head of the council's archives and founded the organization's first periodical publication, *Aframerican Women's*

Journal.[115] Thurman's interest in history played a large role in shaping the contents of the cookbook. Her "pioneering focus on black women's history from all walks of life" is reflected in numerous archival and historical contents of the book.[116] Richly garnished with photographs, ink drawings, newspaper clippings, and historical descriptions, the book tells the story of Black history in America—partly through its food culture and partly through its influential people, organizations, and events, which Thurman weaves together with recipes to recontextualize Black American culture and history. The book thus acts as historical and culinary archive, one that can be widely distributed and referenced by members of a minority community for years to come.

Thurman's "new, unique . . . approach to history" also included an innovative organization of the cookbook's materials, and an unusual feature of the book is that, rather than having sections devoted to specific meals or cooking ingredients, *The Historical Cookbook of the American Negro* takes the reader through the calendar year, with each section representing a single month. Historical and culinary content included often connects to the month it appears in, and by doing so commemorates important dates, people, events, and culinary traditions. The book begins, for instance, with a photograph of Sojourner Truth and Abraham Lincoln, and the recipes listed on the following page are for the January celebrations of New Year's and Emancipation Proclamation Day.[117] The book thus not just provides instructions on how to cook specific recipes but also instructs (or suggests) ways to remember and celebrate African American history, one day at a time.

In addition to its archival and historical functions, the cookbook, as a project, inspired grassroots community action and involvement in the younger generation. Much of the historical material included in *The Historical Cookbook of the American Negro* was found, Thurman writes in the introduction, by young volunteers who went "in search of hidden treasures—into attics and basements; into boxes and chests, pulling out old relics of social, economic and political history."[118] This approach of sending Black youth out in search of forgotten, lost, or endangered knowledge was not unique to *The Historical Cookbook of the American Negro*, and in fact a number of cookbook editors utilized this strategy to foster community engagement and inspire feelings of pride.

The 1970 *Soul Power Cook Book* by students at East Palo Alto's Ravenswood High was initially conceived of by teacher and cookbook compiler

Joan Doyle. The idea for a cookbook arose, Doyle writes in the foreword, out of a concern for "the relevancy of [her] Foods I and II texts in a 97 percent black school like Ravenswood—texts geared on the whole to middle-class white students." As part of the project, the students were required to seek out recipes from their community, test the recipes, and organize and design the book.[119] Students also took a school trip to visit the local publisher that was printing the cookbook. Pride is a central theme of *Soul Power Cook Book*, with the book connecting to soul food and the Black Power movement, the rise of which "contributed to the celebration of foods previously stigmatized because of their association with the slave diet."[120] *Soul Power Cook Book* includes soul food recipes, historical recipes—the recipe for "Creole Grillades," for example, is listed in the book as over a hundred years old—and connections to Black pride in the title as well as the illustration of a raised fist that appears above the table of contents.[121]

The 1968 cookbook *Cooking with Soul: Favorite Recipes of Negro Homemakers* by Rufus King High School in Milwaukee, Wisconsin, also makes the motivation of instilling pride in students explicit. Organized and edited by Ethel Brown Hearon, chairperson of the Home Economics Department, the cookbook project was undertaken to support three main goals: "(1) to share with other cultures foods generally liked by Negroes, (2) to indicate the nutrients in certain 'soul' foods, and (3) to develop a sense of race pride by sharing with others the knowledge and experiences of the Negro in the area of food preparation."[122] In both cases, through gathering and compiling recipes from their friends, families, and community members, students involved in the cookbook projects were able to take up active roles in the soul food and Black Power movements, an involvement that helped preserve and archive underrepresented cultural knowledge. In addition to these benefits, involvement in a cookbook project—seeking out recipes, speaking to family, and engaging with personal histories as well as Black culinary knowledge—was valuable for how it could positively influence students' own perceptions of their race and community.

Interestingly, working at the grassroots in this way not only made radical societal change "at the roots" but also helped spread messages of pride and preservation in cookbooks before mainstream popularity of these trends. According to the "Chronological Bibliography of Cookbooks by African Americans," compiled by Doris Witt with David Walker Lupton, which appears at the end of Witt's book, the first Black American cookbook to use the word "soul" in its title is the community, self-published cookbook by the students at Rufus King High.[123] It could, therefore, be argued that, not only did community cookbooks tap into wider market trends, but they may also have helped create and shape them.

Following on from this and continuing to address the political motivations for self-publishing community cookbooks, the next and final chapter examines cookbooks produced by explicitly feminist organizations. In particular it considers the supposedly contradictory relationship between feminism and food literature and shows that, like the earliest soul food cookbook, community cookbooks produced by feminists were ahead of the mainstream, in particular, for how feminists used cookbooks and traditionally feminine domains to financially and textually support the feminist movement.

CHAPTER FIVE

Food and Feminism

Drawing on the Domestic

FEMINIST FOOD, feminists who cook, and feminist cookbooks are often considered to be paradoxes. During the second wave of feminism, assumptions about feminists and their antagonist relationship to food and cooking were, in some cases, just that: assumptions, which were recycled in "extreme" media depictions and cultural commentary.[1] In other cases these assumptions were fairly accurate of the broad feelings many women had about domesticity and cooking in the second half of the twentieth century. As liberal feminism gained traction and women's liberation began to make a break from "an ideology of femininity as service and selflessness and the insistence that women work for others, not for themselves," cooking as a skill and cultural practice sat uncomfortably close to roles, stereotypes, and gendered structures that many feminists wanted to move away from, even as the field of women's studies aimed to foreground women's historical roles in society and women's traditional knowledge.[2]

This chapter explores these aspects by examining feminist community cookbooks, a number of which have not been seriously addressed or analyzed before. Following an introductory section that describes historical tensions around feminism, food, and cooking, these feminist cookbooks and their compiling organizations are described, to show that community cookbooks were useful to feminists for how they raised funds and provided ways to localize feminist causes to regional audiences. In addition to translating the national movement to local audiences, community cookbooks were also useful as part of feminist revisioning and making connections across the waves of feminism. Although feminist and women's studies scholars were looking to the past to recover and bring greater awareness to the history of women, many nonetheless felt unease at claiming cooking and cooking literature as sites of women's knowledge. The publishing of community cookbooks was, however, one way feminists could connect to and meaningfully recover the histories of first-wave feminists, who themselves used cookbook publishing to further the cause of women's enfranchisement.

Just as the books helped women to look back and make connections to a feminist past, community cookbooks also provided a way to look ahead, imagine new ways of being in the world, and build feminist institutions for the future. As part of a grassroots effort to found and fund a feminist science fiction literary award, named after feminist speculative fiction writer James Tiptree Jr., pen name of Alice B. Sheldon, two community cookbooks were self-published. These cookbooks were part of a playful strategy of feminist writers of speculative fiction to honor books that explored and expanded understandings of gender in science fiction, which the founders hoped would help build a feminist future. As the following shows, although cookbooks are often viewed as a kind of conservative literature that hangs on traditions, community cookbooks self-published and sold by feminists in the second half of the twentieth century were forward-looking and in many ways at the forefront of American feminism.

Cookbooks and Feminist Food Fights

In 1963 Betty Friedan's best-selling book *The Feminine Mystique* arrived like a "bomb" on the American book scene.[3] Discussing such topics as Freud and psychology, Abraham Maslow's hierarchy of needs, and the role of advertising in a woman's life but "couch[ing] them in the language of the women's magazines she had begun writing for in the 1950s," Friedan's book primarily addressed women's feelings of dissatisfaction and isolation.[4] The publishing of *The Feminine Mystique* was a turning point for many women in America, who began to see their experiences as part of a systemic rather than personal problem. Through her book Friedan "helped millions of women comprehend, and then change, the conditions of their lives," and she encouraged women to find ways to lessen or give up the daily household chores that prevented them from entering the paid workforce and exploring their own individual potential.[5]

Among the laundry list of tasks—which often included laundry—that Friedan saw as using up women's time, energy, and creativity was cooking:

"For over fifteen years, the words written for women, and the words women used when they talked to each other, while their husbands sat on the other side of the room and talked shop or politics or septic tanks, were about problems with their children, or how to keep their husbands happy, or improve their children's school, or cook chicken."[6] Cooking was by no means the only task that absorbed women's time and energy, but it was one that perfectly encapsulated the daily, thankless drudgery experienced by women across the country.

Friedan wrote her book for a readership made primarily of suburban homemakers; however, in something of an ironic twist, as the feminist movement gained momentum, it was this figure that many feminists—especially in the 1960s and 1970s—used to define themselves against. Cooking, as a result, became a common metaphor for women's confinement to the home as well as women's wasted potential and was employed by many prominent movement leaders. Gloria Steinem, for example, cofounder of the feminist magazine *Ms.* with Dorothy Pittman Hughes, used cooking as a way to illustrate the differences *Ms.* had with other women's magazines. Unlike the majority of women's magazines, *Ms.* never published recipes in its pages.[7] Steinem described it as a magazine "for the liberated female human being—not how to make jelly but how to seize control of your life."[8] Food and recipes were similarly invoked at the first convention of the Coalition of Labor Union Women (CLUW), an organization described by *Time* magazine as a "pragmatic offshoot of the women's liberation movement." Addressing the high-ranking male union leaders at the meeting, women's labor activist Myra Wolfgang declared, "We have a message for George Meany. We have a message for Leonard Woodcock. We have a message for Frank Fitzsimmons. You can tell them we didn't come here to swap recipes."[9] After this meeting "We didn't come here to swap recipes!" became a well-known CLUW slogan.[10]

References to cooking also appeared in feminist activism. The National Organization for Women (NOW), cofounded by Friedan in 1966, released buttons emblazoned with the words "Don't Assume I Cook" as a way to push back against assumptions about divisions of labor based on gender.[11] In 1968 feminists used aprons as part of their protests, piling the garments in front of the White House and therefore "symbolically rejecting the traditional notion that cooking is women's work."[12] At rallies for the 1970 Women's Strike for Equality, in which women took to the streets in mass protest, cooking was again a part of the rhetoric. In New York one sign at the protest read, "Don't Cook Dinner—Starve a Rat Tonight!"[13] In Chicago a speaker addressed the gathered crowd about the lack of progress in women's issues: "Issues, not recipes. Daycare, not chocolate mousse."[14] Examples such as these from the Women's Strike for Equality rallies support Arlene Voski Avakian and Barbara Haber's claim that, for many women, cooking as a concept was understood as being primarily a "marker of patriarchal oppression."[15]

However, not all women were ready to cut their apron strings. Even women closely aligned with the women's liberation movement sometimes believed that the anticooking rhetoric went too far, feeling that such characterizations played into cultural stereotypes about the lack of importance of meal planning and cooking in broader public life. Humorist and homemaker Erma Bombeck was famous for making a career out of revealing and poking fun at the trials and tribulations of work in the home, but she was also a feminist and fierce supporter of the Equal Rights Amendment (ERA), an ultimately unsuccessful attempt to have gender equality enshrined in the U.S. Constitution. In the 1970s Bombeck went on a two-year national tour to promote ratification of the amendment, using her celebrity but also her (somewhat artificially constructed) position as a homemaker to appeal to women who might still have been uncomfortable with the "feminist" label.[16] Yet, despite her commitment, Bombeck did not always feel welcome in the feminist movement, which largely ignored or ridiculed the suburban women who made up a large portion of her readership. Reflecting on the more hard-line feminists who were the most visible media personalities of the movement, such as Friedan, Bombeck has said, "These women threw a war for themselves and didn't invite any of us. That was very wrong of them."[17]

Jacquelyn Reinach, whose song "Liberation, Now!" became an anthem of the women's movement, was a committed homemaker and mother as well as author. In 1970, the year she penned the song "Liberation, Now!," she also published the cookbook *Carefree Cooking* with Hearthside Press. This supposed contradiction of a feminist committed to and encouraging the act of cooking did not go unnoticed by the press. "Would you believe," Maggie Savoy wrote in her article on *Carefree Cooking* in the *Los Angeles Times*, that "the hand that wrote 'Liberation, Now!' (theme song of the women's lib movement) also wrote a cookbook?" Reinach, it seems, also felt somewhat conflicted, although not about her cookbook. For example, as a "tribute" to her husband and sons, Reinach had the feminist clenched fist removed from the record sleeve of "Liberation, Now!" and noted that she was not "women's lib all the way."[18] And despite her powerful lyrics (written with the help of Betty Friedan), which advocate women's liberation from stereotypical roles, Reinach hoped that the feminist movement could also make a place for women who decided to commit themselves to family and the home.[19]

Second-wave feminist tensions around cooking were, therefore, not universally or equally felt. Although popular cookbooks such as *Betty Crocker's Picture Cookbook* did indeed contribute to a wider media landscape that inundated women with images of the "happy housewife" and the "feminine mystique," cookbooks could also be a way for women to connect to feminism on their own terms.[20] For example, cookbooks might have offered chances to break down the public/domestic dichotomy in a way resonated with feminist ideas, such as "the personal is political."[21] Women on the more radical end of the feminist spectrum made connections between the health-food movement, vegetarianism, and the feminist collective.[22] As for Reinach, she saw her cookbook not as a contradiction to the feminist movement but rather as a way to support it by making women's lives easier. About her "cope-and-cook" cookbook, she commented, "Men make thousands of time-motion studies to lighten their own work; but who thinks of lightening kitchen chores?"[23] By considering the real needs of women in the kitchen and providing helpful solutions, Reinach pursued her own brand of feminism.[24]

Moreover, evidence shows that even main figureheads of the women's liberation movement might not have felt so strongly that cooking was opposed to the goals of women's liberation. In a 1980 interview in *Ms.*, Robin Morgan, editor of the feminist anthology *Sisterhood Is Powerful: An Anthology of Writings from the Women's Liberation Movement*, stated that "a conspirational air does sometimes pervade those conversations in which feminists actually (shhh) trade recipes."[25] And at a 1972 two-day feminist symposium at the University of North Carolina–Chapel Hill, which featured prominent feminist author Kate Millett, a "Women's Liberation Cookbook" was reportedly compiled by speakers and attendees, with one particularly notable recipe for "Norman Mailer Meatballs" calling for a teaspoon of arsenic.[26] Evidence from feminist periodicals shows this was not an isolated instance of interest in cookbooks by women's liberation groups. Anna Leonard of San Francisco put out a call for recipe contributions to the planned *People's Cookbook* in the radical feminist periodical *Off Our Backs*, and an all-women's graphics group from Santa Monica wrote to *Women: A Journal of Liberation* in 1970 to let readers know about their recently completed "A Women's Heritage Almanac and Calendar" as well as their future plans to release a women's liberation cookbook.[27] While there is currently no evidence that the "Women's Liberation Cookbook" or any of the others mentioned in feminist periodicals were ever released, the inclusion of cookbook and recipe content at a feminist symposium attests to Williams's argument that the "standard history of liberal second-wave feminists exaggerates their hatred for domestic tasks."[28]

Although it is often assumed that the strategic distancing from cooking and domestic labor meant that second-wave feminists had a natural dislike for and did not produce cookbooks, feminist organizations did indeed self-publish community cookbooks to raise funds and create local support for feminist causes. Books were made not only in support of second-wave feminist goals but also by a number of feminist organizations, including NOW. As the next section explores, through these cookbooks women supported the women's liberation movement and engaged communities outside of the major feminist centers of New York, Chicago, and San Francisco. Women involved in such cookbook projects tended to take a gentler approach to feminism, a strategy that they hoped would have increased chances of appealing to local communities.

Feeding the Feminist Second Wave

It was not until 1998, well after the second wave of feminism, that the national branch of NOW decided to publish a cookbook. Titled *Don't Assume I Don't Cook*—a play on the slogan that had appeared on so many NOW buttons—the national NOW cookbook was, it seemed, a sign that feminism in America was changing. The supposed irony or paradox of a feminist cookbook was quickly picked up on by media commentators. The article "How Many Feminists Does It Take to Write a Cookbook?," for example, opened with the line, "Did you hear that the National Organization for Women just published a cookbook? No, really. It's no joke."[29] Another article about the book begins in a similar fashion. "Don't laugh," writes Carol Guensburg. "The National Organization for Women . . . has just produced a cookbook."[30] In addition to these mass media quips, the book's editors also seemed aware that a cookbook from NOW would raise a few eyebrows. In the introduction they reference a NOW chapter that was unsure whether the call for recipe contributions was in fact serious or an April Fools' joke, and they also say, "The idea of publishing a NOW recipe book was approached with trepidation, mostly because there were so many stereotypes about the women's rights movement and our supporters."[31]

The NOW cookbook can be seen as part of a third-wave reassessment of second-wave feminists' disinterest in and a changing relationship to femininity, and by extension food. Hidden behind the jokes, these media commentators as well as the NOW cookbook compilers seemed to be saying that a feminist cookbook published in the late 1990s was, in fact, somewhat revolutionary—a surprising kind of book that not only had not been but *could* not have been published before: Whereas earlier feminists might have balked at aligning themselves with anything to do with domestic drudgery, finally, these comments seem to say, feminists could publish a cookbook. In reality, however, women in America had been self-publishing community cookbooks in support of feminist causes for decades.

Whether or not second-wave feminists published and sold community cookbooks is a question that has received very little scholarly attention, and it is often assumed, given the strong anticooking rhetoric of many of the most prominent second-wave feminists and feminist organizations, that these women did not produce cookbooks. In her book on ethnic cooking in America, Donna R. Gabaccia has, for example, addressed community cookbooks from the twentieth century as books that celebrate past generations of women, but she remarked that compilers "acted out of no feminist impulse."[32] These assumptions—that feminists did not create community cookbooks and that community cookbook compilers were not motivated by feminist aims—are seemingly supported by the dearth of second-wave feminist cookbooks, and one of the only researchers to investigate the issue is Stacy J. Williams, who has identified a handful of second-wave feminist community cookbooks, created by both liberal and radical feminist groups.[33]

The following builds on and adds to this work by presenting an updated and expanded list of community cookbooks self-published by explicitly feminist organizations formed as a part of the second wave. The updated list, which was created using library catalog records as well as targeted bookseller and feminist publication searches, brings the number of second-wave feminist community cookbooks to nineteen. (See appendix B for a full list of titles.) Some of these books are not part of any American library collection and are being addressed in an academic work here for the first time. These community cookbooks provide evidence of how feminists across the United States used cookbooks to financially "feed" and support the ongoing feminist movement. Moreover, and in contrast to Gabaccia's claim, the following goes on to show that even women's organizations not directly connected to second-wave feminism supported a select number of feminist goals and initiatives and that the community cookbooks produced by these groups, although usually not labeled as feminist, contributed to both local and national feminist projects.

Perhaps the most well-known organization to come out of the second wave of feminism was NOW, which "emerged as the face of liberal feminism."[34] The goals of NOW were broad—to bring women fully into public life—with more focused initiatives working toward equal opportunities for employment and equal pay.[35] After its founding the organization grew rapidly, with regional chapters appearing across the country.[36] NOW's federated and decentralized organizational structure encouraged chapter freedom and flexibility: Chapters would receive information from the national organization but were free to pursue goals and employ strategies that would be successful in their own area. Although Kelsy Kretschmer has brought into question whether this model created fractures within NOW as a whole, the flexible organizational model undoubtedly aided in popularizing NOW and building a national network of feminist activism.[37] This freedom to act regionally may also help explain the existence of fundraising cookbooks produced and sold by NOW chapters.

Between 1966, the year of the organization's founding, and 1990 at least seven community cookbooks were self-published by NOW chapters across America. Those are *Cooking with Florida Feminist Flair* (1970), by the Broward County Chapter of Florida; a men's recipe book (1978), by the West Palm Beach Chapter of Florida; *A Book of Favorite Recipes* (1978), by the Denton Chapter of Texas; *NOW We're Cooking* (1979), by the Greater Champaign Area Chapter of Illinois; *Everyperson's Cook Book* (ca. 1970s), by the Wichita Chapter of Nebraska; *First Virginia Feminist Cookbook* (1983), by the Lynchburg Chapter of Virginia; and *"Women Are A-Risin'": Feminist Food for Thought Cookbook* (1986), by the Tarrant County Chapter of Texas.[38] The diverse geographic spread of these books, produced in large and small towns across the United States, as well as the fact that several of the books are not held in any major library collection, strongly suggests that this remains a nonexhaustive list of NOW community cookbooks from the given decades.[39] Recent years have shown that rare-book dealers are increasingly acknowledging the value of women's popular cultural materials as well as bringing feminist practice into the rare-book trade, which will hopefully result in the uncovering of more cookbooks produced by feminist groups, including NOW.[40]

One of the main and most popular projects of NOW was the ratification of the ERA, and the use of traditional fundraising methods—like cookbooks—to support feminist aims aligns with statements made by ERA supporters. "Of course we are going to get ERA," one "ratificationist" commented. "If it takes white gloves, we will use white gloves. If it takes combat boots, we will wear combat boots; we'll use both."[41] Taking up this "white gloves" strategy—a concept that chimes with the "tact and velvet gloves" tactic mentioned in the 1915 *Suffrage Cook Book*—regional affiliates of the feminist group ERAmerica were open about their use of cooking and recipes, seeing this as an effective way to raise funds and create support for the amendment. An *ERAmerica Report* from 1980 details, for example, how a South Florida "Great Equality Bake Sale" raised over $3,000 in funds. The sale was described as a "return to bake sale basics—many people making small contributions just the same way they support hospitals, homes for the aged, church missions, synagogue youth groups, banks and endangered whales—because it works."[42]

Readers of the newsletter were asked to participate in an upcoming national Fourth of July bake sale and let customers know that the "ERA is as American as apple pie." To encourage greater fundraising engagement, it was also stated that anyone who sent in their own ideas for future fundraising events to ERAmerica would receive a copy of Liz Carpenter's "Equal Rights Chili" as thanks, a recipe reportedly entered into a Texas chili contest and commended there as being "good for the Constitution."[43] Cookbook creators, it seems, felt similarly. In an advertisement for the feminist community cookbook *The Working Woman's Cookbook: Recipes for a Small Salary*, by Women Employed, the group writes about their fundraising efforts through cookbook sales: "Symphony leagues, friends of the library, Republican wives all do it—why not a direct action organization 'struggling to gain on-the-job equality for women?'"[44]

Traditional fundraising projects were effective in raising meaningful funds but also provided a way to translate national feminist messages into local engagement. Indeed, one of the challenges faced by NOW was its "outside agitator image," and many regional chapters struggled in establishing themselves in communities across the nation. Some NOW chapters could not manage to overcome these communicative and ideological challenges. According to Melissa Estes Blair, the first NOW chapter established in Durham, North Carolina, "never got off the ground" due to the fact that "many activist women in the city were put off by what they saw as NOW's confrontational tactics."[45] Estes Blair gives the example of a NOW flyer that needed to be rewritten to better appeal to the local audience, and, similarly, Florida NOW members used recipes in the hopes of gaining support for the amendment. In their flyer supporting the ERA, the Tallahassee chapter of NOW distributed information on one side and recipes—"Mrs. Carter's ERA Grits Cheese Puffs" and "Mrs. Ford's ERA Desert Relief (Chocolate Ice Box Dessert)"—on the other.[46]

Whereas many feminists used domesticity as something to distinguish themselves against, the tactic of including recipes on an ERA flyer opened up a middle space in between radical and traditional—a space that might appeal to a broader range of Americans still uncertain about the new feminist wave. First Lady Rosalynn Carter stated as much: "I feel it is especially important to explain that women like me support the ERA. I am a relatively traditional person.... I am not threatened by the ERA. I am freed by it."[47]

NOW fundraising cookbooks and ERA bake sales evidence, as Kimberly Wilmot Voss has argued, that "well-behaved" feminists also made significant contributions to the movement.[48] Despite the sometimes strong public opposition NOW presented against domesticity and cooking—such as with their "Don't Assume I Cook" buttons—the use of food and cooking by feminists shows how national NOW tactics and rhetoric were not necessarily as effective in communities outside of the feminist metropolises of New York, Chicago, and San Francisco. In smaller communities outside of the feminist centers, the traditional route of fundraising through cookbooks offered an approach to feminism that was familiar to and favored by many women, and it is noteworthy that of the seven known NOW community cookbooks, five are from regions in the American South. NOW members in these regions needed—and were encouraged by the organizational structure of NOW—to find their own ways of garnering local support. "While grassroots activists took their cues from national leaders," Estes Blair writes, "they developed their own methods of addressing those issues."[49] Fundraising through community cookbooks was one way to address pressing issues for women and raise funds for national causes at the local level.

Outside of NOW several other organizations that were founded as part of and to support the second wave of feminism also produced cookbooks, including the National Women's Political Caucus, the National Abortion Rights Action League, the National Association for Girls and Women in Sport, and—despite their slogan "We didn't come here to swap recipes!"—CLUW, chapters of which produced at least two community cookbooks.[50] Some of these groups produced more cookbooks than others, and the National Women's Political Caucus was particularly open to engaging with cookbooks as fundraisers. At least three caucus chapters across the nation produced cookbooks, those being *Pots and Politics: An Historical Cookbook; From the Suffragists to the Equal Rights Amendment* (1976); *Political Favorites: Featuring Recipes of Oregon Politicians* (1983); and *What's Cooking at the Capitol?* ([1981]). This is perhaps not as surprising when considering that founders of the organization, which was created in 1972 with aims of increasing the number of women holding elected positions in the U.S. government, included Liz Carpenter (previously mentioned in connection to her "Equal Rights Chili") and Dorothy Height, who later edited *The Black Family Dinner Quilt Cookbook*.[51] In contrast, only one cookbook from the National Abortion Rights Action League (NARAL) is currently known to exist: a small and handmade volume called *CHOICE Recipes*, produced by chapter members in Troutdale, Oregon.[52] Similarly, the National Association for Girls and Women in Sport published just one cookbook, titled *Cookies (and Punch, Too!)*, in 1977.[53] Whereas the National Women's Political Caucus chapters seemed to feel more comfortable continuing the gendered practice of publishing community cookbooks for fundraising purposes, *Cookies (and Punch, Too!)* was instead published as a farewell to such practices. In particular the book hoped to signal a break from "the tradition of selling 'cookies and punch' to support sport and athletic programs for girls and women."[54]

Beyond community cookbooks self-published by groups to come out of second-wave feminism and with explicitly feminist aims, there were also numerous fundraising cookbooks produced by women's associations that, while not directly linked to feminism, might be considered part of the feminist movement. In fact, despite some feminist attitudes that "sneered at volunteerism of any kind," many women found their way to the movement through their involvement in voluntary women's clubs and associations.[55] A 1971 news article on women's liberation in Connecticut suburbs, for example, reported that "established organizations in the area are devoting meetings to the changing role of women."[56] The connection to feminism within these groups was often through their support services for women—such as women's shelters, libraries, and family-planning services—as well as through support of the widely popular ERA.

Moreover, and in light of the difficulties NOW chapters had in establishing a firm presence in many communities, these women's voluntary organizations offered in some cases the only feminist networks in a given area. The Young Women's Christian Association (YWCA) in Durham, for example, was the city's main feminist network, supporting feminist ideas and action through its establishment of a Women's Library stocked with feminist periodicals, as well as by hosting women's liberation workshops and feminist speakers.[57] Similarly, the Dallas-area Junior League chapter instigated a program called "Focus" that was described by one writer as a "gentle consciousness-raising group."[58] That preexisting women's organizations took it upon themselves to find ways to support feminism resonates with the overall flexibility offered by women's associations.[59] More than this, it aligns with the liberal feminist belief that meaningful change could be made by "work[ing] through established political and legal channels."[60] Using the existing structure of the women's association allowed groups to incorporate a degree of feminism into their organization without necessitating a complete structural and ideological overhaul.

Organizations that had ties to the women's movement, to greater and lesser degrees, included but were not limited to the YWCA, the American Association of University Women, Planned Parenthood, the National Federation of Business and Professional Women's Clubs, the American Business Women's Association, and the National Council of Jewish Women. Support for the ERA was one cause that brought many women's groups into the feminist fold, and in 1974 there were at least seventy-nine national organizations that supported the proposed amendment, including such diverse groups as the American Nurses Association, the League of American Working Women, and both the Democratic and Republican Parties.[61]

Many of these seventy-nine groups produced community cookbooks for fundraising purposes in numbers that far exceed explicitly feminist cookbooks. To give a sample of some of these numbers, as of November 2025, the global catalog WorldCat lists five community cookbooks published in America between 1950 and 1990 by Planned Parenthood, forty-eight by the YWCA, fifty-three by the American Association of University Women, and eighty-seven cookbooks by chapters of the American Business Women's Association.[62] While certainly not all these chapters used their fundraising cookbooks as a way to support feminist causes, some likely did. Recognizing even a fraction of these cookbooks as feminist would further help to acknowledge the role women's voluntary organizations played in second-wave feminism.

The difficulty, of course, is how to assess feminist alignment or intentions in the production of these books. However, although community cookbooks self-published by preexisting women's organizations typically did not announce their support for feminism—making it difficult to establish just how many feminist community cookbooks were published in America—some books do give clues. In rare cases titles might declare feminist connections, such as with the 1982 *Feminist Food Book*, produced by a coalition of women's clubs in Muskegon, Michigan. In other cases feminist connections appear only in a book's pages, such as in *The Literary Allusions Cookbook*, published in 1982 by the Nashville Chapter of the Women's National Book Association. This book connects to feminism through an included essay on the topic of "Food and Cooking in Feminist Literature." In the essay—one of several literary-themed essays included in the cookbook—Elizabeth Futas and Diane Kadanoff consider the various depictions of food and cooking in recent feminist literature. Providing a list of novels, stories, and poems, the authors encourage the reader to "enjoy your own food and read one of these recommended works of feminist literature!"[63]

The tucked-away essay on feminism in *The Literary Allusions Cookbook* hints that many more community cookbooks with feminist intentions remain to be found and that even women's voluntary associations not directly associated with the women's movement were using community cookbooks as a way to support the second wave of feminism in America. Therefore, by the time the NOW national branch finally published its own community cookbook in 1998, numerous NOW chapters, feminist organizations, and women's groups across the country had already self-published feminist community cookbooks to localize national feminist issues and support the feminist movement.

With this section having established that both second-wave feminist organizations and women's groups more broadly produced community cookbooks to raise funds for the cause of feminism, the following section returns to the books that make their feminist aims explicit, examining how community cookbooks were used to help women make connections to the first wave of feminism.

Recovering a Feminist Past

One of the issues to spark the women's movement in the United States was the deep sense of isolation and alienation many women experienced.[64] While discussions of this phenomenon first began as a kind of diagnosis of suburban, middle-class living in the postwar era, they quickly broadened to include historical and literary disconnects as well. As a result, and overlapping with ideas about the necessity of radical transformations of society, one of the main cultural projects of second-wave feminism became recovering and reconnecting with women's history.

Women, it was argued by many, had been left out of or misrepresented in the historical record and literary canon, with author Joanna Russ framing this silence in her 1983 book *How to Suppress Women's Writing* as a kind of informal censorship, one that had affected women throughout centuries.[65] Feminists contributed to the emerging field of women's studies by actively seeking out and drawing attention to these missing pieces of women's knowledge, tradition, and craft. One striking example of this is Alice Walker's 1976 article in *Ms.* magazine, in which Walker details her attempts to visit Zora Neale Hurston's grave, with the article reviving interest in the largely forgotten author and bringing many of her works back into print.[66] This feminist recovery brought not only forgotten historical figures but also underappreciated women's art forms back into the public light. Books like *Witches, Midwives, and Nurses: A History of Women Healers* (1973) and *The Subversive Stitch: Embroidery and the Making of the Feminine* (1984) reframed traditional women's knowledge and craft from a feminist perspective, through what feminist poet Adrienne Rich labeled "re-visioning," or "entering an old text from a new critical direction."[67] While Rich was addressing mainly literature and writing, the concept of revisioning took on broader implications as part of feminist literacy: a way of "reading" the world from new perspectives.[68]

The recovery of women's knowledge and productions was often mediated through print, in widely distributed mainstream books and magazines as well as more locally distributed ephemeral materials. But although traditional women's crafts like embroidery and scrapbooking received renewed attention as part of second-wave feminism, cooking was one topic that was not as thoroughly addressed by women's studies scholars.[69] And when food was addressed in feminist publications, it was typically in regard to conversations of body image, diet culture, and the politics of vegetarianism. Food, for example, received special attention in a 1987 issue of the feminist magazine *Heresies*; however, the issue looked at food primarily in relation to beauty standards, as well as food cultures outside of the United States. Similarly, books like Susie Orbach's *Fat Is a Feminist Issue* (1979) and Carol J. Adams's *The Sexual Politics of Meat: A Feminist-Vegetarian Critical Theory* (1990) brought greater attention to these issues but often did not connect to the historical implications of cooking and cookbook publishing.

Cookbooks by women and for women in America were almost never part of these feminist recovery efforts, despite the fact that cookbooks are a genre strongly associated with feelings of "nostalgia and loss."[70] Beyond their function as instruction manuals, cookbooks record culinary and cultural traditions, familial ties, and oral traditions. Community cookbooks, perhaps more than professionally published cookbooks, are connected to a "sense of loss and recovery and a fear of disconnection, developing across generations of family members."[71] As historical documents, cookbooks would have offered feminists a natural entry point into learning about women's sometimes subversive engagement with creative culinary expression and, for community cookbooks in particular, with activism and the public sphere.

Commenting on this silence around the subject of cookbooks and food within the second wave of feminism, Avakian and Haber write in their introduction on feminist food studies that food was "a subject that had not appealed to early generations of women's history scholars more interested in setting straight the public record on women's achievements."[72] Anne Bower echoes the sentiment that establishing the legitimacy of cookbooks was slow work: "In gaining academic acceptance, earlier feminists often felt compelled to repress expressions of interests in domestic life for fear that such expression would consign them to an essentialized 'feminine' role."[73] Therefore, although scholars such as Mary A. Procida have commented that women's studies scholars should have recognized the value of cookbooks, many women likely felt discouraged from engaging openly with topics of cooking and cookbooks as part of feminist revisioning "for fear of associating themselves too closely with the domestic drudgery of the kitchen."[74]

But while women's studies scholars were not as interested in claiming cookbooks as historical documents worthy of feminist study, for women otherwise involved in the feminist movement, self-published feminist community cookbooks were useful for how they provided a way for women to revision, engage with, and make connections to past and present in different, productive ways. Through book titles and recipe names that drew on historical figures and by republishing older texts, women created close, communal connections to feminist figures and feminist movements of the past.

The NARAL community cookbook *CHOICE Recipes*, for instance, used its title in an act of revisioning to place the book in a longer timeline of women's grassroots action. The *CHOICE* in *CHOICE Recipes* cleverly references early twentieth-century fundraising cookbooks, which were often named *Choice Recipes* and *Choice Receipts*, with the "choice" indicating that the recipes included had been personally chosen by contributors. Similar to the equally popular titles *Tried and Tested* and *Tried and True*, such cookbook titles highlighted the curation that compilers saw as a main selling point: that recipes had been thoroughly tested in real homes and hand-selected for reliability.[75] NARAL's cookbook creators add a layer of meaning on top of this historical title by referencing the prochoice movement. In drawing on this historical connection, the producers of *CHOICE Recipes* assumed, to use Lisa Mastrangelo's words, a "community literacy"—that is, a readership that both supported the prochoice movement and understood (and perhaps was amused by) the double meaning of the cookbook's title.[76]

The Tarrant County NOW Chapter's *"Women Are A-Risin'": Feminist Food for Thought* cookbook also made humorous connections between past and present, using in this case recipe titles to highlight important feminist figures. In addition to recipes like "A Single Woman's Egg Foo Yong" and "Equality Bagels," playfully named dishes included in the book used the names of contemporary as well as historical female role models, from Tina Turner to Joan of Arc. Part of the humor of the recipes seems to be the unexpected juxtaposition of twentieth-century foods with historical female figures. British eighteenth-century women's rights advocate Mary Wollstonecraft, for example, appears in the recipe for "Wollstonecraft's Stove-Top Barbecue Chicken."[77] However, while recipes are named after prominent female figures—creating entertaining content for readers—a recipe contributor name was also listed at the end of each recipe. While such double sourcing of recipes is common in community cookbooks, they typically describe community connections across family and close friends, where contributors are sharing cherished recipes that have been passed down to them.[78] Bringing historical figures into the books' pages draws them into and makes them part of the cookbook's community, creating, in their own way, a kind of feminist genealogy through food.

Just as Kennan Ferguson has asserted that community cookbooks "intensify" communities through the publishing and distribution of communal recipes, it can be argued that women involved in feminism's second wave used cookbooks to create a sense of community with first-wave feminists.[79] Within *"Women Are A-Risin'"* this strategy is taken up in numerous recipe titles, in which suffragists and first-wave feminists such as Lucy Stone and Sojourner Truth "share" recipes in the book. The "Soups, Salads, Vegetables" section of the book, for instance, begins with a recipe for "Alice Paul's Potato Soup."[80] Paul, along with Crystal Eastman, was one of the initial authors of the Equal Rights Amendment, which was first proposed in 1923. The inclusion of Alice Paul and other first-wave feminists as recipe "contributors" provided the "feminist food for thought" referenced in the cookbook's title and also makes the historical ties across the waves and projects of feminism legible, "literaliz[ing] identity and belonging through the pages of a cookbook."[81]

Indeed, drawing connections across the first two feminist waves was something many feminists of the era were interested in as a way to eliminate feelings of historical isolation. More than this, it was thought to be a way to root the movement in a historical past and frame the women's movement as a timely—if not overdue—event rather than a sudden, radical uprising.[82] By recovering knowledge about the first wave of feminism, second-wave feminists furthermore hoped to learn from and build on the first wave, with Ellen DuBois optimistically writing in the pamphlet *Feminism: Old Wave and New* that "perhaps two waves of feminism will be enough to free us."[83]

Of all the second-wave feminist community cookbooks, the one to most clearly make connections between past and present waves of feminism is the cookbook *Pots and Politics: An Historical Cookbook; From the Suffragists to the Equal Rights Amendment*, by the Washington State Women's Political Caucus. The 1976 cookbook is unusual in how it materially unites the first and second waves of feminism, bringing them into conversation by republishing the entirety of a 1909 suffrage-era community cookbook—*Washington Women's Cook Book*—in the middle of the 1976 cookbook. One of only a handful of known community cookbooks published between 1886 and 1916 to support the women's suffrage movement, the *Washington Women's Cook Book* appears in *Pots and Politics* between pieces of original content, such as sections on speed cooking, a book review, and a "Tongue in Cheek" chapter meant to bring "a snicker to those who read at the table."[84] In republishing the original suffrage cookbook, the compilers of *Pots and Politics* followed the same impulse of (re)discovery and (re)distribution of first-wave knowledge as feminist scholars and presses, even as they took their information from a resource many scholars still seemingly viewed as an out-of-bounds site of feminist inquiry: a cookbook.[85]

Like all community cookbooks, suffrage-era community cookbooks raised funds for the publishing organizations and their chosen causes. For the women's suffrage movement in particular, the books were furthermore useful for how they "advertised the movement, and refuted antisuffrage claims that women's rights advocates abandoned their kitchens, homes, and families."[86] One of the key issues represented in the suffrage cookbook that seems to have impressed compilers of the 1976 cookbook, led by editor Shirlie Kaplan, was the recording of women's names. In the introduction, for example, Kaplan makes note of how the compilers of the 1909 cookbook at first did not plan to attribute recipes with any contributor names. The women, however, later changed their minds, refusing, as Kaplan puts it, "to disappear into anonymity."[87]

As a cookbook that speaks from two periods, *Pots and Politics* has a wide scope, further broadened by the prefacing content of the *Washington Women's Cook Book*. Just as second-wave feminists sought out historical ties for generational anchoring and the validation of women's knowledge, the *Washington Women's Cook Book* compilers placed their own cookbook within a legacy of women's cooking skills, labor, and craft. The dedication acknowledges a "long line" of women's activism (see figure 9), and the editors further write in the preface, "Students of the human race declare that it was woman who first discovered how to build a fire; . . . The inventive genius of those first months made up a cook-book, limited indeed, yet passed on from mother to daughter as the best product of the wisdom of their times.

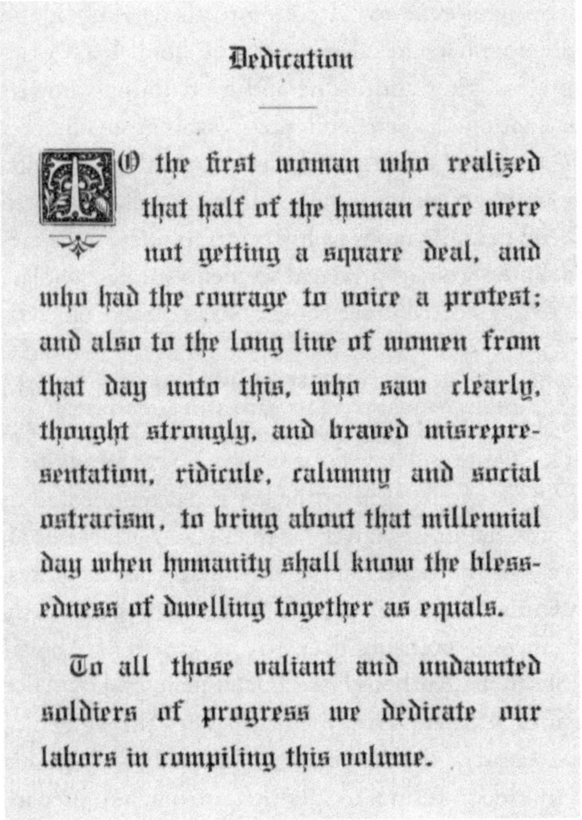

Dedication

To the first woman who realized that half of the human race were not getting a square deal, and who had the courage to voice a protest; and also to the long line of women from that day unto this, who saw clearly, thought strongly, and braved misrepresentation, ridicule, calumny and social ostracism, to bring about that millennial day when humanity shall know the blessedness of dwelling together as equals.

To all those valiant and undaunted soldiers of progress we dedicate our labors in compiling this volume.

FIGURE 9. Dedication, from Linda Deziah Jennings's *Washington Women's Cook Book*, 1909. Manuscripts, Archives, and Special Collections, Washington State University Libraries, Pullman.

We present you these recipes, product of the civilization of our times. In them are represented science, art and the human desire to produce things beautiful."[88] Kaplan and the compilers of *Pots and Politics* echo this in their own introduction, saying that one of their aims in republishing the book was to "demonstrate that while feminism is a revitalized movement, its principles are older."[89]

Pots and Politics participates in feminist recovery—in "setting straight the public record on women's achievements"—not only by republishing and redistributing a first-wave feminist cookbook but also through materially recovering the book: that is, in how it embeds the historical content within contemporary feminist commentary.[90] Through this process of republishing as recovery, the original text becomes timely and "activated in another, historical present."[91] By bringing renewed attention to the cookbook and setting it within a contemporary textual context, the book makes ties between the past and present, thus addressing and overcoming women's feelings of historical alienation. Kaplan and the Washington Chapter members recognized the potential of cookbooks as historical documents, ones that trace the personal lives and economic interventions of women "who might otherwise remain anonymous to historical inquiry."[92] In creating their own cookbook, the women preceded women's studies scholars who would only in later decades come to see cookbooks as objects of "'serious' academic scrutiny."[93]

The focus of the book is not, however, only looking to the past; Kaplan and compilers further use the suffrage-era cookbook to ignite conversations about how far feminism has come and how far it still has to go. In addition to equal pay and education for women, one of the key issues represented in the surrounding, second-wave feminist material is the ERA. With the book published in 1976, the year of the American bicentennial, Kaplan writes, "Will there *be* a Tricentennial? If so, will women be there monotonously repeating identical grievances?—pointing back to the letters of Abigail Adams, the speech of Susan B. Anthony, the amendment of Dr. Alice Paul . . . to be told, wait until next year. How many times can the women of the land take that home instead of their humanity?" In a bid to evade this monotonous and grievance-ridden future, recipes that are quick to prepare are included in the section "Speed Cooking—Recipes for the Busy Political Worker, Elected Official or Candidate (. . . Not Governors Who Have a Staff)," which appears before the republished suffrage cookbook. *Pots and Politics* also encouraged men to take part in kitchen activities, with Kaplan writing that "there ought to be a sharing of the joys of preparation as well as the joys of consumption" and that the recipes in the book "may be recreated by members of either sex."[94] In acknowledging the earlier gender divisions described in the *Washington Women's Cook Book* but expressing a hope that cooking could help society move past these divisions, the book looks not only to the past but to the future.

The next and final section continues this future-looking perspective by examining how community cookbook self-publishing by a group of feminist science and speculative fiction writers helped fund a literary prize focused on expanded understandings of gender and revitalized community interest in feminist science fiction.

Building a Feminist Future

A common thread connecting the feminist community cookbooks examined so far is their flexibility and ability to work well at the grassroots. These are common aspects of all community cookbooks, which are designed and sold in ways that address specific, often local, audiences to raise funds for beneficial causes, and are not unique to feminist cookbooks. However, what is noteworthy about feminist community cookbooks is how they seem, as textual and saleable objects, to eschew both mainstream definitions of feminism as well as pressures to perform feminism in prescribed ways. Second-wave feminist community cookbooks seem, then, to presage the third wave of feminism that began to appear in the early 1990s and that demonstrated a "playfulness within the terrain of femininity."[95] Self-publishing and the ability to act locally at the grassroots gave a diverse range of women (and some men) the opportunity to experiment at and with the boundaries of feminism: engaging with historical culinary sites of women's creativity and ingenuity when others shied away and even, as the following examination of the creation of the 1991 cookbook *The Bakery Men Don't See Cookbook* addresses, creating a literary institution to take feminism into the future.

The Bakery Men Don't See Cookbook was part of a fundraising campaign to establish and support the James Tiptree Jr. Memorial Award, now called the Otherwise Award. Lisa Yaszek has linked the Tiptree Award to other important science fiction feminist "firsts"—including the first academic journal on feminist science fiction studies, *Femspec*, launched in 1999, and the first feminist speculative fiction press, Aqueduct, founded in 2004—citing these collectively as evidence of a renewed interest in feminist science fiction due to digital accessibility and connectivity, which created a kind of "technosocial matrix."[96] But, while the Tiptree Award was indeed the first award of its kind, created to honor works that further the exploration and expansion of gender roles in science fiction and fantasy, the connection to the digital age is overstated.[97] Rather, the award came out of in-person meetings at science fiction conventions and was funded by the grassroots efforts of volunteers, some of whom had long been involved in the feminist fanzine world. Self-published in 1991 with a Macintosh IIx computer by the Society for the Furtherance and Study of Fantasy and Science Fiction (SF^3), *The Bakery Men Don't See Cookbook* bridges these two moments. It also stands slightly outside the general time frame of this work, which has a focus on the years 1950 to 1990. However, as a final case for examination, the book is useful for how it can be seen as reaching across the second and third waves of feminism as well as, in some regards, marking the end of a political and technological era.

The award was first proposed by speculative fiction authors Karen Joy Fowler and Pat Murphy after in-person meetings at WisCon, a feminist science fiction convention held annually in Wisconsin. Another feminist science fiction first, WisCon began in 1977, a time at which "it was considered progressive for most conventions to schedule a single 'Women in SF' panel."[98] Although science fiction has historically been a genre dominated by male authors, women who were connected to feminism began to write in the genre as part of a "new wave of science fiction" in the late 1960s and 1970s.[99] For feminist authors science and speculative fiction was useful, as writer Pamela Sargent put it, as "a questioning of why things are as they are and how they might be different."[100] Similar to the consciousness-raising novel of the 1970s that described women's real lives and thereby offered women readers the chance at a "vicarious 'aha' moment" of understanding their oppression, feminist speculative fiction could also reveal and interrogate societal injustice and gender inequalities.[101] However, unlike the consciousness-raising novel that was firmly based in reality, feminist science fiction was a way for women to "imagine alternatives to patriarchal society."[102] Popular authors of the era included Ursula K. LeGuin, Joanna Russ, Octavia Butler, and, it would later be revealed, Alice B. Sheldon, also known as James Tiptree Jr.

Alice B. Sheldon appeared on the scene in 1968 as part of the new wave of science fiction authors, publishing her stories under the pseudonym James Tiptree Jr. As many female science fiction authors have done, Sheldon chose to write under the guise of a male identity, a tactic that no doubt aided her success.[103] Sheldon herself proved this to be true, later releasing stories under a different, female pseudonym, Raccoona Sheldon, who had to be "recommended by Tiptree before editors would read her submissions."[104] Tiptree was an unusual and mysterious writer, who did not appear at any award ceremonies and did not take telephone calls. All communication with Tiptree had to be done through the mail, which was delivered to a post box, and although Sheldon/Tiptree maintained many close friendships with fellow writers, this was done exclusively through the exchange of letters.[105] Tiptree was also a feminist and made this fact well known, through the incorporation of feminist themes and the exploration of gender in his stories and by contributing to a written Women in Science Fiction symposium in the fanzine

Khatru. As Justine Larbalestier as commented, "At the same time that Tiptree was being critically acclaimed for such stories as 'The Women Men Don't See,' [women writers] were being vociferously attacked and patronized for their feminism."[106] Tiptree withdrew the story from consideration for the 1974 Nebula Award, "so as not to steal votes as a male feminist."[107]

There was, as a result, much speculation about the "real" Tiptree. Theories included that Tiptree was a "a government agent or a great outdoorsman," neither of which were far from the truth; as a child, Sheldon had traveled with her parents on many hunting and scientific expeditions to Africa, and later in life she worked in photo intelligence at the CIA. Others suggested that Tiptree might perhaps be a woman. Friend Robert Silverberg, who complimented the "lean, muscular [and] supple" stories of Tiptree, rejected this theory, writing in the introduction to the 1975 Tiptree collection *Warm Worlds and Otherwise*, "It has been suggested that Tiptree is female, a theory that I find absurd, for there is to me something ineluctably masculine about Tiptree's writing."[108]

Tiptree was, however, publicly revealed to be Alice B. Sheldon in 1977. In correspondence with friends after this unexpected "outing," Sheldon shared her dismay at the loss of Tiptree, suggesting that Tiptree was more than an author's pen name. Rox Samer, addressing the author's complex gender identity, writes, "She wrote to other lesbians of her lifelong love of and desire for women and did so at the same time as she explored masculine and male gender identities alongside female ones, simultaneously reaching out for 'sisterhood' and mourning the loss of Tiptree." For this reason Samer considers Tiptree/Sheldon—or Tip/Alli as the author sometimes referred to him/herself—to be an important figure in not only feminist science fiction but also transfeminist history, one who "caused many cisgender male authors and fans to rethink their gendered presumptions."[109]

It was just this complexity that Pat Murphy and Karen Joy Fowler were drawn to in the creation of the Tiptree Award. The idea for an award for women's writing in science fiction was initially—and jokingly—proposed to Murphy by author and "troublemaker" Richard Kadrey, who thought it would "really piss people off." Murphy, however, who had experienced stereotyping and criticism as a female author of science fiction, thought the idea had merit and brought it up to fellow author Karen Joy Fowler. Together they decided that the award would not honor women writers of science fiction, as originally suggested, but rather the overall exploration of gender within the genre. The two also decided to name the award after a woman, noting that some of the most prominent awards in science fiction—the Hugo Award, the Philip K. Dick Award, and the Arthur C. Clarke Award—were named after men. For these reasons the name James Tiptree Jr. was chosen, honoring both the themes of Tiptree's fiction as well as the irony of the author's history. "It seemed," Murphy stated later, "like such a perfect idea."[110]

Irony and playfulness around the concept of gender were thus built into the award from the very start. There was also a certain playfulness around the idea of a literary award itself, as Tiptree, although a winner of several major science fiction and fantasy awards, had showed a noticeable "reticence about awards and award politics."[111] These elements were on full display at the very first award ceremony, at which Diane Martin dressed as James Tiptree Jr., and the two winners, Gwyneth Jones and Eleanor Arnason, were presented with edible chocolate typewriter trophies. While the founders of the award were interested in "recognis[ing] and reward[ing] value" as well as "bring[ing] relatively unknown writers to recognition," which are common motivations for establishing a literary prize, this was more politically and creatively than economically motivated. Whereas many awards are created to support the publishing industry and "the consumption of literature generally," Tiptree Award founders were concerned with creating a communal space for the exploration and appreciation of diverse narratives within science fiction and fantasy.[112] Writing in *Feminist Bookstore News* in 1995 about the success of the award so far, Susanna J. Sturgis already noted how the very existence of the award seemed to be encouraging the kind of gender exploration in fiction that it was created to celebrate.[113]

Financing the award also presented opportunities for playful engagement with stereotypical gender roles, with one of the earliest financing strategies being bake sales. Murphy writes, "As a political statement, as a means of involving people at the grassroots level, and as an excuse to eat cookies, the award has been financed partly through bake sales at science fiction conventions, organized and supported by fans, writers, and editors."[114] In addition to bake sales, fans in Madison, Wisconsin, came up with the idea for a cookbook almost immediately after the announcement of the award at WisCon in 1991. Jeanne Gomoll recalls that "a bunch of us Madisonians clustered around Pat and began vocalizing such dangerous phrases as 'I'll help,' 'We'd like to publish—,' 'I could do—.'"[115] Gomoll and Diane Martin, who had both been involved with WisCon and editing science fiction fanzines, led the cookbook project, publishing *The Bakery Men Don't See Cookbook* in 1991 and in 1993 a follow-up cookbook, *Her Smoke Rose Up from Supper*, both with "Tiptree puns for titles."[116] Selling at ten dollars and advertised in fanzines such as *Marion Zimmer Bradley's Fantasy Magazine* and *Interzone*, the book was one of the award's earliest fundraising endeavors, which have also included T-shirt sales, auctions, an edited republished edition of *Khatru*, and the sale of a collectively made quilt.[117] At the first Tiptree Award ceremony, a check representing cookbook sales of $1,000 was presented to SF^3.[118]

The cookbook itself can be seen as part of the gender exploration valued by SF^3 members and the award's founders: a traditionally feminine medium used to spotlight and break down gender stereotypes. In a stroke of "delicious irony," the compilers decided to name the book after the withdrawn Nebula-nominated story "The Women Men Don't See," with part of the joke being that, "while men may ignore women, they certainly pay attention to food." At the same time, and though abundant in female voices, the book's compilers were sure to highlight that men as well as women had been involved in the book's creation, and recipes contributed by men are also sprinkled throughout the book. By 1991 the presence of a few men in a community cookbook was not an uncommon sight, even if women continued to be the lead compilers and editors. However, in the case of *The Bakery Men Don't See Cookbook*, the compilers aimed to both help financially fund the Tiptree Award and forward its principles—what they describe as "consciousness- and fund-raising." The participation of men and women in the cookbook was symbolic of the barriers the award meant to break down. "If women and men can work together on projects like cookbooks and cooking without dragging in a lot of counter-productive sexual stereotypes," they write, "maybe we can work together on other projects as well."[119]

Since its founding the award has been an important way to support feminist ideas and the exploration of gender in science fiction and fantasy. Moving away from the literary alone, the award began to honor other forms of stories that explored concepts of gender, sexuality, and identity, and in 2009 Nisi Shawl commented on how the award has paved the way for and brought recognition to many nonbinary and trans members of the science fiction community.[120] In addition to this, Gomoll reflects that the award helped revitalize WisCon and science fiction feminism at a time when antifeminist

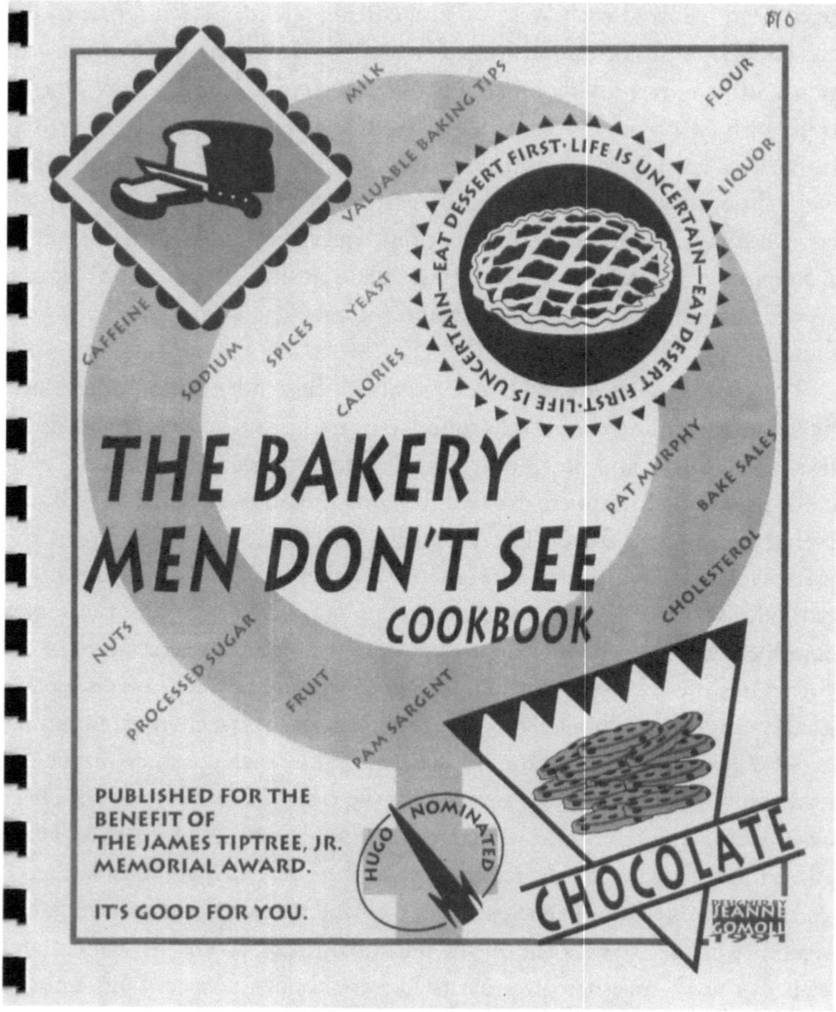

FIGURE 10. Cover of Diane Martin, Jeanne Gomoll, and SF^3's *The Bakery Men Don't See Cookbook*, noting the Hugo Award nomination, 1991. Second printing, 1992. Courtesy of Jeanne Gomoll.

rhetoric was high and when it was feared the gathering was "in the process of losing touch with its feminist mission." WisCon has, since the first award ceremony, consistently hosted the Tiptree—now Otherwise—Award, with each, according to Gomoll, supporting the continued existence of the other.[121] Fundraising activities such as bake sales and producing a cookbook offered opportunities for engagement with and a reinvigoration of feminist science fiction at the local level, supporting a literary award that helped further the aims of science fiction feminism for future generations. Indeed, rather than being part of projects of rediscovery through digital age connectivity, the cookbook and other fundraising efforts connected to the Tiptree Award were an opportunity to engage with feminist science fiction between the second and third waves of feminism, bridging a gap at a time when interest in the genre and its politics was beginning to wane. In another twist of "delicious irony," the cookbook became a phenomenon in its own right: in 1991 the book was nominated for a Hugo Award—one of the many science fiction awards named after a man—a fact displayed on the book's cover (see figure 10).

As this chapter has overall addressed, although it is easy to assume that feminists did not produce cookbooks or that producers of feminist community cookbooks were more traditional, holding onto tasks like cooking as a way to move more slowly into a radically different future, evidence shows that this was not the case. Cookbooks, like bake sales, provided a way for women to localize feminism for regional and suburban communities across America and inspire grassroots action. They could also be sites for doing the work of women's studies, recovering and reactivating historical documents through republishing, and helping to create long-lasting literary institutions that aimed to bring feminism into a new era—doing so in each instance without waiting for approval, permission, or mainstream acceptance.

Conclusion

Liberating the Community Cookbook

THE "LIVING SECTION" of the *New York Times* ran an article in 1977, titled "Cooking with Betty Friedan . . . Yes, Betty Friedan." Written by Friedan herself and headed with a cartoon depicting a woman crawling out of a giant can of Campbell's chicken noodle soup, the article described Friedan's rediscovery of the joys of cooking. Making it clear that she was not "announcing public defection from the women's movement," Friedan used the piece to reflect on how food connects to pleasure, family, care, and creativity.[1] Two weeks later letters from readers commenting on the article were also published. Although the five letters, all from women, had differing opinions on the details of Friedan's piece, none took issue with the idea of a feminist cooking. One disgruntled reader wrote, "You don't speak for us, Betty Friedan. We have never been ashamed of our culinary skills or the pleasures they provide." Another, however, seemed to find the article liberating. "Your article in this morning's Times warmed me and pleased me for many reasons," she writes, "not the least being that I have been vaguely apologetic these last years to my friends in the women's movement because I still love to cook."[2]

These examples show the disconnect that could exist between mainstream feminist rhetoric, amplified by national media, and the lives of women involved in the movement. The "canonization or crucifixion" of feminists by the press motivated many women to create their own channels of communication, such as feminist presses, journals, magazines, fanzines, and newsletters.[3] To date, community cookbooks—compiled recipe books most closely associated with ladies' charitable associations and women's church auxiliaries—have not been considered to be a part of this publishing history. However, as the previous chapters have detailed, community cookbooks were taken up by a wide variety of women to display and learn skills, to connect to other women, to foster support for and fund civil rights, to textually advocate for progressive causes, to inspire grassroots activism, and, not least of all, to support the second-wave feminist movement.

At a time when women were becoming increasingly liberated in the eyes of society from stereotypical gender roles, community cookbooks continued to be produced by women compilers across the country. The popularity of community cookbooks between 1950 and 1990 can be ascribed, at least partially, to accessible and affordable channels for printing. As chapter 2 addresses, the emergence of commercial printers and binders that focused on the community cookbook market as well as the widespread availability of at-home printing technologies opened up self-publishing of community cookbooks for a diverse range of groups. Through—and at times across—self-publishing channels, a number of women's groups were able to put out cookbooks and sell them as fundraising objects.

But while these new printing avenues might have contributed to the ongoing popularity of community cookbooks during these decades, they do not, in isolation, explain sustained and new interest in community cookbooks during such a seemingly unlikely time. Placing the cookbooks within their historical context and looking into specific contradictory themes—women and work, profits and politics, and food and feminism—the previous chapters have attempted to shed light on why so many different women were motivated to self-publish fundraising cookbooks. As was described, women adapted community cookbooks to meet their own social, professional, educational, and political needs. Rather than serving to maintain the status quo, as culinary texts are often thought to do, community cookbooks provided women with a way to influence and change the world around them. The flexible and adaptable genre allowed women to include content specific to their own needs, and, more than this, involvement in the self-publishing cookbook project could be a way to bring vastly different aspects of their lives together.

Although cookbooks are often associated with the home and the domestic sphere, chapter 3 shows that women used the project of the community cookbook to materialize voluntary labor as well as to gain new, potentially employable, skills. Cookbook projects could be a way to make connections, gain experience, and in some cases transition into paid careers, with the self-publishing of cookbooks also being one of many milestones in a woman's voluntary and unpaid career. Although these "invisible careers" were not always recognized or acknowledged as work, they could be incredibly rewarding for the women involved, who published, marketed, distributed, and sold thousands of books outside of traditional publishing channels. Community cookbook projects were also becoming increasingly sophisticated, with women's groups forwarding production and distribution methods that made innovative use of their own talents and networks. As well as working with professional publishers to bring community cookbooks into mainstream markets, cookbook producers ran their own "veritable" cookbook businesses. American Junior League chapters in particular raised significant funds, with their cookbooks selling at speeds that rivaled—or were better than—traditionally published cookbooks.

As chapter 4 details, interest in cookbooks was not limited to women's associations during these decades. Mainstream publishing also experienced a cookbook explosion, with cookbooks taking on more narrative, cultural, and political qualities, as the books moved from instruction manuals to lifestyle guides. Within this market for political cookbooks, women who were involved in new social and political groups of the era began to use the interior space of community cookbooks to advocate for change. Through the addition of extra features—such as forewords, letters of support, and illustrations—politically themed community cookbooks aimed to entice readers who would not normally be interested in the causes of civil rights, integration, and the New Left. Through this content compiling associations hoped to "subtly" engage with readers and influence their political stance. In these cases recipes for food were often secondary to the political cause of the cookbook. The recipes themselves even became spaces that could prompt political action, with activist recipes giving specific instructions for activism—such as organizing a social action group or mailing a congressperson—alongside and part of instructions for cooking food.

In regard to underrepresented groups and racial minorities, the self-publishing of a cookbook could, as a project, itself be a political action. At a time when interest in ethnic and international cookbooks was high, some minority groups felt their own unique culinary traditions were being ignored. Community cookbooks created opportunities to rewrite mainstream culinary narratives about authentic ethnic cooking. Community cookbook projects like *The Historical Cookbook of the American Negro* and *Cooking with Soul* also aimed to affect change not (only) through fundraising but by engaging young people in cookbook making. Through the acts of gathering recipes and speaking to community members, students participated in the preservation and celebration of their own communities. Although some cookbooks had connections to politics and the civil rights movement, such as the *Soul Power Cook Book* by the students of East Palo Alto's Ravenswood High, others were radical for how they used cookbook projects to get to the roots of societal problems.

The final chapter turns to the self-publishing of community cookbooks by feminists to question the "cliché . . . that cookery and feminism are not natural allies."[4] Building off of the work by Stacy J. Williams, the chapter brings to light a greater number—nineteen to date (see appendix B)—of cookbooks created by explicitly feminist groups. Despite the fact that some movement leaders vocally positioned themselves against cooking as a way to distance themselves from stereotypes that served to confine women to the domestic sphere, community cookbooks nonetheless were created to raise funds for the cause of women's liberation. Through these cookbooks, often created by local chapters of national feminist organizations, women brought national feminist ideas to areas outside of the main feminist centers and, by engaging in tried and tested means of fundraising, localized feminist action for smaller communities. In addition to the cookbooks from groups that emerged during women's liberation and the second wave of feminism, such as NOW and NARAL, numerous preexisting women's groups published community cookbooks during these years, some of which make their support of feminism explicit. In these instances the use of existing networks and time-tested strategies was successful at garnering wide support at the local level.

Feminists also used the community cookbook genre as a way to connect to a feminist past. In the case of the National Women's Political Caucus cookbook *Pots and Politics*, the compilers engaged in revisioning by republishing a historical suffrage cookbook and surrounding it with contemporary texts and recipes. In this way, and before women's studies scholars began to take culinary literature seriously, women self-publishers were using the genre of the community cookbook to connect to a feminist past but also, as the final example has shown, to a feminist future. In publishing *The Bakery Men Don't See Cookbook*, science fiction writers came together to financially support a new literary award, one that helped revive a feminist fan community, create a literary institution that supports the exploration of gender in science fiction and fantasy, and bridge a gap between feminist and technological moments.

These chapters explore the extreme edges of community cookbook production to understand why, at a time when community cookbook production seemed most at odds with the new developments in women's lives, women continued to create community-made cookbooks to raise funds. This work, therefore, purposefully foregrounds books and compiling associations related to women's work and political involvement, as well as cookbooks produced by and for the advancement of feminist aims, but there is still much left to be said about community cookbooks from the second half of the twentieth century. *Contradictory Cookbooks* only cursorily addresses women's church and temple auxiliaries, although these groups produced community cookbooks in far greater numbers than many of the groups highlighted here. Future research could look to these organizations to understand their own—possibly shifting—motivations for creating community cookbooks during these years, as well as into the production of community cookbooks by Americans living outside of the United States. The Cookery and Food Collection at the University of Michigan, for instance, includes numerous books produced by women living and working overseas. Books like the 1981 *From the Crocodiles: Recipes from the International Women's Club, Kaduna, Nigeria* and the 1969 community cookbook *¡Buen Provecho!*, by the Women's Society for Christian Service in El Salvador demonstrate the transnational flows of people, material texts, and genre that are rarely addressed. Moreover, closer examination of books by groups such as Native communities—groups of which have been publishing community cookbooks for nearly as long as the American Junior League—gender and sexual minorities, and other American minorities would also help to shift perceptions of twentieth-century community cookbooks away from the idea that the books were produced almost exclusively by and for white Protestant housewives.[5]

Moving beyond the temporal boundaries of this study, an interesting area of research would be community cookbooks in the 1990s, especially in the wake of the many technological changes that occurred in this decade. Indeed, the time frame explored within this work, 1950 to 1990, is as much a cultural as a technological boundary, with community cookbook production having been meaningfully influenced by the inherent flexibility of the compiled cookbook genre but also by the specific printing options available.

The 1990s brought about many changes in American life, and, in publishing, the decade saw the availability of the desktop computer change self-publishing in significant ways. Not long after, the internet allowed for quick and nearly cost-free sharing of content. Self-publishing, as a result, became more accessible than it had ever been, with the necessary agents needed to write, design, edit, and publish a book being as few as one. For community cookbooks this is an important consideration, and it would need to be addressed with a new critical lens that takes the cultural and historical aspects unique to this period into account.

The 1990s also offer the chance to address what seems to be a significant increase in cookbooks sold by and for LGBTQIA+ communities. The 1993 book *Philadelphia Stories: A Dining Out for Life Cookbook* was, for instance, sold to commemorate Philadelphia culinary artists that lost their lives to AIDS, with proceeds supporting "programs for people living with AIDS."[6] The 1995 *Out in the Kitchen: A Cookbook . . . for Those with Non-discriminating Taste* used the fundraising cookbook format to reach voters in Maine, asking them to vote for the protection of antidiscrimination laws.[7] While research into queer cookbooks has been forwarded by Alex Ketchum and Katharina Vester, there is still much to be said about how gender and sexual identity have been part of community cookbooks—through their creators but also in the books' contents, production, distribution, and reception—in the 1990s and beyond.[8]

And what of community cookbooks in the twenty-first century? Cursory examinations seem to indicate that the genre has significantly waned but nonetheless continues on, evolving and changing alongside technological and social conditions. Whereas the second half of the twentieth century saw a proliferation of new commercial printing companies joining a competitive market for community cookbook production, recent decades, however, show a consolidation of these commercial printers, with, for instance, Jumbo Jack's and G&R now part of the company Cookbook Specialists. On the other end of the spectrum, zines—self-published booklets that often come out of underground and oppositional channels—are a popular venue for twenty-first century DIY community cookbooks. These community cookzines take up many genre conventions of community cookbooks but place publication within different artistic and DIY contexts.[9] The 2022 global "anthology of recipes," *You Stir the Pot: Recipes for Change*, for example, resembles the political community cookbooks of the 1960s and 1970s in its use of food and activist recipes, but, instead of collecting recipes locally, contributors can fill out an online form to submit their recipe to the book.[10]

Indeed, it seems that today community cookbooks are now just as likely to be found online and in digital formats as in print, which has had specific benefits. In 2020, as the global COVID-19 pandemic prompted widespread lockdowns and vast social isolation, the community cookbook received renewed attention.[11] A *New York Times* article titled "The Community Cookbook Is Reborn for a Time of Scarcity and Sharing" describes trends in community cookbooks made during quarantine, in which creators used online tools to bring together a potentially global compiling body. With the books "showing up more often on Google Docs than on physical pages" and free to access by online readers, community cookbooks during and after the pandemic are—even more so than their printed predecessors—less about raising funds than bringing people together.[12]

A prime example of the new digital iteration of community cookbooks is the book *The F*ck You Buffet: Secret Family Recipes of Kids Betrayed by Their Homophobic Parents and a Few Recipes from Good and Kind People Because Balance Is Key*. This collection of recipes first appeared as a thread on Tumblr after a user shared a secret family recipe as an impromptu act of culinary revenge against a homophobic family member. Other LGBTQIA+ posters felt inspired to share their own recipes, and the resultant collection was later gathered into a digital book and shared as a Google Doc.[13] While revenge against homophobic family members was the overarching theme, allies also shared recipes and messages of support, and the Tumblr post and resulting book were, in the end, more about togetherness than revenge. The cookbook helped acknowledge a community and its struggles and provided a means through which individuals could share and show their solidarity. Like many of the books produced in the second half of the twentieth century, *The F*ck You Buffet* is only incidentally about recipes and food. On the other hand, there are stark differences between this book and the community cookbooks that came before it. First, *The F*ck You Buffet* is completely digital, and as such lacks the materiality so important to community cookbooks of the twentieth century. Moreover, all contributors to the book are credited using their Tumblr handle, and so it is not clear who exactly contributed or what gender they identify as. This is, for community cookbooks, a significant change, one that not only moves the genre away from the earliest versions of the books that guaranteed "tried and true" recipes from a local community but also, as users remain anonymous, beyond the explicitly gendered constraints of the genre that nineteenth- and twentieth-century creators creatively worked within.

With a digital existence, a lack of economic motivation, and a wide range of contributors—not exclusively or even mainly women—many community cookbooks in the twenty-first century are almost unrecognizable from the charitable cookbooks sold at ladies' aid fairs. Yet community cookbooks do continue. Just as women in the second half of the twentieth century took the existing structure of the community cookbook and adapted it to meet their own specific needs, compilers of today's community cookbooks are adjusting the genre—adding, subtracting, and tinkering with the recipes for the books—to make cookbooks that are valuable and useful to them. And, despite the economic, media, and gendered differences presented in the reborn form of the genre, what remains the same is that community cookbooks, whether on the physical page or digital screen, continue to be a way and reason to bring different—at times contradictory—ideas, eras, causes, and people together.

ACKNOWLEDGMENTS

As with a community cookbook, that this book exists at all is thanks to a collective of people: to Corinna Norrick-Rühl, for taking a big chance on an unusual dissertation topic proposed by a doctoral candidate she hardly knew and for providing invaluable guidance and feedback along the way; to Simon Rosenberg, for bringing the field of book history to life and always asking tough questions; to Erin Kummer, for many things, not least of all always being a voice of encouragement and having the best eye for detail; to my anonymous peer reviewers as well as Leslie Howsam, Chandni Ananth, Erin Kummer, Nayantara Srinivasan, and Laura Ntoumanis, for their helpful comments and corrections at various points of this process; to Silvia Schultermandl, for her supervision and guidance; to Nathaniel Holly, Laura Theobald, Susan Silver, and the University of Georgia Press for bringing this work into being; to my family, for their love and support; and to G, for everything.

For assistance with and support of in-person research visits, I would also like to extend my heartfelt thanks to the following institutions and their staff: the Doris S. Kirschner Cookbook Collection at the University of Minnesota's Magrath Library; the Beatrice McIntosh Cookery Collection housed at the Du Bois Library of the University of Massachusetts, Amherst; the Cookery and Food Collection at Michigan State University; and the Schlesinger Library on the History of Women in America, Radcliffe College, Harvard University. For digital resource access and library assistance, my thanks go to the Schlesinger Library on the History of Women in America, Radcliffe College, Harvard University; the Russell J. Ebeid Library and Resource Center at the Arab American National Museum; and the Kautz Family YMCA Archives, University of Minnesota Libraries. Finally, this research would have hardly been possible without funding provided by two generous research grants: a Michigan State University Libraries Special Collections Visiting Fellowship and a BSA-Pine Tree Foundation Fellowship in Culinary Bibliography.

APPENDIX A: COMMERCIAL PRINTERS AND BINDERS

1. Bev-Ron Publishing Company
2. Circulation Service
3. Cookbook Publishers
4. Favorite Recipes Press
5. Fundcraft Publishing
6. G&R Publishing Company
7. General Publishing and Binding
8. Jumbo Jack's Cookbooks
9. Morris Press
10. North American Press
11. S. C. Toof and Company
12. Walter's Cookbooks
13. Wimmer
14. Women's Clubs Publishing Company

APPENDIX B: COMMUNITY COOKBOOKS BY SECOND-WAVE FEMINISM ORGANIZATIONS

Books marked with * did not appear in the WorldCat Library Database as of September 2025.

1. *Coalition of Labor Union Women, Southeastern Massachusetts Chapter, *CLUW Guide to Cooking: A Book for Men and Women* (North Dartmouth, Mass.: Coalition of Labor Union Women, Southeastern Massachusetts Chapter, n.d.).
2. *Coalition of Labor Union Women, *CLUW's Guide for Gourmets Cookbook* (N.p., 1981).
3. Maya Contenta and Victoria Ramstetter, *The Whoever Said Dykes Can't Cook? Cookbook* (Ohio: Dinah, 1983).
4. *Mary A. Gill, Phyllis W. Stevens, Judith Judson, *First Virginia Feminist Cookbook* (Lynchburg: NOW Virginia, 1983).
5. Vicki Hopman Yates, Portland Area Women's Political Caucus, *Political Favorites: Featuring Recipes of Oregon Politicians* (Portland: Portland Area Women's Political Caucus, 1983).
6. Illinois Women's Political Caucus, *What's Cooking at the Capitol?* ([Springfield]: [Illinois Women's Political Caucus], [1981]).
7. Betty Johnston, Mary Taves, Joyce Purcell, and National Organization for Women, Wichita Chapter, *Everyperson's Cook Book* ([Wichita]: [Wichita NOW], [ca. 1970s]).
8. Shirlie Kaplan, ed., *Pots and Politics: An Historical Cookbook; From the Suffragists to the Equal Rights Amendment* (Tacoma: Washington State Women's Political Caucus, 1976).
9. Muskegon Area Women's Coalition, *Feminist Food Book* (N.p.: Depot Enterprise, 1982).

10. National Association for Girls and Women in Sport, *Cookies (and Punch, Too!)* (Washington, D.C.: National Association for Girls and Women in Sport, 1977).
11. New American Movement, Lucy Parson's Chapter, *Lucy Parsons' Recipes for a Red Planet* (Chicago: New American Movement, Lucy Parsons Chapter, 1970s).
12. *NOW, Broward County, Florida, *Cooking with Florida Feminist Flair* (Broward County: NOW, Broward County, Florida, 1970).
13. NOW Greater Champaign Area Chapter, *NOW We're Cooking* (Champaign: NOW, Greater Champaign Area Chapter, 1979).
14. NOW, Denton, Texas, *A Book of Favorite Recipes* (Shawnee Mission, Kans.: Circulation Service, 1978).
15. *NOW, Tarrant County Chapter, *"Women Are A-Risin'": Feminist Food for Thought Cookbook* (Tarrant County, Tex.: NOW, Tarrant County Chapter, 1986).
16. *NOW West Palm Beach Chapter, Florida, [men's recipe book] ([West Palm Beach]: NOW West Palm Beach Chapter, Florida, 1978).
17. *Oregon NARAL Supporters, *CHOICE Recipes* ([Troutdale]: Oregon NARAL, 1982).
18. *Participants in the Seminar "Politics and Creation: Woolf, Nin and Lessing," *The Dinner Party: A Literary Feast* ([Morgantown, W.Va.], 1979).
19. Women Employed, *The Working Women's Cookbook: Recipes for a Small Salary* (Chicago: Women Employed, 1975).

NOTES

Introduction. Women, Liberation, and the Contradiction of Community Cookbooks

1. L. Gordon, "State Could Lose Them."

2. L. Gordon, "Recipe for Success"; Arthur and Elizabeth Schlesinger Library, "Culinary Holdings," 4.

3. As described by N. Jenkins in the *New York Times*, in 1984, two food-focused scholarly journals were founded. See "History of Food Gains," C1. All articles from the *New York Times* were retrieved from the article archive via the online Times-Machine, https://timesmachine.nytimes.com/.

4. Williams, "Subversive Cooking in Liberal Feminism," 276.

5. Avakian and Haber, "Feminist Food Studies," 1.

6. Potier, "Barbara Haber Brought Books."

7. Chevalier, "Trojan Horse."

8. Bower, *"Our Sisters' Recipes,"* 137; DuSablon, *America's Collectible Cookbooks*, 139.

9. Guensburg, "Delicious Irony."

10. Julian, "There's a Lot of History," A51. All articles from the *Boston Globe* were retrieved via https://www.proquest.com/historical-newspapers.

11. Weinraub, "Legacy of the Charitable Cookbook," E8. All articles from the *Washington Post* were retrieved via https://www.proquest.com/historical-newspapers.

12. As was sometimes the case. Ferguson, for instance, has argued that community cookbooks were part of a "political battle against feminism," whose authors "saw 'women's lib' as demeaning their place in the home." *Cookbook Politics*, 77.

13. Two in-person library visits to Michigan State University and Harvard University's Schlesinger Library were generously funded by the Michigan State University Libraries Special Collections Visiting Fellowship and a BSA-Pine Tree Foundation Fellowship in Culinary Bibliography, respectively. Other in-person research trips were taken to the University of Massachusetts Amherst and the University of Minnesota, Twin Cities, and a number of digital cookbook collections were consulted for this work, many of which are hosted by the Internet Archive.

14. Kelly, "Choice Receipts from American Housekeepers," 31.

15. Not all scholars agree on the terminology for the books. While Bower uses the term "community cookbook" in her influential edited compilation, *Recipes for Reading*, in her contribution to the volume, Longone uses the term "charities" to discuss the books. "Tried Receipts," 18.

16. See, for example, Bower, "Bound Together," 6; Gabaccia, "Food, Recipes, Cookbooks," 21; and Derleth, "Kneading Politics," 453.

17. Kelly, "Choice Receipts from American Housekeepers," 31.

18. Le Dantec-Lowry, "Reading Women's Lives in Cookbooks," 100. See also Boles, "Stirring Constantly," 33.

19. See, for example, Elias, *Food on the Page*; Bower, *"Our Sisters' Recipes"*; and Walden, *Tasteful Domesticity*.

20. For instance, Cook's bibliography *America's Charitable Cooks* addresses a period of 1861 to 1915, and Brown and Brown's *Culinary Americana* addresses the years 1860 to 1960.

21. Bower, "Bound Together," 6.

22. Wilmot Voss, *Women Politicking Politely*, 32.

23. Fox, "Community Cookbooks Trace Culinary Trends."

24. For example, community cookbooks may lack title pages or even identifiable titles. These features are described in more detail in chapter 2 of this volume.

25. Rasmussen, "Cataloging Community Cookbooks."

26. Iacovetta et al., introd. to *Edible Histories, Cultural Politics*, 5–6.

27. Ireland, "Compiled Cookbook as Foodways Autobiography," 108.

28. Boles, "Stirring Constantly."

29. "Cookbook" (emphasis added).

30. For more specific detail on print run numbers, see chapter 3 of this volume.

31. Howsam, "Study of the Book," 1.

32. Driver, "Cookbooks as Primary Sources," 258.

33. Murray, *Introduction to Contemporary Print Culture*, 2.

34. Price, *What We Talk About*, 11.

35. Price, *What We Talk About*, 72, 52.

36. Finkelstein and McCleery, *Introduction to Book History*, vii.

37. Darnton, "What Is the History?," 67.

38. Howsam, "In My View," 2; Ezell, "Laughing Tortoise," 336.

39. These strides can be seen, for example, with the publication of Eichhorn's *Adjusted Margin*, Lyons's *Typewriter Century*, and Rich Dana's 2022 book *Cheap Copies!*, as well as the 2023 course "Identifying and Understanding Twentieth-Century Duplicating Technologies" offered at the Rare Book School.

40. See, for instance, Reyes Elizondo and Cole, "On Decolonising Book History." See also Goldsby and McGill, "What Is 'Black'?"; Spires, "On Liberation Bibliography"; and Noble and Pyke, "Queer Bibliography."

41. These ways include but are not limited to Beins, "Publishing Assemblage"; Ozment, "Rationale for Feminist Bibliography"; Travis, "Women in Print Movement"; and Wilson et al., *Edinburgh Companion to Women.*

42. See Coker and Ozment, "Building the *Women in Book.*"

Chapter One. "What Else Can We Women Do?": Women's Clubs and Community Cookbooks

1. Longone and Longone, *American Cookbooks and Wine Books*, 32.

2. Ireland, "Compiled Cookbook as Foodways Autobiography," 107.

3. Appleby et al., *Encyclopedia of Women in American History*, xv, 256.

4. *Six Hundred Dollars a Year*, 45–46. Also partially included in Cook, *America's Charitable Cooks*, 6.

5. *Six Hundred Dollars a Year*, 46.

6. Scott, *Natural Allies*, 59–62, 58.

7. Scott, *Natural Allies*, 61.

8. Kirshenblatt-Gimblett, "Moral Sublime," 142.

9. See B. Gordon, "Playing at Being Powerless."

10. Kirshenblatt-Gimblett, "Moral Sublime," 142.

11. Scott, *Natural Allies*, 62.

12. Kirshenblatt-Gimblett, "Moral Sublime," 137.

13. B. Gordon, "Playing at Being Powerless," 146; Kirshenblatt-Gimblett, "Moral Sublime," 142.

14. B. Gordon, "Playing at Being Powerless," 147, 154. See also Kirshenblatt-Gimblett, "Moral Sublime," 150.

15. Scott, *Natural Allies*, 67.

16. Harbour, "I Earn by My Own."

17. Moores, *Lincoln*, 203–204.

18. Longone, "Tried Receipts," 21.

19. Other examples of the different kinds of books sold at Sanitary Fairs include Metropolitan Fair, *Catalogue of the Art Exhibition*; Jarvis, *Sophia*; and United States Sanitary Commission, *Book of Bubbles.*

20. Those books are Wittenmyer's *United States Christian Commission* and *Camp Cookery and Hospital Diet* and Cook's America's Charitable Cooks, 77, 173.

21. Moss, *Poetical Cook-Book*, 48–49, 103. Longone has noted that community cookbooks and women's magazine are both excellent sources for turn-of-the-century "rhyming recipes," and Miller and Hardman have more recently addressed the use of poetry in twentieth-century vegetarian and vegan cookbooks. Longone, "Mince Pie That Launched," 86; Miller and Hardman, "Lyrical Cookbook."

22. An exception to this is DuSablon, who lists the 1861 *Camp Cookery* cookbook as the first charity cookbook sold in the United States; however, the title clearly states that the book was produced and sold for volunteer use in hospitals rather than for fundraising. *America's Collectible Cookbooks*, 145.

23. Moss, *Poetical Cook-Book*, 1.

24. Fisher and Fisher, *Pot Roast, Politics, and Ants*, 28.

25. Longone, "Tried Receipts," 24.

26. Moss, *Poetical Cook-Book*.

27. A few examples include Alpha Phi, *Our Mothers' Recipes*; Members of the Ann Arbor, *Fare Thee Well*, 3; and Flora Macdonald Highland Games, *Flora's Fare*, 104. In Szathmary's 1972 introduction to *Poetical Cook-Book*, he makes the claim that because of this cookbook "the quotation became very famous."

28. Croly, *Sorosis*, 6.

29. Croly, *Sorosis*, 7.

30. Croly, *History of the Women's Club*.

31. Croly, *History of the Women's Club*.

32. Decker, "Meaning of the Woman's Club," 2.

33. Longone, "Tried Receipts," 26, 18.

34. Longone, "Tried Receipts," 21.

35. Kirshenblatt-Gimblett, "Moral Sublime," 151.

36. Kelly, "Choice Receipts from American Housekeepers," 31; Cook, *America's Charitable Cooks*. Longone has asserted that this number likely represents only half the amount of community cookbooks produced in these years. "Tried Receipts," 20.

37. Lyons, *History of Reading and Writing*, 187.

38. Casper, introd. to *History of the Book*, 7, 11, 15.

39. Appleby et al., *Encyclopedia of Women in American History*, 257.

40. Bower, "Bound Together," 5.

41. Long, "Aflame with Culture," 4:477.

42. Pawley, *Organizing Women*, 6; Long, "Aflame with Culture," 4:486, 478, 482; Felsenstein and Connolly, *What Middletown Read*, 168.

43. Long, "Aflame with Culture," 4:483, 484.

44. Long writes that, as women's skills in literary analysis increased, "clubs began to expect more original compositions." "Aflame with Culture," 4:482.

45. McHenry, "Reading and Race Pride," 4:494.

46. According to the bibliography of cookbooks by African Americans included as an appendix to Witt's book *Black Hunger*, at least three community cookbooks were compiled by Black women's groups between 1910 and 1936, one from the Negro Culinary Art Club of Los Angeles (221–222).

47. Schenone, *Thousand Years*, 120.

48. For example, see the case with the letter and recipe for "Roast Duck" from Jack London included in Kleber, *Suffrage Cook Book*, 45–46.

49. Kelly, "Choice Receipts from American Housekeepers," 37.

50. Indian Women's Club of Tulsa, *Indian Cook Book*, 3–5.

51. Sterling, *Alumnae Cookbook*.

52. Longone, "Tried Receipts," 20.

53. Lady Lytton's presence is noteworthy, not least of all because it was her father, Robert Bulwer-Lytton, first Earl of Lytton, who under the pen name Owen Meredith wrote the poem that has appeared in so many community cookbooks over the years. In fact, Lytton opens her handwritten recipe for "Hasty Pudding" in the *Suffrage Cook Book* with the first four lines of this poem. Kleber, *Suffrage Cook Book*, 153.

54. Kleber, *Suffrage Cook Book*, 7.

55. Longone, "Tried Receipts," 20; Derleth, "Kneading Politics," 452.

56. Scott, *Natural Allies*, 180.

57. See Dale, "Fundraising as Women's Work?," 4.

58. Scott, *Natural Allies*, 175.

59. Fisher and Fisher, *Pot Roast, Politics, and Ants*, 45.

60. Scott, *Natural Allies*, 175.

61. Mackintosh, "My Life and Hard Times."

62. Kaplan Daniels, *Invisible Careers*, 195, 17.

63. Cholesterol and Banks, "On the Picket Line," 6.

64. Schlafly, foreword to *Flavored with Freedom*; Ferguson, *Cookbook Politics*, 77.

65. Croly, *History of the Women's Club*, x.

66. Kleber, *Suffrage Cook Book*, 147.

67. Bradley, *Mass Media*, 41–42.

68. For a detailed description of the inequalities faced by women in America in the 1950s and 1960s, see Coontz, *Strange Stirring*, 5–18.

69. Neuhaus, "Way to a Man's Heart," 537.

70. Coontz, *Strange Stirring*, 61, 59.

71. Crowell, "Civil Rights Movement," 518.

72. Pandia Health Editorial Team, "Birth Control Throughout History."

73. Yellen, "History of Women's Work."

74. The "wave" metaphor of feminism has faced criticism, particularly for its focus on white, middle-class women, and also for its seemingly linear, progressive account of history. While the critiques of the metaphor are justified, it is nonetheless a common and useful shorthand for what Evans describes as a "tidal wave" of changes that took place as a result of women's activism in the second half of the twentieth century. *Tidal Wave*, 1.

75. Evans, *Tidal Wave*, 16.

76. Kretschmer, *Fighting for NOW*, 48.

77. Evans, "Women's Movement," 67, 66.

78. Cowan, *More Work for Mother*, 202–203; K. Jenkins, "Year of the Woman," 510.

79. Specific examples of this anticooking rhetoric within second-wave feminism are given in chapter 5 of this volume.

80. See Lane-McKinley, "Notes on Utopian Failure."

81. McMillian, "Our Founder, the Mimeograph Machine," 92.

82. Hayden and King, "Sex and Caste," 99.

83. "Revival of Feminism."

84. Williams, "Recipes for Resistance," 196.

85. Cannon, *Can-Opener Cookbook*, 1.

86. Endrijonas, "Processed Foods from Scratch," 157.

87. Estes Blair, "Dynamic Force in Our Community," 32.

Chapter Two. From Cookie Cutter to DIY: Cookbook Printing After World War II

1. Fox, "Community Cookbooks Trace Culinary Trends"; Guensburg, "Delicious Irony"; Julian, "There's a Lot of History," A51.

2. There were also increasing overlaps between these two areas in the given decades, a somewhat surprising trend that is addressed more comprehensively in chapter 3 of this volume.

3. Darnton, "What Is the History?," 67–68.

4. Levy, "Do Women Have a Book?," 298.

5. K. Melvin, "History of Neglect." This was originally published on the *Vida: Women in Literary Arts* website, which is no longer available. An archived version can be found through the Internet Archive's Wayback Machine.

6. Coser, "Publishers as Gatekeepers of Ideas," 15.

7. Adams and Barker, "New Model," 15; Malik, "Horizons of the Publishable."

8. For example, see McGrath, "Comping White."

9. K. Melvin, "History of Neglect."

10. In the introduction to *Oxford Handbook of Publishing*, for instance, Bhaskar and Phillips write that publishing is a "host of industries" (3).

11. Skains, *Digital Authorship*, 17.

12. Harker and Konchar Farr, "Outrageous, Dangerous, and Unassimilable," 2.

13. See Rasmussen, "Cataloging Community Cookbooks"; Kumin, "On Turn-of-the-Century Suffrage Cookbooks"; Bower, "Cooking Up Stories," 38; and Tye, *Baking as Biography*, 211.

14. Fisher and Fisher, *Pot Roast, Politics, and Ants*, 33.

15. Milford New Century Club, *Blue Hen's Chickens' Cook Book*; Women of Central Congregational Church, *Central Congregational Church Cook Book*; Stiefel and Jacobs, *St. Pauls Bazaar Kochbuch*.

16. Ireland, "Compiled Cookbook as Foodways Autobiography," 112.

17. "About Us."

18. Jumbo Jack's Cookbooks, *Let Us Help You Prepare*, 6, 3.

19. Wintermute, "Joy of Cataloging Community Cookbooks," 199.

20. Vance, "Walter's Publishing."

21. "About" (Jumbo Jack's).

22. "Our History" (Morris).

23. Wintermute, "Joy of Cataloging Community Cookbooks," 199; Hays, Rolfes and Associates, *How to Write and Publish*, 47 (emphasis in original).

24. "Ephemerals."

25. "Community and Church Cookbooks."

26. Longone, "Tried Receipts," 28.

27. "Our History" (Cookbook).

28. American Lutheran Church Women, *Bergen Cook Book*, 69, 29.

29. See, for example, Oxford United Methodist Church, *Art of Cooking in Oxford*.

30. "Our History" (Cookbook).

31. Women's Society St. Luke's Union, *Midlothian Woman's Cook Book*, 3.

32. Ross, "Ella Smith's Unfinished Community Cookbook," 168.

33. Hays, Rolfes and Associates, *How to Write and Publish*, 120.

34. Fisher and Fisher, *Pot Roast, Politics, and Ants*, 33.

35. Hays, Rolfes and Associates, *How to Write and Publish*, 122–123.

36. See Hawley, "Revaluing Mimeographs as Historical Sources," 41; "Antique Copying Machines"; Banham, "Printing to 1970," 107–108.

37. Tallman, "Out of the Red," 205–206.

38. Banham, "Printing to 1970," 96, 107; Eble, "Exquisite Balance of Nature," 280.

39. Hawley, "Revaluing Mimeographs as Historical Sources," 44.

40. Hawley, "Revaluing Mimeographs as Historical Sources," 44.

41. Although often understood as a disadvantage, the smell of spirit duplication has taken on a nostalgic quality, with Hawley writing that "many people of a certain age recall—perhaps too fondly—the smell of spirit duplicating from course assignments printed in the school duplicating office." "Revaluing Mimeographs as Historical Sources," 43.

42. Banham, "Printing to 1970," 108

43. Although these print processes have key differences, mimeograph eventually became an umbrella term for both stencil and spirit duplication. Hawley, "Revaluing Mimeographs as Historical Sources," 41.

44. Jennings, "Pirating Pound," 91.

45. Clay and Phillips, *From a Secret Location.*

46. As the final section of chapter 5 of this volume shows, there were also overlaps between community cookbook and fanzine creators.

47. Home Economics Alumnae, *Taste It Supper.*

48. An example of this is the Friendship Club, which is addressed in the following chapter of this volume.

49. "Cookbook Sales Buy Church Windows."

50. Fairview Parents and Teachers Association, *Green Book*, 229.

51. See, for example, Women's Architectural League, *Blueprint for the Cook.*

52. Morrison, "Versatility, Economy and Speed," 199–201.

53. This information is based on information in the front matter of three different editions of the book included in the South Dakota Community Cookbook Collection. See "South Dakota Community Cookbook Collection."

54. National Council of Jewish Women, *Blue Denim Cook Book.*

Chapter Three. Women and Work: Between Paid and Unpaid Careers

1. Davidson and Hatcher, introd. to *No More Separate Spheres!*, 10; Coontz, *Strange Stirring*, 59.

2. Quoted in Fox, "Community Cookbooks Trace Culinary Trends."

3. Driver, "Cookbooks as Primary Sources," 270.

4. Hays, Rolfes and Associates, *How to Write and Publish*, xi.

5. Ferguson, *Cookbook Politics*, 77; St. Michael's Home School Association, *Children's Choices.*

6. Ferguson, *Cookbook Politics*, 77.

7. J. H. Kelson Bible Class, *Cookbook.*

8. Prince of Peace ALCW, *Not Bread Alone.*

9. Crabtree and Tobiassen, *"Will the Gentlemen Yield?,"* 31. Bower notes a similar example from the 1920s cookbook, in which the women "present themselves as 'professional' housewives." "Cooking Up Stories," 40.

10. Kaplan Daniels, *Invisible Careers*, xxviii.

11. Tyler, *Silk Stockings and Ballot Boxes*, 6.

12. Wilmot Voss, *Women Politicking Politely*, 35.

13. Chambré, "Parallel Power Structures," 181, 184. A common perception was that the work women engaged in as part of volunteer associations was an extension of household duties—a kind of "municipal housekeeping" (172). See also McCarthy, "Parallel Power Structures."

14. Davidson and Hatcher, introd. to *No More Separate Spheres!*, 8.

15. "Teacher in Space Cookbook."

16. For a list of some of these professional women's associations, see Roe, *Trouble with Women Is Men*, 128.

17. Women Strike for Peace, *Peace de Resistance*, vol. 1.

18. Swan, *Fundraising for the Small Public*, 161.

19. Amos, *Fundraising Ideas*, 40.

20. Driver, "Cookbooks as Primary Sources," 271.

21. Miller, "Some Advice," 8.

22. Flanagan, *Grass Roots Fundraising Book*, 129.

23. Hays, Rolfes and Associates, *How to Write and Publish*, 233–234.

24. Coontz notes that "head and master" laws meant that some men were in a position to forbid their wives to go to work, and specific jobs, such as airline attendants, expected women to resign once they married. *Strange Stirring*, 5, 9.

25. Roe, *Trouble with Women Is Men*, 124.

26. Waunakee Wisconsin Centennial Committee, *People Pleasing Recipes*; Staub, "Community Creates a Cookbook," 70.

27. Bower, "Bound Together," 14.

28. Wilmot Voss, *Women Politicking Politely*, 73–74, 71.

29. See, for example, the articles published in the *Evening Star*: Beale, "Exclusively Yours," B–3, B–5; Lewine, "Mystery Solved," F–4; and "Press Club Cookbook," D–8.

30. "Press Club Cookbook," D–8.

31. Swan, *Fundraising for the Small Public*, 40.

32. Flanagan, *Successful Volunteer Organization*, 150.

33. See Kirshenblatt-Gimblett, "Moral Sublime," 137.

34. Swan, *Fundraising for the Small Public*, 36.

35. Shefferman, "Friendship Club," 3.

36. At least three articles related to O'Rourke and *Westchester County Tricentennial Cookbook* were published in the *New York Times*. These and a number of other community cookbook articles appearing in the paper from the 1960s attest to the national interest the cookbooks were beginning to receive. See D. Greene, "Alice O'Rourke Again Sets Aside," 31; Kriss, "Wanted," 17; T. Melvin, "Mrs. O'Rourke Busy on Cookbook," 14.

37. T. Melvin, "Mrs. O'Rourke Busy on Cookbook," 14.

38. "Press Club Cookbook," D–8.

39. Congregation Beth Yeshurun, "*Let My People . . . Eat!*"

40. Shefferman, "Friendship Club," 3.

41. Staub, "Community Creates a Cookbook," 43, 42, 70.

42. Mackintosh, "My Life and Hard Times."

43. Flanagan, *Grass Roots Fundraising Book*, 129.

44. It is interesting to note the authors' use of the term "career" in regard to voluntary work, two years before the publishing of Kaplan Daniels's *Invisible Careers*; Roe also uses the word "career" to describe both full-time jobs and housework. Hays, Rolfes and Associates, *How to Write and Publish*, 8; Roe, *Trouble with Women Is Men*, 22.

45. Eichhorn, *Adjusted Margin*, 169.

46. McMillian, "Our Founder, the Mimeograph Machine," 92.

47. Roe, *Trouble with Women Is Men*, 125.

48. C. McKinney, *Information Activism*, 30.

49. Wilmot Voss, *Women Politicking Politely*, 36.

50. See, for example, Flanagan, *Grass Roots Fundraising Book*, 129.

51. More work can certainly be done in mapping these connections, with one interesting potential connection being the sharp increase in women who began to work in professional fundraising. According to Dale, by the end of the 1980s, "women represented a majority of members in the top three professional organizations of fundraisers in the United States"; see "Fundraising as Women's Work?" 4.

52. "Employment," 10.

53. Biltmore United Methodist Church, *What's Cook'n at Biltmore.*

54. Huey, "Cookbook Business Is Good," 74.

55. Stiltner, *Al Hasa Saudi Arabia Cookbook.*

56. Coon Valley Lutheran Church ALCW, *Our Daily Bread.*

57. Sass, "PW Special Report," 50. All articles from *Publishers Weekly* were retrieved via the Publishers Weekly digital archives, https://digitalarchives.publishersweekly.com/.

58. Szathmary, "Cupboardful of Charitable Cookbooks," 93.

59. "Cookbooks for Every Taste," E6.

60. According to Makos and Morse, in 1989 "65% of the selections from [the Book-of-the-Month Club's] HomeStyle Club" were cookbooks. "Cookbook Sales Beyond the Bookstore," 32. For a definition of book clubs, see Norrick-Rühl, *Book Clubs and Book Commerce*, 5–7.

61. Saunders, "Flavor of a Place," 28.

62. Hays, Rolfes and Associates, "Hays, Rolfes and Associates Announces."

63. Hays, Rolfes and Associates, *How to Write and Publish*, xi (emphasis in original.).

64. Hays, Rolfes and Associates, *How to Write and Publish*, xi–xii.

65. Saunders, "Flavor of a Place," 26; Weinraub, "It Takes a Cookbook."

66. See Luey, "Modernity and Print III," 568–570.

67. Kirshenblatt-Gimblett, "Moral Sublime," 152.

68. Nordheimer, "Cookbook Profits Pay," 32.

69. More amateur and DIY books could also exceed sales expectations, although often in smaller numbers. The 1959 cookbook *Our Favorite Cookies*, for instance, by the Bethany Lutheran Ladies' Aid of Mohawk, Michigan, is bound with yarn, and both covers are made using strips of wallpaper, cut straight from the roll. While it would be easy to assume that such an obviously homemade book brought in only limited fundraising sales, the 1959 version was actually a second printing, created, one can assume, in response to sustained demand. Bethany Lutheran Ladies' Aid, *Our Favorite Cookies*.

70. "McIlhenny Hall of Fame Award."

71. James, "Recipes for Success," C1.

72. *Cookbook Committee Annual Report*.

73. Elder, "Fund-Raising Cookbooks Are More."

74. McDowell, "Name It and You'll Find," NA14.

75. Miller, "Local Cookbooks," C1.

76. Time-Life Books, "Permission Agreement"; General Mills, "Letter to the Junior League."

77. Nelson, "Letter to All."

78. Brownson, "Illinois' Best," G10.

79. McDowell, "Name It and You'll Find," NA14.

80. Fabricant, "L. I. Group's Cookbook Goes National," 6.

81. Yankee Candle, "Letter to the Mrs. Rebecca."

82. Hansen, "Recipe for a New Cookbook," 24.

83. Anderson, "Cookbook Market," 42.

84. Quoted in Hansen, "Recipe for a New Cookbook," 24.

85. One of the earliest known Junior League community cookbooks was published in 1930 in Los Angeles. Lindgren and Germer, *UNXLD*, 92–94.

86. See Barnes, "Junior League Eleven," 47, 46, 47–48.

87. Another way sales figures of community cookbooks have been recorded is through the Tabasco Community Cookbook Awards, which ran from 1990 to 2010. In addition to the yearly national and regional awards, books were also entered into the Walter S. McIlhenny Hall of Fame, which honored community cookbooks that had sold more than one hundred thousand copies, no matter the year of publication. In 1990, the founding year of the Tabasco Community Cookbook Awards, at least twelve books were inducted into the McIlhenny Hall of Fame. For these books it

can be firmly stated that each had sold at least one hundred thousand copies before the year 1990. "McIlhenny Hall of Fame Award."

88. Sheraton, "Regional Cookbooks at Their Best," C6.

89. Miller, "Local Cookbooks," C1.

90. Fisher and Fisher, *Pot Roast, Politics, and Ants*, 46.

91. Miller, "Local Cookbooks," C1.

92. In addition to this, the Junior League of Baton Rouge also released three revised editions of the book, with two of these editions—as well as the original—having sold the one hundred thousand copies needed to be inducted into the McIlhenny Hall of Fame. *River Road Recipes*.

93. Miller "Local Cookbooks," C1.

94. Junior League of South Bend, "Letter to Dear Madam President."

95. Wilmot Voss, *Women Politicking Politely*, 70, 71.

96. Norrick-Rühl, *Book Clubs and Book Commerce*, 7.

97. "Press Club Cookbook," D–8.

98. Staub, "Community Creates a Cookbook," 71.

99. Tyler, *Silk Stockings and Ballot Boxes*, 7.

100. Kaplan Daniels, *Invisible Careers*, 181; Hays, Rolfes and Associates, *How to Write and Publish*, 7.

101. Withers, "Politics of the Workshop," 217, 218, 217.

102. D. Greene, "Alice O'Rourke Again Sets Aside," 31.

103. T. Melvin, "Mrs. O'Rourke Busy on Cookbook," 14.

104. Tyler, *Silk Stockings and Ballot Boxes*, 6.

Chapter Four. Profits and Politics: Fundraising Cookbooks at the Grassroots

1. Nussel, "Heating Up the Sources," 958. See also West, "Performing Resistance," 373.

2. The majority of the cookbooks discussed in this chapter were viewed in person during a special collection summer research fellowship at Michigan State University.

3. See Gabaccia, *We Are What We Eat*; Inness, *Secret Ingredients*; West, "Performing Resistance"; Zafar, "Signifying Dish."

4. Seligson, "What We Need Now," BR8.

5. "Publishers 1956 Title Output Analyzed," 32; Anderson, "Cookbook Market," 42.

6. Sass, "PW Special Report," 42, 41.

7. Seligson, "What We Need Now," BR8.

8. Elias, *Food on the Page*, 113; Sass, "PW Special Report," 48.

9. See, for example, Dyer, *Perfect Dinner Party Cookbook*.

10. The book was later renamed *The Ebony Cookbook*. See DeKnight, *Ebony Cookbook*, 13.

11. Dennis, "From Apicus to Gastroporn," 9.

12. Seligson, "What We Need Now," BR8.

13. Dennis, "From Apicus to Gastroporn," 9.

14. Sass, "PW Special Report," 48.

15. Elias, *Food on the Page*, 146.

16. Women's National Book Association, *Literary Allusions Cookbook*, 16.

17. McDowell, "Name It and You'll Find," NA14.

18. Elias, *Food on the Page*, 178.

19. Leonardi, "Recipes for Reading," 342. Compare with Bower, "Cooking Up Stories," 36.

20. Quoted in Leonardi, "Recipes for Reading," 345.

21. Zafar, "Signifying Dish," 451.

22. Belasco, *Appetite for Change*, 95–96.

23. Howsam, "Culture of Food," vii.

24. Elias, *Food on the Page*, 155–158.

25. Larsen and Singer, *Beat Generation Cook Book*.

26. Elias, *Food on the Page*, 158.

27. Belasco, *Appetite for Change*, 45, 97; Schenone, *Thousand Years*, 330.

28. Gregory, *Dick Gregory's Natural Diet*, 15.

29. Smart-Grosvenor, *Vibration Cooking*, 1, 31.

30. See Miller and Hardman, "By the Pinch"; and Derleth, "Kneading Politics."

31. Miller and Hardman, "By the Pinch," 121.

32. "Waiting Is Over," 216.

33. Mastrangelo, "Community Cookbooks," 73.

34. Elias, *Food on the Page*, 111.

35. Fritschner, "Junior League Jackpot."

36. Saunders, "Flavor of a Place," 28.

37. Hays, Rolfes and Associates, "Hays, Rolfes and Associates Announces."

38. Hays, Rolfes and Associates, *How to Write and Publish*, 20, 12, 12–15. It's also worth noting that the two ran popular community cookbook seminars, where they might have offered similar advice to attendees.

39. Hays, Rolfes and Associates, *How to Write and Publish*, 15–16.

40. American Business Women's Association, *We Knead Dough*; Crippled Children's Hospital and School, *Stay for Lunch*.

41. Ferguson, *Cookbook Politics*, 3.

42. Gattuso, "Eat Like a 1970s Radical."

43. Doley et al., *People's Philadelphia Cookbook*, ii–iii; Ostrander, *Money for Change*, 57.

44. Doley et al., *People's Philadelphia Cookbook*, ii.

45. Gattuso, "Eat Like a 1970s Radical"; Doley et al., *People's Philadelphia Cookbook*, ii.

46. Kuffman, *West Oakland Soul Food*, 5; Atkinson, "Oakland Peter Maurin House," 4.

47. Kauffman, "West Oakland." Kuffman's name appears in this journal with a typographical error.

48. "Southern Conference Educational Fund"; Klibaner, "Travail of Southern Radicals," 181.

49. Southern Conference Educational Fund, *SCEF Recipes*, 13, 18. An example of a SCEF calendar can be viewed in the Civil Rights Movement Archive: SCEF, "Struggle in Today's South."

50. *Annual Report, 1968–1976.*

51. "Meeting Minutes, Jun. 1969–Dec. 1970."

52. "Treasurer's Reports, 1968–1974."

53. "Meeting Minutes, Jan. 1971–Jan. 1974."

54. "Treasurer's Reports, 1968–1974."

55. Nielson, "Inventing a Space to Speak," 63.

56. See Genette, *Paratexts*; Nielson, "Inventing a Space to Speak," 64.

57. Doley et al., *People's Philadelphia Cookbook*, 4, iii, 25–26, 29.

58. Southern Conference Educational Fund, *SCEF Recipes*, 41.

59. Citizens United for Racial Equality, *Integrated Cook Book*, 68, 122, 144, 2, 16(B).

60. Citizens United for Racial Equality, *Integrated Cook Book*, 53, 73, 150 (emphasis in original).

61. The flyer lists politicians Alan Cranston, Daniel Inouye, Hubert Humphrey, Edward Brooke, and Abraham Ribicoff; singer Vikki Carr; and Tom Smothers, of the comedy duo Smothers Brothers. *Integrated Cookbook.*

62. Kauffman, "West Oakland." All articles from the *Catholic Worker* were retrieved via https://thecatholicnewsarchive.org/. Advertisement, Pepper et al., *Berkeley Barb*, 8.

63. J. McKinney's article is one of very few sources that provide a timeline for this cookbook, which is undated, and is generally thought to have been produced some time in the 1960s or early 1970s. WorldCat lists the earliest appearance of the book as 1963, although no other sources have been found to support that date. "Luncheon with 'Soul,'" 31.

64. Tipton-Martin, *Jemima Code*, 98.

65. Advertisement, Pepper et al., *Berkeley Barb*, 8.

66. Atkinson, "Oakland Peter Maurin House," 4.

67. Chester, "Sex, Race and Class," 617–618; Danky, "Oppositional Press," 272–273.

68. Swan, *Fundraising for the Small Public*, 21.

69. See Inness, *Dinner Roles*; Neuhaus, "Way to a Man's Heart."

70. "Newsletters, 1968–1976."

71. *Annual Report, 1968–1976.*

72. Michigan Metro Girl Scouts Council, *Arab/American Girl Scout Cookbook*, 1.

73. New Arrivals at the Eglin, *Happy in My Stomach.*

74. Milholland, "Brief History."

75. Derleth, "Kneading Politics," 450. Williams also uses this term to describe liberal feminist cookbooks. "Recipes for Resistance," 239.

76. Doley et al., *People's Philadelphia Cookbook*, ii.

77. J. McKinney, "Luncheon with 'Soul,'" 31; "Newsletters, 1968–1976."

78. Ferguson, *Cookbook Politics*, 1.

79. See Derleth, "Kneading Politics"; and Inness, *Secret Ingredients.*

80. Derleth, "Kneading Politics," 462.

81. "Palczewski Suffrage Postcard Archive."

82. Chevalier, "Trojan Horse."

83. Kleber, *Suffrage Cook Book.*

84. Evans, "Women's Movement," 63.

85. West, "Performing Resistance," 369, 371.

86. West, "Performing Resistance," 360.

87. Friends of Children of Vietnam, *"Chosen Moms" Cook Book*, 2.

88. Chester, "Sex, Race and Class," 618.

89. Doley et al., *People's Philadelphia Cookbook*, 4.

90. Allen, "Artist as Bookmaker," 14.

91. Dubisar, "If I Can't Bake," 8.

92. Citizens United for Racial Equality, *Integrated Cook Book*, 127, 134, 151.

93. Women Strike for Peace, *Peace de Resistance*, 2:35, 103 (emphasis in original), 125.

94. Howsam, "Culture of Food," iii.

95. Sarachild, "Consciousness-Raising," 144.

96. Chen, "Recreating the Chinese American Home," 494.

97. Those cookbooks are Turner, *Federation Cookbook*; Montana Federation, *Cook Book*; and Negro Culinary Art Club, *Eliza's Cook Book*. See Witt, *Black Hunger*, 221–228.

98. Inness, *Secret Ingredients*, 40.

99. Higgs and Richards, "Roll Over, Gutenberg!," 102–103.

100. Barth, "Chronological Bibliography."

101. Navajo Curriculum Center, *Ch'iyáán 'íít'iní binaaltsoos*, vi.

102. Witt, *Black Hunger*, 5.

103. For example, see Mecklenberg-Faenger, "Hear the Table Call." Bower also addresses the use of this stereotype in an early twentieth-century cookbook. See "*Our Sisters' Recipes*." Commercial cookbook printer and binders Bev-Ron also featured the "mammy" figure on their Kitchen Secrets cover option into the 1950s.

104. Zafar, "Signifying Dish," 450.

105. Witt, *Black Hunger*, 215.

106. Spiegel, "Yes, It Matters."

107. Gvion, "What's Cooking in America?," 66, 67.

108. Japanese American Citizens' League, *East-West Flavors*; Japanese American Citizens' League, *Nisei Kitchen*.

109. Inness, *Secret Ingredients*, 59.

110. Japanese American Citizens' League, *Nisei Kitchen*.

111. Milholland, "Brief History."

112. Eves, "Recipe for Remembrance," 281.

113. Chiltoskey and Beck, *Cherokee Cooklore*, 2–41.

114. Azaransky, *This Worldwide Struggle*, 2.

115. Smith, *Black Firsts*, 415.

116. Azaransky, *This Worldwide Struggle*, 26.

117. Thurman, *Historical Cookbook*.

118. Thurman, *Historical Cookbook*.

119. Ravenswood High School, *Soul Power Cook Book*, 3.

120. Witt, *Black Hunger*, 6.

121. Ravenswood High School, *Soul Power Cook Book*, 15.

122. Rufus King High School, *Cooking with Soul*, 5.

123. Witt, *Black Hunger*, 223.

Chapter Five. Food and Feminism: Drawing on the Domestic

1. Wilmot Voss, *Women Politicking Politely*, 68.

2. Parker, *Subversive Stitch*, 6.

3. Menand, "Books as Bombs."

4. Coontz, *Strange Stirring*, 21.

5. Horowitz, *"Feminine Mystique,"* 38.

6. Friedan, *Feminine Mystique*, 11.

7. Farrell, "Like a Tarantula," 58.

8. "For the Liberated Female," 52. Also quoted in Farrell, "Like a Tarantula," 53.

9. "Ms. Blue Collar," 80.

10. This slogan was again picked up for the twenty-fifth anniversary conference theme: "We Didn't Come Here to Swap Recipes—Not Then, 1974—not now, 1999." "About CLUW."

11. The National Women's Political Caucus released similar buttons with the text, "Women! Make policy, not coffee." Guensburg, "Delicious Irony."

12. Williams, "Feminist Guide to Cooking," 59.

13. Williams, "Subversive Cooking in Liberal Feminism," 269.

14. Dore, *She's Beautiful When She's Angry*, 1:19:51–54.

15. Avakian and Haber, "Feminist Food Studies," 2.

16. Wilmot Voss, *Women Politicking Politely*, 68.

17. Skow, "Erma in Bomburia," 64. Also quoted in Wilmot Voss, *Women Politicking Politely*, 68.

18. Savoy, "Jacquelyn Reinach Mixes Cookbook," D1.

19. Swinth, *Feminism's Forgotten Fight*, 25; Savoy, "Jacquelyn Reinach Mixes Cookbook," D1.

20. See Inness, *Dinner Roles*, 144–145; Horner, "*Betty Crocker's Picture Cookbook*," 332–333.

21. This has been explored by Elias, who discusses how cookbooks like *I Hate to Cook Book* and *Mastering the Art of French Cooking* offer "proto-feminist" views. *Food on the Page*, 108.

22. See, for example, the Bloodroot Collective's cookbook *Political Palate*, in which the authors write, "Our choices in furniture, pictures, the music we play, the books we sell, and the food we cook all reflect and express our feminism. Our food is vegetarian because we are feminists" (xi).

23. Savoy, "Jacquelyn Reinach Mixes Cookbook," D1.

24. Reinach was not the only feminist to release a cookbook. In 1973 Esther Lewin and Birdina Lewin published *The Women's Lib Cookbook: Or, Whose Place Is in the Kitchen?*, with recipes that include "Consciousness-Raising Souffle," "Wrap Sessions," and "Feminine Mousstique." There is also a connection between this cookbook and activist community cookbooks, as Esther Lewin was responsible for the Women Strike for Peace community cookbook *Peace de Resistance*, vol. 1, and Lewin and Lewin, *Women's Lib Cookbook*, 30, 59, 92.

25. Quoted in Williams, "Feminist Guide to Cooking," 59.

26. "Poet Kizer Meeting with Women," 7.

27. "Droppings"; "Guide to the Movement," 62.

28. Williams, "Recipes for Resistance," 203.

29. "How Many Feminists?"

30. Guensburg, "Delicious Irony."

31. National Organization for Women, *Don't Assume I Don't Cook*, 6.

32. Gabaccia, *We Are What We Eat*, 184.

33. See Williams, "Feminist Guide to Cooking"; Williams, "Subversive Cooking in Liberal Feminism."

34. Kretschmer, *Fighting for NOW*, 10.

35. NOW, "National Organization."

36. Barakso, *Governing NOW*, 13; Kretschmer, *Fighting for NOW*, 42.

37. Kretschmer, *Fighting for NOW*, 8, 16.

38. The men's recipe book was sold to fund the establishment of a domestic-assault shelter. The exact title of this book could not be established, but it was referenced as already being sold in a Tallahassee NOW newsletter in 1978. "Florida NOW News," 5.

39. NOW chapters also continued to produce community cookbooks after 1990; for example, in 1998 the South Jersey NOW Alice Paul Chapter published the cookbook *A Taste of Feminism*.

40. See, for example, Romney, "On Feminist Practice."

41. Mathews and De Hart, *Sex, Gender, and the Politics*, 91.

42. ERAmerica, *ERAmerica Report*.

43. ERAmerica, *ERAmerica Report*.

44. "Spokeswoman Review," 14.

45. Estes Blair, "Dynamic Force in Our Community," 40, 35–36.

46. Hunt, "Kitchen Politics?"

47. Hunt, "Kitchen Politics?" (ellipses in original).

48. Wilmot Voss, *Women Politicking Politely*, 3.

49. Estes Blair, "Dynamic Force in Our Community," 30, 31.

50. *A CLUW Guide to Cooking* was listed on the University of Amherst's no longer accessible *New England Cookery at the Grass Roots* blog. Coalition of Labor Union Women, "Papers, 1972–1994 (Predominantly, 1974–1990)"; *New England Cookery*.

51. Other founders include well-known feminist politicians, political advisers, and activists, such as Bella Abzug, Gloria Steinem, and Shirley Chisholm. "About" (National Women's Political Caucus).

52. Oregon NARAL Supporters, *CHOICE Recipes*.

53. The copy of the book held by the Schlesinger Library was donated as part of Betty Friedan's papers, and the book contains a recipe donated by Friedan.

54. National Association for Girls, *Cookies (and Punch, Too!)*, 1.

55. Robertson, "Betty Friedan Ushers," 10.

56. "Look at Women's Lib in Suburbia," 28.

57. Estes Blair, "Dynamic Force in Our Community," 37–38.

58. Mackintosh, "My Life and Hard Times."

59. Black women in North Carolina similarly used preexisting women's groups as places to explore and support the civil rights movement. C. Greene, *Our Separate Ways*, 27.

60. Williams, "Subversive Cooking in Liberal Feminism," 268.

61. Kaplan, *Pots and Politics*, 102. The same list of these organizations can also be found at "Appendix D."

62. The figures were obtained through searches on WorldCat, https://www.worldcat.org/, which consolidates bibliographic records from libraries across the globe. While these numbers do not encompass all cookbooks produced by the groups in question—for instance, my own private collection includes a community cookbook from Planned Parenthood that is not indexed in WorldCat—they can provide a useful overview.

63. Women's National Book Association, *Literary Allusions Cookbook*, 117, 121.

64. Friedan, *Feminine Mystique*, 85.

65. Russ, *How to Suppress Women's Writing*, 2.

66. Walker, "In Search of Zora Neale."

67. Rich, "When We Dead Awaken," 18. A somewhat similar attempt to reclaim the history of women's clubs as feminist was made by Blair in *Clubwoman as Feminist*. Reviewers, however, were critical of Blair's attempts to assert feminist intentions to earlier decades of women's clubs. See, for example, Jeffrey, "Reviewed Work," 232.

68. McBean, "Feminist 1970s," 354.

69. Cooks's 1971 bibliography of charitable cookbooks could possibly be seen as connected to the renewed interest in women's history; however, Cook does not make any such aim explicit. *America's Charitable Cooks*.

70. Appadurai, "Make a National Cuisine," 18.

71. Gabaccia, "Food, Recipes, Cookbooks," 20.

72. Avakian and Haber, "Feminist Food Studies," 6.

73. Bower, "Bound Together," 9.

74. Procida, "No Longer Half-Baked," 198.

75. Recipes in early community cookbooks were, to quote a 1912 cookbook, "not to fill space, and may be relied on." Quoted in Longone, "Tried Receipts," 22.

76. Mastrangelo, "Community Cookbooks," 76.

77. Tarrant County NOW Chapter, *"Women Are A-Risin',"* 11, 21, 13.

78. An important exception to this is the many recipes sourced from enslaved people and Black household staff included in community cookbooks in the nineteenth century, which were co-opted by or attributed to the white women who contributed the recipes to the book. In so doing, these white women made claim to Black women's creative and culinary talents while also participating in the public erasure of Black culinary heritage.

79. Ferguson, *Cookbook Politics*, 79.

80. Tarrant County NOW Chapter, *"Women Are A-Risin',"* 5.

81. Ferguson, *Cookbook Politics*, 80.

82. Withers, *Virago Reprints and Modern Classics*, 16.

83. DuBois, *Feminism: Old Wave and New*, 4.

84. Kaplan, *Pots and Politics*, 9.

85. See, for example, the biography of women's suffrage leader Elizabeth Cady Stanton published by the Feminist Press. Oakley, *Elizabeth Cady Stanton*.

86. Derleth, "Kneading Politics," 461–462.

87. Kaplan, *Pots and Politics*, 7.

88. Jennings, *Washington Women's Cook Book*.

89. Kaplan, *Pots and Politics*, 9.

90. Avakian and Haber, "Feminist Food Studies," 6.

91. Withers here is addressing reprints of women's texts put out by the British feminist publisher Virago. *Virago Reprints and Modern Classics*, 1.

92. Nussel, "Heating Up the Sources," 957.

93. Le Dantec-Lowry, "Reading Women's Lives in Cookbooks," 100.

94. Kaplan, *Pots and Politics*, 101, 5 (emphasis and ellipses in original).

95. Piepmeier, *Girl Zines*, 45.

96. Yaszek, "On the Occasion," 16.

97. Murphy, "Illusion and Expectation," 348. This article is also found in the introductory material of Martin, Gomoll, and SF^3, *Bakery Men Don't See Cookbook*.

98. "History."

99. Samer, *Lesbian Potentiality and Feminist Media*, 186.

100. Martin, Gomoll, and SF^3, *Bakery Men Don't See Cookbook*, 14.

101. Harker and Konchar Farr, "Outrageous, Dangerous, and Unassimilable," 4.

102. McBean, "Feminist 1970s," 361.

103. Lefanu, *Feminism and Science Fiction*, 2.

104. Martin, Gomoll, and SF^3, *Bakery Men Don't See Cookbook*, 2.

105. Samer, *Lesbian Potentiality and Feminist Media*, 187.

106. Larbalestier, *Battle of the Sexes*, 201.

107. Samer, *Lesbian Potentiality and Feminist Media*, 190, 191.

108. Quoted in Hicks, "Whatever It Is," 72.

109. Samer, *Lesbian Potentiality and Feminist Media*, 185, 184, 185.

110. Murphy, "Illusion and Expectation," 347, 348.

111. Samer, *Lesbian Potentiality and Feminist Media*, 209.

112. Squires, *Marketing Literature*, 97.

113. Sturgis, "Inventing the Tiptrees," 52.

114. Murphy, "Illusion and Expectation," 349.

115. Martin, Gomoll, and SF^3, *Bakery Men Don't See Cookbook*, 4–5.

116. Samer, *Lesbian Potentiality and Feminist Media*, 206.

117. Murphy, "Illusion and Expectation," 349. There is an interesting connection between community cookbooks and patchwork quilts. Not only did a number of community cookbooks make use of embroidery and quilting imagery on their covers and in their titles, such as with *The Black Family Dinner Quilt Cookbook* (1993), but Bower draws closer connections between the forms, particularly for the ways scholars have been slow to appreciate these works of women's material culture and see them as "readable." "Bound Together," 4.

118. Gomoll, "History of WisCon."

119. Martin, Gomoll, and SF^3, *Bakery Men Don't See Cookbook*, 3.

120. Samer, *Lesbian Potentiality and Feminist Media*, 209.

121. Gomoll, "History of WisCon." The change in the name of the award was brought about due to "questions raised on social media about whether the name of the Tiptree Award should be reconsidered" in light of the fact that, in 1987, Sheldon "shot first her husband, Huntington Sheldon, and then herself." While this event is widely understood to have been the fulfillment of a suicide pact, others have interpreted it as a case of a caregiver killing a disabled dependent. For more on the background of this name change, see Lothian, "Alice Sheldon and the Name."

Conclusion: Liberating the Community Cookbook

1. Friedan, "Cooking with Betty Friedan," 68.

2. "Letters," 49.

3. "Women's Movement," 1.

4. Schenone, *Thousand Years*, 107.

5. Current knowledge is that the first Native American community cookbook was published in 1933 and that one of the earliest Junior League community cookbook was published in 1930. Barth, "Chronological Bibliography"; Lindgren and Germer, *UNXLD*, 92–94.

6. ActionAIDS, *Philadelphia Stories*.

7. Maine Won't Discriminate, *Out in the Kitchen*, ii.

8. See Ketchum, "Recipe for a Queer Cookbook"; Vester, "Queering the Cookbook."

9. For a book historical analysis of vegan cookzines, see Miller and Hardman, "By the Pinch," 123–129.

10. "About" (*You Stir the Pot*).

11. Givens, "Creating Community."

12. Krishna, "Community Cookbook Is Reborn."

13. Tastefullyterrible and contributors, *F*ck You Buffet*.

BIBLIOGRAPHY

Archival Sources

Annual Report, 1968–1976. MS-0087. Box 4. Virtual folder 9. Citizens United for Racial Equality (CURE) Records, MS-0087. Special Collections and University Archives, San Diego State University. https://archives.sdsu.edu/repositories/2/archival_objects/104168.

"Appendix D: National Organizations Supporting the Equal Rights Amendment." 1975. Box 47. Folder "Women in 1974: Citizen's Advisory Council on the Status of Women." Betty Ford White House Papers, 1973–1977. Gerald R. Ford Presidential Library, Ann Arbor, Mich. https://www.fordlibrarymuseum.gov/library/document/0018/81556915.pdf.

Coalition of Labor Union Women Collection. "Papers, 1972–1994 (Predominantly, 1974–1990)." Box 28. Folder 7. Walter P. Reuther Library, Archives of Labor and Urban Affairs, Wayne State University. https://reuther.wayne.edu/files/LR000664.pdf.

Cookbook Committee Annual Report. Circa 1976. MC 787. Box 213. Folder 9. Additional Records of the Junior League of Boston, Circa 1907–2010. Schlesinger Library, Radcliffe Institute, Harvard University, Cambridge, Mass.

General Mills. "Letter to the Junior League of Boston." April 15, 1981. MC 787. Box 213. Folder 11. Additional Records of the Junior League of Boston, Circa 1907–2010. Schlesinger Library, Radcliffe Institute, Harvard University, Cambridge, Mass.

Hays, Rolfes and Associates. "Hays, Rolfes and Associates Announces the Community Cookbook Seminar." 1981. MC 595. Box 22. Folder 8. Records of the Fishermen's Wives of Gloucester, 1950–2009 (inclusive), 1977–2004 (bulk). Schlesinger Library, Radcliffe Institute, Harvard University, Cambridge, Mass.

Integrated Cookbook. 1976. MS-0087. Box 6. Virtual folder 4. Citizens United for Racial Equality (CURE) Records, MS-0087. Special Collections and University Archives, San Diego State University. https://archives.sdsu.edu/repositories/2/archival_objects/104248.

Junior League of South Bend. "Letter to Dear Madam President." Circa 1976–1981. MC 787. Box 213. Folder 9. Additional Records of the Junior League of Boston,

Circa 1907–2010. Schlesinger Library, Radcliffe Institute, Harvard University, Cambridge, Mass.

"Meeting Minutes, Jan. 1971–Jan. 1974." MS-0087. Box 8. Virtual folder 1. Citizens United for Racial Equality (CURE) Records, MS-0087. Special Collections and University Archives, San Diego State University. https://archives.sdsu.edu/repositories/2/archival_objects/104164.

"Meeting Minutes, Jun. 1969–Dec. 1970." MS-0087. Box 1. Virtual folder 6. Citizens United for Racial Equality (CURE) Records, MS-0087. Special Collections and University Archives, San Diego State University. https://archives.sdsu.edu/repositories/2/archival_objects/104156.

Nelson, Cynthia. "Letter to All Participating Eastern Junior Leagues." May 22, 1980. MC 787. Box 213. Folder 10. Additional Records of the Junior League of Boston, Circa 1907–2010. Schlesinger Library, Radcliffe Institute, Harvard University, Cambridge, Mass.

New England Cookery at the Grass Roots. Special Collections and University Archives, UMass Amherst Libraries. Accessed June 1, 2019. http://scua.library.umass.edu/cookbooks/.

"Newsletters, 1968–1976." Citizens United for Racial Equality (CURE) Records, MS-0087. Box 6. Virtual folder 12. Special Collections and University Archives, San Diego State University. https://archives.sdsu.edu/repositories/2/archival_objects/104264.

Time-Life Books. "Permission Agreement for Use of Copyright Material." April 21, 1921. MC 787. Box 214. Folder 1. Additional Records of the Junior League of Boston, Circa 1907–2010. Schlesinger Library, Radcliffe Institute, Harvard University, Cambridge, Mass.

"Treasurer's Reports, 1968–1974." MS-0087. Box 8. Virtual folder 1. Citizens United for Racial Equality (CURE) Records, MS-0087. Special Collections and University Archives, San Diego State University. https://archives.sdsu.edu/repositories/2/archival_objects/104292.

Yankee Candle. "Letter to the Mrs. Rebecca Bernie." July 11, 1979. MC 595. Box 22. Folder 7. Records of the Fishermen's Wives of Gloucester, 1950–2009 (inclusive), 1977–2004 (bulk). Schlesinger Library, Radcliffe Institute, Harvard University, Cambridge, Mass.

Cookbooks

ActionAIDS. *Philadelphia Stories: A Dining Out for Life Cookbook: A Collection of Remembrances About Philadelphia Culinary Artists Who Have Died of AIDS, with Recipes from Some of the Restaurants They Shaped*. Philadelphia: ActionAIDS, 1993.

Alpha Phi, Iota Chapter (University of Wisconsin). *Our Mothers' Recipes.* Madison: Alpha Phi, n.d.

American Business Women's Association, Grand Charter Chapter. *We Knead Dough.* Kansas City: North American Press, n.d.

American Lutheran Church Women, Bergen Lutheran Church. *Bergen Cook Book.* Iowa Falls: General Publishing and Binding, 1973.

American Women's Club of Korea. *Passing Through.* Seoul: Korea Computer, 1987.

Bethany Lutheran Ladies' Aid. *Our Favorite Cookies.* Mohawk, Mich.: Bethany Lutheran Ladies' Aid, 1959.

Biltmore United Methodist Church. *What's Cook'n at Biltmore.* Waterloo, Iowa: G&R Publishing, 1975.

Bloodroot Collective. *The Political Palate: A Feminist Vegetarian Cookbook.* Bridgeport, Conn.: Sanguinaria, 1980.

Cannon, Poppy. *The Can-Opener Cookbook.* Kingsport: Kingsport, 1953.

Chiltoskey, Mary Ulmer, and Samuel E. Beck, eds. *Cherokee Cooklore: Preparing Cherokee Foods.* Cherokee: Chiltoskey, 1951.

Church of the Ascension. *Parish Cookbook: Festival '77, Garden of Eatin'.* Virginia Beach: Church of the Ascension, 1977.

Citizens United for Racial Equality. *The Integrated Cook Book.* San Diego: Citizens United for Racial Equality, 1970.

Cleveland Sorosis. *The Cleveland Sorosis Cook Book.* Cleveland: Kneale, 1916.

Coon Valley Lutheran Church ALCW. *Our Daily Bread.* Iowa Falls: General Publishing and Binding, 1976.

Crabtree, Paulette, and Audrey Tobiassen, eds. *"Will the Gentlemen Yield?": Or, What's Cookin' 'Round the Capitol!* Pensacola: Crabtree and Tobiassen, 1973.

Crippled Children's Hospital and School. *Stay for Lunch: Luncheon Recipes from the Files of the Members of the Crippled Children's Hospital and School Auxiliary, Sioux Falls, South Dakota.* Sioux Falls, 1982.

DeKnight, Freda. *The Ebony Cookbook.* Chicago: Johnson, 1973.

Doley, Ann, Jim Quinn, Harvey Finkle, Eliza Drake, and People's Fund Membership. *The People's Philadelphia Cookbook.* Philadelphia: People's Fund, 1976.

Eagle Forum, Lubbock, Texas. *Flavored with Freedom.* Lubbock, Tex.: West, 1986.

Fairview Parents and Teachers Association. *The Green Book: Kitchen Tested Recipes from Fairview Area.* Fairview, Mich.: Fairview Parents and Teachers Association, 1970.

Flora Macdonald Highland Games. *Flora's Fare: Cookbook.* Hartwell, Ga.: Calico Kitchen, 1992.

Friendship Club. *Friendship Club Cook Book.* Madison: Friendship Club, 1951.

Friends of Children of Vietnam. *"Chosen Moms" Cook Book*. Ashland, Ore.: Friends of Children of Vietnam, [1970s].

Gregory, Dick. *Dick Gregory's Natural Diet for Folks Who Eat: Cookin' with Mother Nature*. New York: Harper and Row, 1974.

Home Economics Alumnae of Mississippi Southern College. *Taste It Supper: Recipes from Forrest County Home Economics Alumnae of Mississippi Southern College*. Forrest County: Home Economics Alumnae of Mississippi Southern College, 1961.

Indian Women's Club of Tulsa, Oklahoma. *Indian Cook Book*. Tulsa: Indian Women's Club of Tulsa, Oklahoma, 1933.

Japanese American Citizens' League. *East-West Flavors*. Los Angeles: Auxiliary, n.d.

———. *Nisei Kitchen*. Saint Louis: Saint Louis Chapter, Japanese American Citizens League, 1975.

Jennings, Linda Deziah, ed. *Washington Women's Cook Book*. Seattle: Washington Equal Suffrage Association, 1909.

J. H. Kelson Bible Class, Bethel Baptist Church. *Cookbook*. Scranton: Bethel Baptist Church, n.d.

Kaplan, Shirlie, ed. *Pots and Politics: An Historical Cookbook; From the Suffragists to the Equal Rights Amendment*. Tacoma: Washington State Women's Political Caucus, 1976.

Kleber, L. O., ed. *Suffrage Cook Book*. Pittsburgh: Equal Franchise Federation of Western Pennsylvania, 1915.

Kuffman, Dorothy, ed. *West Oakland Soul Food Cook Book*. 2nd. ed. Oakland: Maurin Neighborhood House, 1968.

Lappé, Frances Moore. *Diet for a Small Planet*. New York: Ballantine Books, 1971.

Larsen, Carl, and James Singer, eds. *The Beat Generation Cook Book*. New York: 7 Poets, 1961.

Lewin, Esther, and Birdina Lewin. *The Women's Lib Cookbook: Or, Whose Place Is in the Kitchen?* N.p.: Ritchie, 1973.

Maine Won't Discriminate. *Out in the Kitchen: A Cookbook . . . for Those with Non-discriminating Taste*. Lenexa, Kans.: Cookbook Publishers, 1995.

Martin, Diane, Jeanne Gomoll, and SF^3. *The Bakery Men Don't See Cookbook*. Madison: SF^3, 1991.

Members of the Ann Arbor Wellesley Club. *Fare Thee Well*. Iowa Falls: General Publishing and Binding, 1974.

Michigan Metro Girl Scouts Council. *The Arab/American Girl Scout Cookbook*. Dearborn: Michigan Metro Girl Scout Field Department, 1988.

Milford New Century Club. *Blue Hen's Chickens' Cook Book*. Milford, Del.: *Milford Chronicle*, 1921.

Montana Federation of Negro Women's Clubs. *Cook Book*. Billings: Montana Federation of Negro Women's Clubs, 1927.
Moss, Maria J. *A Poetical Cook-Book*. Philadelphia: Caxton Press of C. Sherman, Son and Company, 1864.
Muskegon Area Women's Coalition. *Feminist Food Book*. N.p.: Depot Enterprise, 1982.
National Association for Girls and Women in Sport. *Cookies (and Punch, Too!)* Washington, D.C.: National Association for Girls and Women in Sport, 1977.
National Council of Jewish Women, Greensboro Section. *The Blue Denim Cook Book*. Greensboro, N.C.: Greensboro Section, National Council of Jewish Women, 1975.
National Organization for Women. *Don't Assume I Don't Cook: Recipes for Women's Lives: National Organization for Women Cookbook*. Washington, D.C.: National Organization for Women, 1998.
Navajo Curriculum Center at Rough Rock Demonstration School. *Ch'iyáán 'íít'íní binaaltsoos*. Rough Rock, Ariz.: Navajo Curriculum Center at Rough Rock Demonstration School, 1986.
Negro Culinary Art Club of Los Angeles. *Eliza's Cook Book*. Los Angeles: Wetzel, 1936.
New Arrivals at the Eglin Refugee Reception Center. *Happy in My Stomach / Tôi Vui Trong Lòng*. New York: YMCA Refugee and Resettlement Services, 1975.
NOW, Tarrant County Chapter. *"Women Are A-Risin'": Feminist Food for Thought Cookbook*. Tarrant County, Tex.: NOW, Tarrant County Chapter, 1986.
Oregon NARAL Supporters. *CHOICE Recipes*. [Troutdale]: Oregon NARAL, 1982.
Oxford United Methodist Church. *The Art of Cooking in Oxford*. Chicago: Women's Clubs Publishing Company, 1970.
Prince of Peace ALCW. *Not Bread Alone*. La Crescent, Minn.: Prince of Peace ALCW, 1976.
Ravenswood High School. *Soul Power Cook Book*. Menlo Park, Calif.: Doyle / Lane Magazine and Book Company, 1970.
Reinach, Jacquelyn. *Carefree Cooking*. New York: Hearthside, 1970.
Republican Women's Club Lubbock, Texas. *GOP Cookbook*. Lubbock: Lubbock Company / Republican Women's Club, 1967.
Rufus King High School. *Cooking with Soul: Favorite Recipes of Negro Homemakers*. Milwaukee: Rufus King High School, 1968.
Sisterhood of the Temple Beth Hillel-Beth El. *Passoverama: A Collection of Favorite Recipes*. 2nd ed. Wynnewood, Pa.: Sisterhood of Temple Beth Hillel–Beth El, 1978.
Smart-Grosvenor, Vertamae. *Vibration Cooking, or The Travel Notes of a Geechee Girl*. 3rd ed. New York: Ballantine, 1991.

Southern Conference Educational Fund. *SCEF Recipes: A Radical Cookbook*. Louisville: Southern Conference Educational Fund, 1973.

Sterling, Mary D. Eldridge, ed. *The Alumnae Cookbook: Well-Tested Recipes for Table Dainties, Contributed by Graduates of the Girls' High and Normal School Philadelphia*. Philadelphia: Burk and McFetridge, 1891.

Stiefel, Ida, and Minnie Jacobs, eds. *St. Pauls Bazaar Kochbuch und Geschæftsfuehrer.* Chicago: Kressmann and Brother, 1892.

Stiltner, Karen, ed. *Al Hasa Saudi Arabia Cookbook*. Iowa Falls: General Publishing and Binding, 1976.

St. Michael's Home School Association. *Children's Choices*. Gastonia, N.C.: Good Will, 1970.

Tastefullyterrible and contributors. *The F*ck You Buffet: Secret Family Recipes of Kids Betrayed by Their Homophobic Parents and a Few Recipes from Good and Kind People Because Balance Is Key*. N.p., 2020. Accessed August 30, 2023. https://drive.google.com/file/d/1WjcDfZrPMroPw9f5GfEyoaTs2KEx4Pub/view.

Thurman, Sue Bailey, ed. *The Historical Cookbook of the American Negro*. Washington, D.C.: National Council of Negro Women, 1958.

Turner, Bertha, comp., *The Federation Cookbook: A Collection of Tested Recipes, Contributed by the Colored Women of the State of California*. Pasadena, Calif., 1910.

Waunakee Wisconsin Centennial Committee. *People Pleasing Recipes, 1871–1971*. Waunakee: Centennial, 1971.

Westchester Tricentennial Cookbook Committee. *Westchester County Tricentennial Cookbook, 1683–1983*. Westchester County, N.Y.: Westchester Tricentennial Cookbook Committee, 1983.

Women of Central Congregational Church. *Central Congregational Church Cook Book*. Topeka: Trapp Print-Shop, 1913.

Women's Architectural League. *Blueprint for the Cook*. 2nd ed. Kansas City: Cookbook Publishers, 1976.

Women's National Book Association, Nashville Chapter. *Literary Allusions Cookbook*. Nashville: Women's National Book Association, 1982.

Women's National Press Club. *Who Says We Can't Cook!* Washington, D.C.: McIver Art and Publications, 1955.

Women's Society St. Luke's Union Church. *Midlothian Woman's Cook Book*. Blue Island, Ill.: Blue Island, 1925.

Women Strike for Peace. *Peace de Resistance: A Cook Book*. Edited by Esther Lewin. Los Angeles: Women Strike for Peace, n.d.

———. *Peace de Resistance*. Vol. 2. 2nd ed. Los Angeles: Women Strike for Peace, n.d.

Print, Internet, and Film Sources

"About CLUW." Coalition of Labor Union Women. Accessed October 28, 2024. http://www.cluw.org/?zone=/unionactive/view_page.cfm&page=About-20CLUW.

"About." Jumbo Jack's. Accessed May 18, 2020. http://www.jumbojacks.com/about/.

"About." National Women's Political Caucus. Accessed November 17, 2024. https://www.nwpc.org/history/.

"About Us." Fundcraft. Accessed November 17, 2024. https://fundcraft.com/fundraising-cookbooks/1-cookbook-book-publishing.asp.

"About." *You Stir the Pot: Recipes for Change.* 2022. Accessed November 17, 2024. https://www.youstirthepot.com/about.

Adams, Thomas R., and Nicolas Barker. "A New Model for the Study of the Book." In *A Potencie of Life: Books in Society; The Clark Lectures, 1986–1987*, edited by Nicholas Barker, 5–43. London: British Library, 1993.

Allen, Gwen. "The Artist as Bookmaker." In *The Thing: The Book*, edited by John Herschend and Will Rogan, 13–24. San Francisco: Chronicle Books, 2014.

Amos, Janell Shride. *Fundraising Ideas: Over 225 Money Making Events for Community Groups, with a Resource Directory.* Jefferson: McFarland, 1995.

Anderson, Jean. "Is the Cookbook Market Simmering Down?" *Publishers Weekly*, August 19, 1974, 42–44.

"Antique Copying Machines." Early Office Museum. Accessed November 17, 2024. https://www.officemuseum.com/copy_machines.htm.

Appadurai, Arjun. "How to Make a National Cuisine: Cookbooks in Contemporary India." *Comparative Studies in Society and History* 30, no. 1 (1988): 3–24.

Appleby, Joyce, Eileen K. Cheng, and Joanne L. Goodwin, eds. *Encyclopedia of Women in American History.* Abingdon, Oxon: Routledge, 2015.

Arthur and Elizabeth Schlesinger Library on the History of Women in America. "Culinary Holdings Enhanced by AIWF Collection." *Schlesinger Library Newsletter*, Fall 1990.

Atkinson, Harriette S. "Oakland Peter Maurin House." *Catholic Worker* 31, no. 1 (1964): 3–4.

Avakian, Arlene Voski, and Barbara Haber. "Feminist Food Studies: A Brief History." In *From Betty Crocker to Feminist Food Studies: Critical Perspectives on Women and Food*, edited by Arlene Voski Avakian and Barbara Haber, 1–28. Amherst: University of Massachusetts Press, 2005.

Azaransky, Sarah. *This Worldwide Struggle: Religion and the International Roots of the Civil Rights Movement.* Oxford: Oxford University Press, 2017.

Banham, Rob. "Printing to 1970." In Eliot and Rose, *Companion to the History*, 95–109.

Barakso, Maryann. *Governing NOW: Grassroots Activism in the National Organization for Women*. Ithaca: Cornell University Press, 2004.

Barnes, Paula C. "The Junior League Eleven: Elite Women of Little Rock Struggle for Social Justice." *Arkansas Historical Quarterly* 57, no. 1 (1998): 46–61.

Barth, Ellen. "Chronological Bibliography of Indigenous American Cookbooks." University of Münster. January 2, 2025. https://www.uni-muenster.de/imperia/md/content/englischesseminar/bookstudies/barth_chronological_bibliography_of_indigenous_american_cookbooks.pdf.

Beale, Betty. "Exclusively Yours: Press Club Cookbook Party Is Autographer's Heaven." *Evening Star* (Washington, D.C.), November 16, 1955.

Beins, Agatha. "A Publishing Assemblage: Building Book History Methodology Through Feminist Periodicals." *American Periodicals: A Journal of History and Criticism* 28, no. 2 (2018): 105–122. https://muse.jhu.edu/article/702110.

Belasco, Warren. *Appetite for Change: How the Counterculture Took on the Food Industry*. 2nd ed. Ithaca: Cornell University Press, 2007.

Bhaskar, Michael, and Angus Phillips. Introduction to *The Oxford Handbook of Publishing*, edited by Angus Phillips and Michael Bhaskar, 1–18. Oxford: Oxford University Press, 2019.

Blair, Karen J. *The Clubwoman as Feminist: True Womanhood Redefined, 1868–1914*. New York: Holmes and Meier, 1980.

Boles, Frank. "'Stirring Constantly': 150 Years of Michigan Cookbooks." *Michigan Historical Review* 32, no. 2 (2006): 33–62. https://doi.org/10.1353/mhr.2006.0039.

Bower, Anne. "Bound Together: Recipes, Lives, Stories, and Readings." In Bower, *Recipes for Reading*, 1–14.

———. "Cooking Up Stories: Narrative Elements in Community Cookbooks." In Bower, *Recipes for Reading*, 29–50.

———. "*Our Sisters' Recipes*: Exploring 'Community' in a Community Cookbook." *Journal of Popular Culture* 31, no. 3 (1997): 137–151.

———, ed. *Recipes for Reading: Community Cookbooks, Stories, Histories*. Amherst: University of Massachusetts Press, 1997.

Bradley, Patricia. *Mass Media and the Shaping of American Feminism, 1963–1975*. Jackson: University Press of Mississippi, 2003.

Brown, Eleanor Parker, and Robert Carlton Brown. *Culinary Americana: Cookbooks Published in the Cities and Towns of the United States of America During the Years from 1860 Through 1960*. New York: Roving Eye, 1961.

Brownson, JeanMarie. "Illinois' Best: Duo Travels the State for the Best Its Cookbooks Have to Offer." *Chicago Tribune*, October 11, 1995.

Camp Cookery and Hospital Diet for the Use of the U.S. Volunteers Now in Service. New York: Brady, 1861.

Casper, Scott E. Introduction to *A History of the Book in America*. Vol. 3, *The Industrial Book*, edited by David D. Hall and Scott E. Casper, 1–39. Chapel Hill: University of North Carolina Press, 2007.

Chambré, Susan M. "Parallel Power Structures, Invisible Careers, and the Changing Nature of American Jewish Women's Philanthropy." In *Women, Philanthropy, and Civil Society*, edited by Kathleen D. McCarthy, 169–189. Indianapolis: Indiana University Press, 2001.

Chen, Yong. "Recreating the Chinese American Home Through Cookbook Writing." *Social Research* 81, no. 2 (2014): 489–500.

Chester, Gail. "Sex, Race and Class: The Radical, Alternative, and Minority Book Trade in Britain." In *The Cambridge History of the Book in Britain*. Vol. 7, *The Twentieth Century and Beyond*, edited by Andrew Nash, Claire Squires, and I. R. Willison, 616–645. Cambridge: Cambridge University Press, 2019.

Chevalier, Andre. "Trojan Horse of the Women of Suffrage." Rare Books Digest. April 18, 2014. https://rarebooksdigest.com/2014/04/18/trojan-horse-of-the-women-of-suffrage/.

Cholesterol, Virginia, and Mrs. Theodore William Banks. "On the Picket Line with Ladies Against Women." In "Satire." Special issue, *Heresies: A Feminist Publication on Art and Politics* 5, no. 2 (1985): 6–8.

Clay, Steve, and Rodney Phillips. *From a Secret Location: Poetry, Little Mags, Small Presses, and Transient Documents from the Mimeo Era and Beyond*. Granary Books. Accessed November 17, 2024. https://fromasecretlocation.com/introduction/.

Coker, Cait, and Kate Ozment. "Building the *Women in Book History Bibliography*, or Digital Enumerative Bibliography as Preservation of Feminist Labor." *Digital Humanities Quarterly* 13, no. 3 (2019). http://www.digitalhumanities.org/dhq/vol/13/3/000428/000428.html.

"Community and Church Cookbooks from Northeastern PA." Scranton Public Library. Accessed November 17, 2024. https://digitalarchives.powerlibrary.org/papd/islandora/object/papd%3Apscrl-cccfnepa.

Cook, Margaret. *America's Charitable Cooks: A Bibliography of Fund-Raising Cook Books Published in the United States (1861–1915)*. Kent, 1971.

"Cookbook." In *The Oxford Companion to the Book*, edited by Michael F. Suarez and H. R. Woudhuysen, 2:637–638. Oxford: Oxford University Press, 2010.

"Cookbook Sales Buy Church Windows, Office Equipment." *Church Management* 30, no. 11 (1954): 68.

"Cookbooks for Every Taste." *Washington Post*, January 14, 1982. https://www.proquest.com/historical-newspapers/cookbooks-every-taste/docview/147452691/se-2.

Congregation Beth Yeshurun. "*Let My People . . . Eat!*" *Message* (Houston) 4, no. 9 (1976): 2. https://texashistory.unt.edu/ark:/67531/metapth1288001/.

Coontz, Stephanie. *A Strange Stirring: The Feminine Mystique and American Women at the Dawn of the 1960s*. New York: Basic Books, 2011.

Coser, Lewis. "Publishers as Gatekeepers of Ideas." *Annals* 421 (1975): 14–22.

Cowan, Ruth Schwartz. *More Work for Mother: The Ironies of Household Technology from the Open Hearth to the Microwave*. New York: Basic Books, 1983.

Croly, Jane Cunningham. *The History of the Women's Club Movement in America*. New York: Allen, 1898.

———. *Sorosis: Its Origin and History*. New York: Little, 1886.

Crowell, Elsie Bradwell. "The Civil Rights Movement." In Appleby, Cheng, and Goodwin, *Encyclopedia of Women*, 517–520.

Dale, Elizabeth J. "Fundraising as Women's Work? Examining the Profession with a Gender Lens." *Journal of Philanthropy and Marketing* 22 (2017): 1–10.

Dana, Rich. *Cheap Copies! The Obsolete Press Guide to DIY Hectography, Mimeography and Spirit Duplication*. Iowa City: Obsolete, 2022.

Danky, James P. "The Oppositional Press." In *A History of the Book in America*. Vol. 5, *The Enduring Book: Print Culture in Postwar America*, edited by David Paul Nord, Joan Shelley Rubin, and Michael Schudson, 269–285. Chapel Hill: University of North Carolina Press, 2009.

Darnton, Robert. "What Is the History of Books?" *Daedalus* 111, no. 3 (1982): 65–83.

Davidson, Cathy N., and Jessamyn Hatcher. Introduction to *No More Separate Spheres! A Next Wave American Studies Reader*, edited by Cathy N. Davidson and Jessamyn Hatcher, 7–26. Durham: Duke University Press, 2002.

Decker, Sarah S. Platt. "The Meaning of the Woman's Club Movement." *Annals of the American Academy of Political and Social Science* 28 (1906): 1–6.

Dennis, Abigail. "From Apicus to Gastroporn: Form, Function, and Ideology in the History of Cookery Books." *Studies in Popular Culture* 31, no. 1 (2008): 1–17.

Derleth, Jessica. "'Kneading Politics': Cookery and the American Woman Suffrage Movement." *Journal of the Gilded Age and Progressive Era* 17 (2018): 450–474. https://doi.org/10.1017/S1537781418000063.

Dore, Mary, dir. 2016. *She's Beautiful When She's Angry*. Chicago: Music Box Films. DVD.

Driver, Elizabeth. "Cookbooks as Primary Sources for Writing History: A Bibliographer's View." *Food, Culture and Society* 12, no. 3 (2009): 257–274.

"Droppings." *Off Our Backs* 1, no. 14 (1970): 12.

Dubisar, Abby. "'If I Can't Bake, I Don't Want to Be Part of Your Revolution': CODEPINK's Activist Literacies of Peace and Pie." *Community Literacy Journal* 10, no. 2 (2016): 1–18.

DuBois, Ellen. *Feminism: Old Wave and New.* Chicago: Chicago Women's Liberation Union, 1971.

DuSablon, Mary Anna. *America's Collectible Cookbooks: The History, the Politics, the Recipes.* Athens: Ohio University Press, 1994.

Dyer, Ceil. *The Perfect Dinner Party Cookbook.* New York: McKay, 1974.

Eble, Kenneth E. "An Exquisite Balance of Nature." *Journal of Higher Education* 32, no. 5 (1961): 280–281.

Eichhorn, Kate. *Adjusted Margin: Xerography, Art, and Activism in the Late Twentieth Century.* Cambridge: MIT Press, 2016.

Elder, Lisa. "Fund-Raising Cookbooks Are More Than Recipes." *Oklahoman*, February 22, 1983. https://eu.oklahoman.com/story/news/1983/02/22/fund-raising-cookbooks-are-more-than-recipes/62855394007/.

Elias, Megan J. *Food on the Page: Cookbooks and American Culture.* Philadelphia: University of Pennsylvania Press, 2017.

Eliot, Simon, and Jonathan Rose, eds. *A Companion to the History of the Book.* 2nd ed. Hoboken: Wiley-Blackwell, 2020.

"Employment: Women." *Indianapolis Star*, December 2, 1951.

Endrijonas, Erica. "Processed Foods from Scratch: Cooking for a Family in the 1950's." In *Kitchen Culture in America: Popular Representations of Food, Gender and Race*, edited by Sherrie A. Inness, 157–173. Philadelphia: University of Pennsylvania Press, 2001.

"Ephemerals: Cookbooks, Event Programs, and Directories." Internet Archive. Accessed November 17, 2024. https://archive.org/details/ncephemerals.

ERAmerica. *ERAmerica Report.* University of South Carolina University Libraries Digital Collection. 1–4. June 1980. https://digital.tcl.sc.edu/digital/collection/era/id/2045.

Estes Blair, Melissa. "'A Dynamic Force in Our Community': Women's Clubs and Second-Wave Feminism at the Grassroots." *Frontiers* 30, no. 3 (2009): 30–51.

Evans, Sara M. *Tidal Wave: How Women Changed America at Century's End.* New York: Free Press, 2003.

———. "The Women's Movement in the United States in the 1960s." In *Challenging Times: The Women's Movement in Canada and the United States*, edited by Constance Backhouse and David H. Flaherty, 61–71. Montreal: McGill-Queen's University Press, 1996.

Eves, Rosalyn Collings. "A Recipe for Remembrance: Memory and Identity in African-American Women's Cookbooks." *Rhetoric Review* 24, no. 3 (2003): 280–297.

Ezell, Margaret J. M. "The Laughing Tortoise: Speculations on Manuscript Sources and Women's Book History." *English Literary Renaissance* 32, no. 2 (2008): 331–355.

Fabricant, Florence. "L. I. Group's Cookbook Goes National." *New York Times*, October 19, 1980.

Farrell, Amy. "'Like a Tarantula on a Banana Boat': *Ms.* Magazine, 1972–1989." In *Feminist Organizations: Harvest of the New Women's Movement*, edited by Myra Marx Ferree and Patricia Yancey Martin, 53–68. Philadelphia: Temple University Press, 1995.

Felsenstein, Frank, and James J. Connolly. *What Middletown Read: Print Culture in an American Small City*. Amherst: University of Massachusetts Press, 2015.

Ferguson, Kennan. *Cookbook Politics*. Philadelphia: University of Pennsylvania Press, 2020.

Finkelstein, David, and Alistair McCleery. *An Introduction to Book History*. 2nd ed. Abingdon, Oxon: Routledge, 2005.

Fisher, Carol, and John Fisher. *Pot Roast, Politics, and Ants in the Pantry: Missouri's Cookbook Heritage*. Columbia: University of Missouri Press, 2008.

Flanagan, Joan. *The Grass Roots Fundraising Book: How to Raise Money in Your Community*. Chicago: Contemporary Books, 1982.

———. *The Successful Volunteer Organization: Getting Started and Getting Results in Nonprofit, Charitable, Grass Roots, and Community Groups*. Chicago: Contemporary Books, 1981.

"Florida NOW News: National Organization for Women." *Florida NOW News* 6, no. 6 (1978): 1–8. http://purl.flvc.org/fsu/fd/FSU_MSS2008003_B17_F05_005.

"Food Is a Feminist Issue." Special issue, *Heresies: A Feminist Publication on Art and Politics* 6, no. 1 (1987).

"For the Liberated Female." *Time* 98, no. 25 (1971): 52.

Fox, Deanna N. "Community Cookbooks Trace Culinary Trends, Recipes." Times Union. July 26, 2017. https://www.timesunion.com/living/article/Community- cookbooks-trace-culinary-trends-recipes-11437968.php.

Friedan, Betty. "Cooking with Betty Friedan . . . Yes, Betty Friedan." *New York Times*, January 5, 1977, 68, 77.

———. *The Feminine Mystique*. 1963. Reprint, New York: Dell, 1974.

Fritschner, Sarah. "A Junior League Jackpot." *Washington Post*, January 14, 1983. https://www.washingtonpost.com/archive/lifestyle/food/1982/01/14/a-junior-league-jackpot/aadd82ee-12a4-42f6-a0aa-abfc17ea98e5/.

Gabaccia, Donna R. "Food, Recipes, Cookbooks, and Italian-American Life." *Italian Americana* 16, no. 1 (1998): 5–23.

———. *We Are What We Eat: Ethnic Food and the Making of Americans*. Cambridge: Harvard University Press, 1998.

Gattuso, Reina. "Eat Like a 1970s Radical with 'The People's Philadelphia Cookbook.'" Atlas Obscura. January 24, 2020. https://www.atlasobscura.com/articles/philadelphia-food-history.

Genette, Gérard. *Paratexts: Thresholds of Interpretation*. Translated by Jane E. Lewin. Cambridge: Cambridge University Press, 1997.

Givens, Charity. "Creating Community, One Byte at a Time: Digital Community Cookbooks During the COVID-19 Pandemic." *Explorations in the History and Culture of Human Nourishment* 13, no. 3 (2023): 200–218. https://doi.org/10.1080/07409710.2023.2228035.

Goldsby, Jacqueline, and Meredith L. McGill. "What Is 'Black' About Black Bibliography?" *Papers of the Bibliographical Society of America* 116, no. 2 (2022): 161–189. https://doi.org/10.1086/719985.

Gomoll, Jeanne. "A History of WisCon." Nerds of a Feather, Flock Together. November 12, 2018. http://www.nerds-feather.com/2018/11/feminist-futures-history-of-wiscon.html.

Gordon, Beverly. "Playing at Being Powerless: New England Ladies Fairs, 1830–1930." *Massachusetts Review* 27, no. 1 (1986): 144–160.

Gordon, Larry. "Recipe for Success: UC San Diego Benefits from a Cookbook Compromise." *Los Angeles Times*, December 24, 1990. https://www.latimes.com/archives/la-xpm-1990-12-24-mn-5288-story.html.

———. "State Could Lose Them: Universities Licking Lips for Recipes." *Los Angeles Times*, August 31, 1988. https://www.latimes.com/archives/la-xpm-1988-08-31-mn-1214-story.html.

Greene, Christina. *Our Separate Ways: Women and the Black Freedom Movement in Durham, North Carolina*. Chapel Hill: University of North Carolina Press, 2005.

Greene, Donna. "Alice O'Rourke Again Sets Aside 'More Normal Life.'" *New York Times*, June 8, 1986.

Guensburg, Carol. "Delicious Irony: The NOW Cookbook." *Tampa Bay Times*, June 24, 1999. https://www.tampabay.com/archive/1999/06/24/delicious-irony-the-now-cookbook/.

"Guide to the Movement." *Women: A Journal of Liberation* 1, no. 4 (1970): 62–63.

Gvion, Liora. "What's Cooking in America? Cookbooks Narrate Ethnicity: 1850–1990." *Food, Culture and Society* 12, no. 1 (2009): 54–76.

Hansen, Barbara. "Recipe for a New Cookbook." *Los Angeles Times*, June 7, 1979.

Harbour, Jennifer. "'I Earn by My Own Labor from Day to Day:' African American Women's Activism in the Wartime Midwest." *Journal of the Illinois*

State Historical Society 108, nos. 3–4 (2015): 347–373. https://doi.org/10.5406/jillistathistsoc.108.3-4.0347.

Harker, Jaime, and Cecilia Konchar Farr. "Outrageous, Dangerous, and Unassimilable: Writing the Women's Movement." In *This Book Is an Action: Feminist Print Culture and Activist Aesthetics*, edited by Jaime Harker and Cecilia Konchar Farr, 1–19. Urbana: University of Illinois Press, 2016.

Hawley, E. Haven. "Revaluing Mimeographs as Historical Sources." *RBM: A Journal of Rare Books, Manuscripts, and Cultural Heritage* 15, no. 1 (2014): 40–55.

Hayden, Casey, and Mary King. "Sex and Caste." In *The Movements of the New Left, 1950–1975: A Brief History with Documents*, edited by Van Gosse, 99–102. Cham, Switzerland: Palgrave Macmillan, 2005.

Hays, Rolfes and Associates. *How to Write and Publish a Classic Cookbook.* New York: Plume, 1986.

Hicks, Heather J. "'Whatever It Is That She's Since Become': Writing Bodies of Text and Bodies of Women in James Tiptree, Jr.'s 'The Girl Who Was Plugged in' and William Gibson's 'The Winter Market.'" *Contemporary Literature* 37, no. 1 (1996): 62–93.

Higgs, Colleen, and Moira Richards. "Roll Over, Gutenberg!" *Agenda: Empowering Women for Gender Equity* 60 (2004): 100–104.

"History." WisCon. Accessed November 17, 2024. https://wiscon.net/about/history/.

Horner, Jennifer R. "*Betty Crocker's Picture Cookbook*: A Gendered Ritual Response to Social Crises of the Postwar Era." *Journal of Communication Inquiry* 24, no. 3 (2000): 332–345.

Horowitz, Daniel. "*The Feminine Mystique* and the Feminist Movement." In *The Turbulent 60s: 1963*, edited by William S. McConnel, 37–42. Farmington Hills, Mich.: Greenhaven, 2004.

"How Many Feminists Does It Take to Write a Cookbook?" *Greensboro News and Record*, June 6, 1999. https://greensboro.com/how-many-feminists-does-it-take-to-write-a-cookbook/article_3185aa5b-953c-52f8-80ef-979e096bf33d.html.

Howsam, Leslie. "Culture of Food / Food as Culture." In *Food, Cookery and Culture*, edited by Leslie Howsam, i–xi. Working Papers in the Humanities 7. 1998. https://hdl.handle.net/20.500.14776/15246.

———. "In My View: Women and Book History." *SHARP News* 7, no. 4 (1998): 1–2.

———. "The Study of the Book." In *The Cambridge Companion to the History of the Book*, edited by Leslie Howsam, 1–13. Cambridge: Cambridge University Press, 2015.

Huey, Pamela. "Cookbook Business Is Good." *Independent*, November 18, 1976.

Hunt, Adam. "Kitchen Politics? Grits in the American South and the Equal Rights Amendment." Illuminations. January 29, 2021. https://fsuspecialcollections.wordpress.com/2021/01/29/kitchen-politics-grits-in-the-american-south-and-the-equal-rights-amendment/.

Iacovetta, Franca, Valerie J. Korinek, and Marlene Epp. Introduction to *Edible Histories, Cultural Politics: Towards a Canadian Food History*, edited by Franca Iacovetta, Valerie J. Korinek, and Marlene Epp, 3–28. Toronto: University of Toronto Press, 2012.

Inness, Sherrie A. *Dinner Roles: American Women and Culinary Culture*. Iowa City: University of Iowa Press, 2001.

———. *Secret Ingredients: Race, Gender, and Class at the Dinner Table*. Cham, Switzerland: Palgrave Macmillan, 2006.

Ireland, Lynne. "The Compiled Cookbook as Foodways Autobiography." *Western Folklore* 40, no. 1 (1981): 107–114.

James, Caryn. "Recipes for Success in New Cookbooks." *New York Times*, March 27, 1985.

Jarvis, Samuel G. *Sophia, or The Reign of Woman*. New York: Holman, 1864.

Jeffrey, Kirk. "Reviewed Work: The *Clubwoman as Feminist: True Womanhood Redefined, 1868–1914*, by Karen J. Blair." *New York History* 62, no. 2 (1981): 230–232.

Jenkins, Krista. "Year of the Woman." In *Encyclopedia of Women and American Politics*, edited by Lynne E. Ford, 510–511. New York: Facts on File, 2008.

Jenkins, Nancy. "The History of Food Gains a Scholarly Pedigree." *New York Times*, May 1984.

Jennings, Chelsea. "Pirating Pound: Drafts and Fragments in 1960s Mimeograph Culture." *Journal of Modern Literature* 40, no. 1 (2016): 88–108.

Julian, Sheryl. "There's a Lot of History in Those Cookbooks: Study of Food Paints Picture of American Family Life." *Boston Globe*, November 25, 1990.

Jumbo Jack's Cookbooks. *Let Us Help You Prepare a Successful Cookbook*. Audubon, Iowa: Jumbo Jack's Cookbooks, 1996.

Kaestle, Carl F., and Janice A. Radway, eds. *A History of the Book in America*. Vol. 4, *Print in Motion: The Expansion of Publishing and Reading in the United States, 1880–1940*. Chapel Hill: University of North Carolina Press, 2009.

Kaplan Daniels, Arlene. *Invisible Careers: Women Civic Leaders from the Volunteer World*. Chicago: University of Chicago Press, 1988.

Kauffman, Dorothy. "West Oakland." *Catholic Worker* 34, no. 12 (1969): 8.

Kelly, Alison P. "Choice Receipts from American Housekeepers: A Collection of Digitized Community Cookbooks from the Library of Congress." *Public Historian* 34, no. 2 (2012): 30–52.

Ketchum, Alex. "Recipe for a Queer Cookbook." In *Queering Nutrition and Dietetics: LGBTQ+ Reflections on Food Through Art*, edited by Phillip Joy and Megan Aston, 127–134. New York: Routledge, 2022.

Kirshenblatt-Gimblett, Barbara. "The Moral Sublime: The Temple Emanuel Fair and Its Cookbook, Denver, 1888." In Bower, *Recipes for Reading*, 136–153.

Klibaner, Irwin. "The Travail of Southern Radicals: The Southern Conference Educational Fund, 1946–1976." *Journal of Southern History* 49, no. 2 (1983): 179–202.

Kretschmer, Kelsy. *Fighting for NOW: Diversity and Discord in the National Organization for Women*. Minneapolis: University of Minnesota Press, 2019.

Krishna, Priya. "The Community Cookbook Is Reborn for a Time of Scarcity and Sharing." *New York Times*, April 27, 2020. https://www.nytimes.com/2020/04/28/dining/community-cookbooks-coronavirus.html.

Kriss, Gary. "Wanted: 300 Recipes." *New York Times*, September 12, 1982.

Kumin, Laura. "On Turn-of-the-Century Suffrage Cookbooks, Trojan Horse for Women's Equality." Lit Hub. November 4, 2024. https://lithub.com/on-turn-of-the-century-suffrage-cookbooks-trojan-horse-for-womens-equality/.

Lane-McKinley, Madeline. "Notes on Utopian Failure in the Commune Kitchens." In *Nourishing Resistance: Stories of Food, Protest, and Mutual Aid*, edited by Wren Awry, 131–137. Oakland: PM, 2023.

Larbalestier, Justine. *The Battle of the Sexes in Science Fiction*. Middletown, Conn.: Wesleyan University Press, 2002.

Le Dantec-Lowry, Hélène. "Reading Women's Lives in Cookbooks and Other Culinary Writings: A Critical Essay." *Revue française d'études américaines* 2, no. 116 (2008): 99–122. https://doi.org/10.3917/rfea.116.0099.

Lefanu, Sarah. *Feminism and Science Fiction*. Bloomington: Indiana University Press, 1989.

Leonardi, Susan J. "Recipes for Reading: Summer Pasta, Lobster à la Riseholme, and Key Lime Pie." *PMLA* 104, no. 3 (1989): 340–347.

"Letters." *New York Times*, January 19, 1977.

Levy, Michelle. "Do Women Have a Book History?" *Studies in Romanticism* 53 (2014): 297–317.

Lewine, Frances. "Mystery Solved: Cook First Lady's Recipe How Long 'Till It's Done.'" *Evening Star* (Washington, D.C.), October 17, 1962.

Lindgren, Don, and Mark Germer. *UNXLD: American Cookbooks of Community and Place*. Vol. 1. Biddeford, Maine: Rabelais, 2018.

Long, Elizabeth. "Aflame with Culture: Reading and Social Mission in the Nineteenth-Century White Women's Literary Club Movement." In Kaestle and Radway, *History of the Book*, 4:476–490.

Longone, Janice B., and Daniel T. Longone. *American Cookbooks and Wine Books, 1797–1950*. Ann Arbor, Mich.: Wine and Food Library, 1984.

Longone, Janice Bluestein. "The Mince Pie That Launched the Declaration of Independence, and Other Recipes in Rhyme." *Gastronomica* 2, no. 4 (2002): 86–89. https://www.jstor.org/stable/10.1525/gfc.2002.2.4.86.

———. "'Tried Receipts': An Overview of America's Charitable Cookbooks." In Bower, *Recipes for Reading*, 17–28.

"A Look at Women's Lib in Suburbia: The Emphasis Is Different." *New York Times*, April 7, 1971.

Lothian, Alexis. "Alice Sheldon and the Name of the Tiptree Award." Otherwise Award. September 2, 2019. https://otherwiseaward.org/2019/09/alice-sheldon-and-the-name-of-the-tiptree-award.

Luey, Beth. "Modernity and Print III: The United States 1890–1970." In Eliot and Rose, *Companion to the History*, 559–572.

Lyons, Martyn. *A History of Reading and Writing in the Western World*. Basingstoke: Palgrave, 2009.

———. *The Typewriter Century: A Cultural History of Writing Practices*. Toronto: University of Toronto Press, 2021.

Mackintosh, Prudence. "My Life and Hard Times in the Junior League." *Texas Monthly*, 1979. https://www.texasmonthly.com/being-texan/my-life-and-hard-times-in-the-junior-league/.

Makos, Jeff, and Libby Morse. "Cookbook Sales Beyond the Bookstore." *Publishers Weekly*, September 8, 1989, 30–33.

Malik, Rachel. "Horizons of the Publishable: Publishing in/as Literary Studies." *ELH* 75, no. 3 (2008): 707–735.

Mastrangelo, Lisa. "Community Cookbooks: Sponsors of Literacy and Community Identity." *Community Literacy Journal* 10, no. 1 (2015): 73–86.

Mathews, Donald G., and Jane Sherron De Hart. *Sex, Gender, and the Politics of ERA: A State and the Nation*. Oxford: Oxford University Press, 1990.

McBean, Sam. "The Feminist 1970s." In *American Literature in Transition, 1970–1980*, edited by Kirk Curnutt, 352–364. Cambridge: Cambridge University Press, 2018.

McCarthy, Kathleen D. "Parallel Power Structures: Women and the Voluntary Sphere." In *Lady Bountiful Revisited: Women, Philanthropy, and Power*, edited by Kathleen D. McCarthy, 1–31. New Brunswick: Rutgers University Press, 1990.

McDowell, Edwin. "Name It and You'll Find a Cookbook on It." *Chicago Tribune*, October 18, 1981. https://www.proquest.com/historical-newspapers/reading/docview/170554051/se-2.

McGrath, Laura B. "Comping White." *Los Angeles Review of Books*, January 21, 2019. https://lareviewofbooks.org/article/comping-white/.

McHenry, Elizabeth. "Reading and Race Pride: The Literary Activism of Black Clubwomen." In Kaestle and Radway, *History of the Book*, 4:491–510.

"McIlhenny Hall of Fame Award." Favorite Recipes Press. Accessed August 30, 2023. https://www.frpbooks.com/about/award_details.aspx?cat=4.

McKinney, Cait. *Information Activism: A Queer History of Lesbian Media Technologies*. Durham: Duke University Press, 2020.

McKinney, Joan. "A Luncheon with 'Soul.'" *Oakland Tribune* (California), December 17, 1968.

McMillian, John. "'Our Founder, the Mimeograph Machine': Participatory Democracy in Students for a Democratic Society's Print Culture." *Journal for the Study of Radicalism* 2, no. 2 (2008): 85–110. https://www.jstor.org/stable/41887605.

Mecklenberg-Faenger, Amy. "'Hear the Table Call of the South:' White Supremacist Rhetoric and the 1950 *Charleston Receipts* Junior League Cookbook." *Peitho Journal* 20, no. 2 (2018): 212–232.

Melvin, Katrina. "A History of Neglect." *Vida: Women in Literary Arts*, October 2, 2011. https://www.vidaweb.org/a-history-of-neglect/.

Melvin, Tessa. "Mrs. O'Rourke Busy on Cookbook." *New York Times*, March 20, 1983.

Menand, Louis. "Books as Bombs." *New Yorker*, January 24, 2011. https://www.newyorker.com/magazine/2011/01/24/books-as-bombs.

Metropolitan Fair, United States Sanitary Commission. *Catalogue of the Art Exhibition at the Metropolitan Fair in Aid of the U.S. Sanitary Commission*. New York: Metropolitan Fair, 1864.

Milholland, Lola. "A Brief History of Japanese American Cookbooks: The Evolution of West Coast Spiral Bounds from the 1960s to the 1990s." *Stained Page News*, March 19, 2021. https://www.stainedpagenews.com/p/a-brief-history-of-japanese-american.

Miller, Bryan. "Local Cookbooks: A Regional Touch for Fund-Raising." *New York Times*, September 1, 1982.

———. "Some Advice on How to Produce a Cookbook." *New York Times*, September 1, 1982.

Miller, Laura J., and Emilie Hardman. "By the Pinch and the Pound: Less and More Protest in American Vegetarian Cookbooks from the Nineteenth Century to the Present." In *Protest on the Page: Essays on Print and the Culture of Dissent*, edited by James P. Danky, Jennifer Ratner-Rosenhagen, and James L. Baughman, 111–136. Madison: University of Wisconsin Press, 2015.

———. “The Lyrical Cookbook: Expressive Forms Connecting Vegetarian Communities.” *Amerikastudien/American Studies* 70, no. 3 (2025), 285–301. https://doi.org/10.33675/AMST/2025/3/6.

Moores, Charles W., ed. *Lincoln: Addresses and Letters*. New York: American Book Company, 1914.

Morrison, Don. “Versatility, Economy and Speed Spur Growth of Plastic Binding.” In *ODR Reproductions Reference Guide*, edited by Samuel D. Wolff Jr., Nanney Thomas Grady, and Albert Prioletta, 199–201. Offset Duplicator Review, 1960.

“Ms. Blue Collar.” *Time* 103, no. 18 (1974): 80.

Murphy, Pat. “Illusion and Expectation: The Baking of an SF Award.” In *Women of Other Worlds: Excursions Through Science Fiction and Feminism*, edited by Helen Merrick and Tess Williams, 342–369. Nedlands: University of Western Australia Press, 1999.

Murray, Simone. *Introduction to Contemporary Print Culture: Books as Media*. Abingdon, Oxon: Routledge, 2021.

Neuhaus, Jessamyn. “The Way to a Man’s Heart: Gender Roles, Domestic Ideology, and Cookbooks in the 1950s.” *Journal of Social History* 32, no. 3 (1999): 529–555.

Nielson, Danielle. “Inventing a Space to Speak: Ethos, Agency and United States’ Woman Suffrage Cookbooks (1886–1916).” *Gender and History* 34, no. 1 (2022): 59–76.

Noble, Malcolm, and Sarah Pyke. “Queer Bibliography: A Rationale.” *Papers of the Bibliographical Society of America*, 118, no. 2 (2024): 147–169. https://doi.org/10.1086/730427.

Nordheimer, Jon. “Cookbook Profits Pay for a Water Main.” *New York Times*, December 15, 1975.

Norrick-Rühl, Corinna. *Book Clubs and Book Commerce*. Cambridge: Cambridge University Press, 2019.

NOW. “The National Organization for Women’s 1966 Statement of Purpose.” National Organization for Women. October 29, 1966. https://now.org/about/history/statement-of-purpose/.

Nussel, Jill. “Heating Up the Sources: Using Community Cookbooks in Historical Inquiry.” *History Compass* 4, no. 5 (2006): 956–961.

Oakley, Mary Ann B. *Elizabeth Cady Stanton*. Old Westbury, N.Y.: Feminist Press, 1972.

Ostrander, Susan A. *Money for Change: Social Movement Philanthropy at Haymarket People’s Fund*. Philadelphia: Temple University Press, 1995.

“Our History.” Cookbook Publishers. Accessed August 27, 2024. https://cookbookpublishers.com/about/our-history/.

"Our History." Morris Printing Group. Accessed November 17, 2024. https://www.morrisprintinggroup.com/history/.

Ozment, Kate. "Rationale for Feminist Bibliography." *Textual Cultures* 13, no. 1 (2020): 149–178. https://doi.org/10.14434/textual.v13i1.30076.

"Palczewski Suffrage Postcard Archive, Anti-suffrage Sub-collection." University of Northern Iowa. Accessed November 17, 2024. https://scholarworks.uni.edu/suffrageanti_images/.

Pandia Health Editorial Team. "Birth Control Throughout History." Pandia Health. Accessed November 17, 2024. https://www.pandiahealth.com/resources/birth-control-throughout-history/.

Parker, Rozsika. *The Subversive Stitch: Embroidery and the Making of the Feminine*. London: Women's Press, 1984.

Pawley, Christine. *Organizing Women: Home, Work, and the Institutional Infrastructure of Print in Twentieth-Century American*. Amherst: University of Massachusetts Press, 2022.

Pepper, Sgt, De, Lf, et al., eds. Advertisement. *Berkeley Barb* 7, no. 24 (1968): 1–28. https://jstor.org/stable/community.28033200.

Piepmeier, Alison. *Girl Zines: Making Media, Doing Feminism*. New York: New York University Press, 2009.

"Poet Kizer Meeting with Women." *Daily Tar Heel*, January 13, 1972.

Potier, Beth. "Barbara Haber Brought Books and Cooks to Schlesinger Library: Made Schlesinger a Home for Good Taste." *Harvard Gazette*, January 16, 2003. https://news.harvard.edu/gazette/story/2003/01/barbara-haber-brought-books-and-cooks- to-schlesinger-library/.

"Press Club Cookbook Is Now 'Best Seller.'" *Evening Star* (Washington, D.C.), February 12, 1956.

Price, Leah. *What We Talk About When We Talk About Books*. New York: Basic Books, 2019.

Procida, Mary A. "No Longer Half-Baked: Food Studies and Women's History (Review)." *Journal of Women's History* 16, no. 3 (2004): 197–205.

"Publishers 1956 Title Output Analyzed." *Publishers Weekly*, January 21, 1957, 31–33.

Rasmussen, Hans. "Cataloging Community Cookbooks." *Primary Source* 27, no. 2 (2008). https://aquila.usm.edu/theprimarysource/vol27/iss2/3.

"The Revival of Feminism." Click: The Revival of Feminism; The Feminist Movement. Accessed November 17, 2024. https://www.cliohistory.org/click/politics-social/revival.

Reyes Elizondo, Andrea, and Jean Lee Cole, "On Decolonising Book History." *SHARP News*, October 8, 2020. https://www.sharpweb.org/sharpnews/2020/10/08/on-decolonising-book-history/.

Rich, Adrienne. "When We Dead Awaken: Writing as Re-vision." *College English* 34, no. 1 (1972): 18–30.

River Road Recipes. Junior League of Baton Rouge. Accessed November 7, 2025. https://www.juniorleaguebr.org/fundraisers/river-road-recipes/.

Robertson, Nan. "Betty Friedan Ushers in a 'Second Stage.'" *New York Times*, October 19, 1981.

Roe, Dorothy. *The Trouble with Women Is Men*. Englewood Cliffs, N.J,: Prentice-Hall, 1961.

Romney, Rebecca. "On Feminist Practice in the Rare Books and Manuscripts Trade: Buying, Cataloguing, and Selling." *Criticism* 64, no. 3–4 (2022): 413–432.

Ross, Alice. "Ella Smith's Unfinished Community Cookbook: A Social History of Women and Work in Smithtown, New York, 1884–1922." In Bower, *Recipes for Reading*, 154–172.

Russ, Joanna. *How to Suppress Women's Writing*. Austin: University of Texas Press, 2005.

Samer, Rox. *Lesbian Potentiality and Feminist Media in the 1970s*. Durham: Duke University Press, 2022.

Sarachild, Kathie. "Consciousness-Raising as a Radical Weapon." In *Feminist Revolution: An Abridged Edition with Additional Writings*, edited by Kathie Sarachild and Redstockings, 144–150. New York: Random House, 1975.

Sass, Lorna J. "A PW Special Report: What's Cooking in Cookbooks?" *Publishers Weekly*, September 20, 1985, 41–58.

Saunders, Lucy. "The Flavor of a Place: Community and Regional Cookbooks Combine Hometown Cooking with Fund-Raising Ventures." *Publishers Weekly*, September 8, 1989, 26–28.

Savoy, Maggie. "Jacquelyn Reinach Mixes Cookbook and Women's Lib." *Los Angeles Times*, August 30, 1970. https://www.proquest.com/news/docview/156490807/373AA079CA8F46BFPQ/1?accountid=14597.

SCEF. "Struggle in Today's South: SCEF 1975 Calendar." Civil Rights Movement Archive. Accessed November 7, 2025. https://www.crmvet.org/docs/scef_calendar-r.pdf.

Schenone, Laura. *A Thousand Years over a Hot Stove: A History of American Women Told Through Food, Recipes, and Remembrances*. New York: Norton, 2003.

Schlafly, Phyllis. Foreword to *Flavored with Freedom*, by Eagle Forum.

Scott, Anne Firor. *Natural Allies: Women's Associations in American History*. Urbana: University of Illinois Press, 1993.

Seligson, Marcia. "What We Need Now Is Another French Cookbook." *New York Times*, November 9, 1969.

Shefferman, Eleanor. "Friendship Club Puts Out Friendly Cook Book: Recipes Give International Flavor to It." *Wisconsin State Journal*, December 16, 1951.

Sheraton, Mimi. "Regional Cookbooks at Their Best." *New York Times*, January 5, 1977.

Six Hundred Dollars a Year: A Wife's Effort at Low Living, Under High Prices. Boston: Ticknor and Fields, 1867.

Skains, R. Lyle. *Digital Authorship: Publishing in the Attention Economy*. Cambridge: Cambridge University Press, 2019.

Skow, John. "Erma in Bomburia." *Time* 124, no. 1 (1984): 56–65.

Smith, Jessie Carney. *Black Firsts: 4,000 Ground-Breaking and Pioneering Historical Events*. 2nd ed. Detroit: Visible Ink, 2003.

"South Dakota Community Cookbook Collection." South Dakota State University. Accessed November 17, 2024. https://openprairie.sdstate.edu/sd_cookbooks/.

"Southern Conference Educational Fund (SCEF)." Digital SNCC Gateway. Accessed November 17, 2024. https://snccdigital.org/inside-sncc/alliances-relationships/scef/.

Spiegel, Tamio. "Yes, It Matters: Nisei Cuisine and Japanese American Identity." Discover Nikkei. October 6, 2017. www.discovernikkei.org/en/journal/2017/10/6/yes-it-matters/.

Spires, Derrick R. "On Liberation Bibliography: The 2021 BSA Annual Meeting Keynote." *Papers of the Bibliographical Society of America* 116, no. 1 (2022): 1–20. https://doi.org/10.1086/718342.

"The Spokeswoman Review." *Spokeswoman* 6, no. 10 (1976): 11–14.

Squires, Claire. *Marketing Literature: The Making of Contemporary Writing in Britain*. Cham, Switzerland: Palgrave, 2009.

Staub, Shirley. "A Community Creates a Cookbook." *Wisconsin State Journal*, 1971, 42–46, 69–75, 80. https://content.mpl.org/digital/collection/WaunakeePL/id/415.

Sturgis, Susanna J. "Inventing the Tiptrees: Reinventing the Agenda." *Feminist Bookstore News* 18, no. 1 (1995): 51–52.

Swan, James. *Fundraising for the Small Public Library: A How-To-Do-It Manual for Librarians*. New York: Neal-Schuman, 1990.

Swinth, Kirsten. *Feminism's Forgotten Fight: The Unfinished Struggle for Work and Family*. Cambridge: Harvard University Press, 2018.

Szathmary, Louis. "A Cupboardful of Charitable Cookbooks." *Boston Globe*, December 7, 1983.

———. Introduction to *A Poetical Cook-Book*, by Maria J. Moss. New York: Arno, 1972.

Tallman, Marion L. "Out of the Red: Five Years with a School Paper and a School Annual: On a Budget!" *Clearing House* 30, no. 4 (1955): 205–207.

Teacher in Space Cookbook: Compiled by the Teacher in Space National Finalists, the "'Class of 51l,'" United Space Shuttle Challenger Mission Scheduled for Launch, January 22, 1986 and Other Parties Interested in Space Education. Raptis Rare Books. Accessed November 17, 2024. https://www.raptisrarebooks.com/product/teacher-in-space-cookbook-first-edition-signed/.

Tipton-Martin, Toni. *The Jemima Code: Two Centuries of African American Cookbooks.* Austin: University of Texas Press, 2015.

Travis, Trysh. "The Women in Print Movement: History and Implications." *Book History* 11 (2008): 275–300. https://doi.org/10.1353/bh.0.0001.

Tye, Diane. *Baking as Biography: A Life Story in Recipes.* Montreal: McGill Queen's University Press, 2010.

Tyler, Pamela. *Silk Stockings and Ballot Boxes: Women and Politics in New Orleans, 1920–1963.* Athens: University of Georgia Press, 1996.

United States Sanitary Commission. *The Book of Bubbles: A Contribution to the New York Fair in Aid of the Sanitary Commission.* New York: Endicott, 1864.

Vance, Daniel. "Walter's Publishing." *Connect Business Magazine*, September 1, 2005. https://connectbiz.com/2005/09/walters-publishing/.

Vester, Katharina. "Queering the Cookbook." In *The Cambridge Companion to Literature and Food*, edited by J. Michelle Coghlan, 131–145. Cambridge: Cambridge University Press, 2020.

"The Waiting Is Over . . . Mollie Katzen's New Cookbook Is Here!" *Publishers Weekly*, August 27, 1982.

Walden, Sarah W. *Tasteful Domesticity: Women's Rhetoric and the American Cookbook, 1790–1940.* Pittsburgh: University of Pittsburgh Press, 2018.

Walker, Alice. "In Search of Zora Neale Hurston." *Ms.*, March 1976, 74–89.

Weinraub, Judith. "It Takes a Cookbook." *Washington Post*, June 4, 1997. https://www.washingtonpost.com/archive/lifestyle/food/1997/06/04/it-takes-a-cookbook/57337067-ffdb-4a92-8929-c8be810fd642/.

———. "The Legacy of the Charitable Cookbook." *Washington Post*, June 4, 1997. https://www.proquest.com/historical-newspapers/legacy-charitable-cookbook/docview/1453417839/se-2.

West, Isaac. "Performing Resistance in/from the Kitchen: The Practice of Maternal Pacifist Politics and La WISP's Cookbooks." *Women's Studies in Communication* 30, no. 3 (2007): 358–373.

Williams, Stacy J. "A Feminist Guide to Cooking." *Contexts* 13, no. 3 (2014): 59–61. https://doi.org/10.1177/1536504214545763.

———. "Recipes for Resistance: Feminist Political Discourse About Cooking, 1870–1985." PhD diss., University of California, San Diego, 2008.

———. "Subversive Cooking in Liberal Feminism, 1963–1985." In *Gender and Food: From Production to Consumption and After*, edited by Marcia Texler Segal and Vasilikie P. Demos, 265–286. Bingley: Emerald Group, 2016.

Wilmot Voss, Kimberly. *Women Politicking Politely: Advancing Feminism in the 1960s and 1970s*. Lanham, Md.: Lexington Books, 2017.

Wilson, Nicola, Claire Battershill, Sophie Heywood, et al, eds. *The Edinburgh Companion to Women in Publishing*. Edinburgh: Edinburgh University Press, 2024.

Wintermute, Harriet E. "The Joy of Cataloging Community Cookbooks." *Cataloging and Classification Quarterly* 55, no. 4 (2017): 197–228.

Withers, D-M. "The Politics of the Workshop: Craft, Autonomy and Women's Liberation." *Feminist Theory* 21, no. 2 (2020): 217–234. https://doi.org/10.1177/1464700119859756.

———. *Virago Reprints and Modern Classics: The Timely Business of Feminist Publishing*. Cambridge: Cambridge University Press, 2021.

Witt, Doris. *Black Hunger: Soul Food and America*. Minneapolis: University of Minnesota Press, 1999.

Wittenmyer, Annie. *A Collection of Recipes for the Use of Special Diet Kitchens in Military Hospitals*. Saint Louis: Studley, Printers and Binders, 1864.

"The Women's Movement: What the Hell Is Happening." *Pandora: A Washington Women's News Journal*, December 1, 1976, 1, 8.

Yaszek, Lisa. "On the Occasion of *Femspec*'s Twentieth Anniversary." *Femspec* 20, no. 1 (2020): 16–17, 80.

Yellen, Janet L. "The History of Women's Work and Wages and How It Has Created Success for Us All." Brookings. May 2020. https://www.brookings.edu/articles/the-history-of-womens-work-and-wages-and-how-it-has-created-success-for-us-all/.

Zafar, Rafia. "The Signifying Dish: Autobiography and History in Two Black Women's Cookbooks." *Feminist Studies* 25, no. 2 (1999): 449–469.

INDEX

www.ingramcontent.com/pod-product-compliance
Lightning Source LLC
LaVergne TN
LVHW040505011026
849280LV00024B/227